For Nina and Frances

Contents

Acknowledgements

Among the many people who assisted us with the research for this book, we would like to thank: Hernán Benítez, Ramón Cereijo, Teresa Adelina Fiora, Héctor J. Cámpora, Atilio Renzi, Benito Llambi, Pedro Gagliardo, Fermín Chavez, José Espejo, Delia Degliuomini de Parodi, Emma Nicolini, Ricardo Guardo, Liliane Lagomarsino de Guardo, Juana Larrauri de Abrami, Ana C. Macri, Maria Rosa Calviño de Gomez, Valentin Thiébaud, Rodolfo Puiggros, Sara Gatti, Celina R. de Martinez Payva, José María Castineira de Dios, Alberto F. Bolaños, Carlos Aloé, Jorge Spotti, Angel Miel Asquía, Pierina Dealessi, Eduardo Colom, Luis F. Gay, Cipriano Reyes, Leonardo Vidal, Guillermo de Prisco, Palmira Repetti, Roberto Petinato, María Eugenia Alvarez and Pilar Madirolas.

We would also like to thank: Robert Cox, Bob and Nina Lindley, Julie Taylor, Antonio Molinari, Louise Doyon, Mario Soffici, Fanny Yest, Julio Korn, Antonio Marquez, David Viñas, Roberto Vacca, Otelo Borroni, all of whom gave generously of their time and assistance. In Buenos Aires we were helped by the staffs of the Biblioteca Nacional, the Archivo Gráfico de la Nación, *La Nación,* and the archives of Congress; in Hanover by the staff of Baker Library and in London by the staff of the *Sunday Times* reference library.

Lastly, we would like to thank, among our many friends who gave us support: León Pomer, Liliane Isler, Rogelio García Lupo, Michael Carter, Leo Spitzer, Alberto Alvarez Pereira, Claudio Armegol, Gregorio Selser, Victor Claiman, Ramon Garriga and Murdoch Morrison.

Photograph on page 2 of illustrations by courtesy of Anne-Marie Heinrich; on pages 3, 4, 5, 6, 7, 8, 9, 10, 11 by courtesy of Archivo Gráfico de la Nación.

Introduction

When this book was written almost twenty years ago, Argentina was suffering from the worst military dictatorship in its history. Everywhere one could find sombre evidence of 'disappearances' – the mass murder of political dissidents in the name of stability. Peronism – the political movement created by Juan Perón, and his wife Evita – was outlawed, and many of the guerillas who had supported the old dictator in the final days of his rule had been kidnapped or killed. Although Perón's reputation had faded with the catastrophic period in power of his second wife Isabel, the memory of his first wife Evita remained undiminished.

I discovered that her myth burnt most brightly among poor people, who could be seen placing flowers each Sunday on her tomb at the Recoleta; but she was also capable of instilling fear among those who had conspired to remove her embalmed body after her death, hiding it for twenty-odd years. Such people – generals or admirals, men habituated to obedience – remembered that a Prime Minister of Argentina had been kidnapped only five years before, tried for his role in the disappearance of Evita's body, and summarily executed. Sitting in darkened apartments beneath photographs of themselves as moustached cadets, bodyguards standing at the door, they were nervous when they discussed their own relationship to 'that woman', afraid that she would somehow come back to take revenge on them.

Evita has, of course, returned, as she promised to her *descamisados* that she would do; but her subsequent 'lives' have confounded all expectations. In her own country her story is at last part of history, arousing the sort of peaceful controversy one might expect from so astonishing a career. In the rest of the world, however, she has attained the condition of apotheosis – becoming a deity in the new world pantheon of electronic celebrity.

To date, the 'rock opera' by Andrew Lloyd Webber and Tim Rice that bears her name has earned over $1 billion, playing in Africa, South America and Japan, as well as Europe and the United States. The choice of Madonna to play Evita in a film version is not only inevitable but somehow fitting – a tribute from the ambiguous idol of one age to the equally ambiguous cult object of an earlier one.

Evita's life, short as it was, is one of the most absorbing of the twentieth century, but the way in which it was imaginatively annexed and, in some cases literally, fought over, is just as interesting. There have been few major discoveries in relation to Evita's life in the past fifteen years, and I have added an Epilogue to take account of events since this book was first published. Otherwise the book, like Evita herself, I hope, has been left intact – a piece of historical reportage made at a time when the possibility of tranquil definitiveness was remote indeed.

Nicholas Fraser
London, 1995

1

The House of Doña Juana

Even in the centre of the village the streets were unsurfaced, dusty in the dry season, impassable during the winter rains. The plaza was nothing more than a large space of crushed brick surrounded by crude likenesses of nymphs, war heroes, the Virgin, and the national emblem. On one side was the church, on the other the two stores. The houses were low, one-storey brick boxes identical in structure and arranged on a grid. Some were whitewashed, some light brown, and all were without porches and shut off from the dust of the streets. The regularly spaced trees were severely pollarded, and thus diminished to the houses' stunted scale. Where the village ended, three or four blocks away from the plaza in each direction, the land went straight to the horizon, a vast space, with a vaster sky, fenced into enclosures too large to see across. In the distance were cattle, standing singly or in groups, and trees, which had been planted as windbreaks for the isolated farms.

The level and featureless plain west of Buenos Aires is called the *pampa*. It is one of the richest agricultural areas in the world and Los Toldos, which is one hundred and fifty miles from the capital of Argentina, is little different from the other small and utterly isolated settlements set down across the pampa.

'It is not so much that the houses are small,' the Argentine writer Ezequiel Martínez Estrada observed in 1933[1]

'as the fact that they are dwarfed by the immensity of their surroundings. Their smallness is an optical illusion; it is the pampa that makes them seem so.

'These villages are like meteorites, pieces of inhabited stars fallen to earth in the countryside. One can enter one of them and believe one is entering the village one has just left and that the whole voyage was an illusion. One can ask the name of the village and be rewarded with a smile, since the inhabitants believe that this is "*the* village", a place with a name in the midst of a place with no name. There is no real distinction between the village and the countryside; the village just depends on the latter and that is all. It is there but it could be to the right or to the left, indeed, it could even not be there at all . . .

There used to be Indians on the plain, but many of them were slaughtered in the frontier wars of the 1880s. Los Toldos had been the site of one of their encampments, as its name, 'The Tents', signifies. A few Indians now lived in hovels outside the village and on feast days they would dress up in white berets and ponchos, ride horses and carry lances. But the people of the village had come during the wars or afterwards, when the land, empty and open, was colonized. The first wire fence was set up in 1844, the first Aberdeen Angus arrived in 1876, and the first refrigerated ship came from England in 1877.[2] By the 1890s, English money and English technology had created a fan of railways across the plain from the capital, Buenos Aires, and the villages grew up as points on the railway lines, halts at which cattle were loaded. The villagers who had come to Argentina from Spain or Italy worked as labourers or sold things to the region's farmers. They were never hungry, but they had little other than food. They could not own land since it had been parcelled into huge holdings and given to native Argentines after the Indian wars. Although their wages were low, they did not think of themselves as poor. With the great distances and the roads turned to mud for so much of the year, they travelled little and when they did, found only villages like their own. They had few standards of comparison.

At five o'clock on 7 May 1919, an Indian woman went on foot to a house west of the village to deliver a child. It was a simple, low house constructed around a patio bordered with trees, with outhouses some distance away. The child's father, Juan Duarte, was important in the neighbourhood. He was forty-three years old and came from Chivilcoy, a town twenty miles away. There he had married Estela Grisolía, who bore him three daughters. Eighteen years previously he had left his wife and daughters in Chivilcoy and come to Los Toldos to work as estate manager on behalf of the Malcolm family who owned the land. He received a portion of whatever profits he made working the land and he was deeded small portions of property by the owners. This, in a rural society of such great simplicity, was enough to earn him the much coveted title of *estanciero*. The farm had two horse-drawn reapers and it was successful. Duarte had an automobile, and in 1908 he was made Justice of the Peace in recognition of the local influence he had by then acquired. He liked to have people in his house and they liked to be there because he was convivial.

The mother of the child was Juana Ibarguren, his mistress in Los Toldos, and it was said that her grandmother had come to the village with the soldiers during the Indian campaign. Her mother, Petronia Núñez, had lived for a while with a Basque carter called Ibarguren and it was his name that the daughter took. She met Duarte when she was very young, fifteen or sixteen years old. Even after Juana's children were born, Duarte's wife came frequently to see him, and it was probably for this reason that the ménage was circumspect. The children – Blanca, Elisa, Juan, Erminda and now Eva María – lived with their mother in a house on the main street of the village and thus, though the whole village was aware of the true situation, an outward propriety was maintained. Yet Juana Ibarguren did not behave as if she was simply Duarte's mistress. She adopted the name Duarte. She had dark eyes and strong features, dressed well, and even used perfume, which was unusual for the time. In the village she was envied, which is perhaps why she was also despised. It was said that she had inherited her stubbornness and arrogance from her Basque father.

There are no existing birth certificates or baptismal records for the youngest child. Those who claim to have seen these documents before they were destroyed say that she was baptized with her sister Erminda and her brother Juan, on 21 November 1919.[3] Her first names were given as Eva María, her surname as Ibarguren. Her father's name was not entered on either document and since the six months' interval between birth and baptism was longer than usual, village gossip said there had been some argument between the father and mother over what names the children should be given. None of them ever used their legal surname, preferring to call themselves by their father's name.

Duarte's 'second marriage' was not unusual. The circumstances of war, the imperatives of the frontier and the complete absence of records meant that in nineteenth-century rural Argentina settlers took Indian women and left them and their children behind as they moved onwards, from settlement to settlement and region to region. These children, it has been suggested by the writer Ezequiel Martínez Estrada, 'might well adopt the customs of their fathers, but in their hearts they could not be satisfied by them. They had no home, they were the pariahs of the plain; more like animals without masters than men.'[4] In the early twentieth century, though manners were softer, there were still many such informal arrangements.

Duarte seems to have been kind to his mistress and children while he was in Los Toldos. They had a home in the village, and a maid, and more than a semblance of family life. But as the question of the naming of his children and his subsequent behaviour towards them would seem to indicate, his sense of paternity had its limits.

In the early months of 1920, when his youngest child was less than a year old, Duarte left his farm and doña Juana and returned to his first family in Chivilcoy. He may have decided that the farm was not making enough money or he may have resolved to go back to his wife; he did not make his reasons clear and no one in the village seems to have felt he had any obligation to do so. His departure left doña Juana impoverished. She and her five children left the house on the main street and moved to Calle Francia 1021, a two-room house near the railway with a shed at the back for cooking, and a yard. It is now a decrepit rural slum, smelling of stale cooking and crowded with children. When the Duartes lived there it was probably not much better and must have been a humiliating home even in Los Toldos where nothing amounts to very much. In order not to starve, doña Juana sewed clothes for the people of the village. Yet she continued to be regarded as a kept woman; that reputation would stay with her whatever she did and it probably caused her more pain than the family's new poverty. It was whispered for example, that doña Juana had become intimate with a Carlos Rosset and that Rosset was indeed not her only protector. 'In the village, the gossips spoke about Eliseo Calviño, who gave the family chickens, of Elías Tomasse, who provided them with meat, of Miguel Lizazo, Juan Gilabert, Amadeo Garín and many more . . .', said a man who was at school with the elder daughters.[5] It is remembered that the sort of thing said behind doña Juana's back was said openly to her daughters. Juan, the only son, became their protector as he got older and threatened those who insulted them. It was the family's reputation, rather than the way they actually lived, that counted. 'You could say anything you liked to those girls,' the same man said, 'but they weren't *chicas buscadoras*, they weren't tarts at all, though all the village said they were.'

On 8 January 1926, doña Juana and her family heard that Duarte had been killed in a car accident near Chivilcoy. Doña Juana resolved to attend the funeral, though legally she and her family did not exist for the dead man's family and their presence according to the conventions of the time could only be interpreted as an affront. She dressed the children in mourning. Blanca was then eighteen years old, Elisa sixteen, Juan twelve, Erminda ten and Eva María only six. They arrived at Chivilcoy when the wake was already in progress and when they came to the door and identified themselves, Estela Grisolía de Duarte, the legal wife, said they could not come in. A violent argument about who they were and why they had come ensued. Doña Juana had to plead with the wife's brother, the Mayor of Chivilcoy, and it was only after he had spoken to his sister that the five children could enter the house.

There was food on the tables and a lot to drink. The dead man, dressed in his best clothes, was displayed in an open coffin surrounded by flowers. They were led in by the brother and while the other guests watched in silence, they looked briefly at the man who had been part of their family, crossed themselves in prayer and went outside. They waited in the car; it was a hot and dusty summer day. When the wake ended, the coffin was brought out and placed on a horse-drawn hearse decorated with black and silver velvet. They were allowed to walk behind the hearse, not immediately behind it, for that was where the real Duartes walked, but behind them, to the rear of the undifferentiated crowd of mourners. The cemetery was some distance outside the village, walled off from the road, and the red-brown dust rose up around the column of mourners and discoloured their black clothes. The mother and the children watched the priest at the graveside, the sprinkling, then the shovelling of the earth, and then they walked back to the village behind the mourners and returned to Los Toldos.

Neither Evita nor her sisters could ever confront the question of illegitimacy. As late as 1972 Erminda, the second youngest, would write that her mother and father were happily married, that he kissed her and her younger sister Eva María goodnight the night before he left the village on a business trip, and died. As for the 'legitimate' Duartes, Erminda simply suggests that they were her step-sisters and that they 'were more sad than we were, because with the death of their father they were orphans, since they had lost their mother some years before.'[6] *La Razón de mi Vida*, the book in which the adult Evita gave some account of her life and acts, contains no dates, no mention of childhood occurrences; the past is subsumed under the flat image of what she had then become, and the character of her acts represented as something outside her personality, a 'mission' mysteriously implanted rather than evolved. The nearest Evita came to speaking about her feelings was to evoke '*a sense of outrage against injustice*. As far as I can remember the existence of injustice has hurt my soul as if a nail was being driven into it. From every period of my life I retain the memory of some injustice tormenting me and tearing me apart.'[7]

Evita had been too young to have any memory of her often-absent father's departure, but she can never have forgotten the funeral. She had never left the village before, never before seen her family through the eyes of other people. While she could not have understood the noise and the passions aroused by her mother's wish to see the body, nor indeed why she should see it, she did understand that there were people who hated her mother and hated her, and she was perhaps angry with her mother for having exposed her to that hatred.

Eva María was small and thin and quiet, with black hair and large, staring brown eyes. She had attacks of rage which seemed strange to her family; when her grandmother died a year after her father she threw herself to the ground and cried inconsolably. Her family called her *la flaca*: skinny. She was closest to her sister Erminda, whom everyone called Chicha, and to a dog called León. She played with Chicha and León on a piece of land with willows and a mulberry tree beside the railway line. From the house there was the sound of the sewing machine, for her mother worked all day and sometimes in the evenings. The children had few toys, only second-hand or damaged dolls, and in this respect they were poor. But there was always enough to eat, *pucheros* or *polentas*, the beef and corn stews of the Argentine working class, and because doña Juana earned her living making clothes, they were well-dressed, probably better than most of the village children. Doña Juana was proud of them and had high standards. She 'wouldn't allow the slightest degree of slovenliness, on any occasion, in her four daughters; and she taught [them] to take care of [them]selves, to behave like the little girls [they] were.'[8] It was she who gave her children the sense that they were poor because they had been unfairly made so and that by rights they should not be. 'What hurt us most,' Erminda wrote, 'was to see how our mother was getting sores on her legs from her varicose veins. But she never gave in to the pain, she went on working . . . Every morning we had to help her out of bed. When the doctor told her to rest, she said sharply to him, "I don't have the time. If I rest how shall I work and how will they live?"'

When she was eight years old, Eva María put on a pinafore and walked with Chicha down the main street, Calle Mitre, past the plaza and the stores to the small elementary school at the other end of the village. There was only one teacher, but the children were taught an ambitious variety of subjects, including chemistry, zoology and mineralogy. Eva María was quiet and good and according to her marks an average student. She was often absent from school. Her teacher could not remember much about her except her enormous eyes.

The second year at school, all the children took part in a

ceremony attended by the Governor of Buenos Aires.[9] The visit of an important politician was so rare that the Mayor took advantage of the occasion to stage a pageant representing the origins and evolution of the village. The Indians that remained in Los Toldos were the first to enter the square, followed by the schoolchildren. The Mayor, dressed in a shabby frock-coat, made a long speech about Progress and Democracy. Then Micaela García Cisneros, a sad-faced little girl with white shoes, white stockings, a white dress and a white bow in her hair followed him: 'I who feel in my blood the heat of legendary and historic acts,' she said, 'who was born in the silence of an Indian encampment and nursed in the rough but strong arms of an innocent woman . . . I feel truly great, humbled and purified by this strong sense of Argentineness . . .. May this day's spirit of unity last forever.' The children sang the national anthem; there were more speeches, banquets, a football match, and then the politician went home by train, the children waving on the platform, while a biplane flew overhead behind him.

The Mayor who organized the ceremony was a member of the Radical Party and had only recently been elected. Duarte had been a Conservative and it was through his friends, also Conservatives, that Elisa, the eldest daughter, had got a job at the post office. Doña Juana asked the Mayor if he would keep her daughter in her job and when he said he could not, she asked him if he would find her one somewhere else.[10] He found her one in Junín, twenty miles away, and it was thus, some time in the early months of 1930, that the Duartes hired a truck, packed their belongings and left Los Toldos. It is said that they left at night because they owed money in the village.

People had moved a great deal in nineteenth-century Argentina, but predominantly, away from the coast in search of land. Now, in the 1930s, as the slump in food prices took effect, some of them were moving back again. Junín, where the Duartes settled, was originally a fort, then a railway centre, but it was now becoming a way-station between the land and Buenos Aires. Around the perimeter of nineteenth-century Junín were unsafe and hastily-constructed *barrios* with names like Tierra del Fuego and Villa Italia. It was to these slums that the migrants came. The fortunate ones found work in the railway workshops, smelting or uphol-stering, but most of them would find nothing and take the train to Buenos Aires.

The Duarte family was part of this migratory movement in search of work, but because of Elisa's job at the post office they were more fortunate than many. Junín, with its palm trees and caramel-and-pistachio-coloured cathedral, is full of small shuttered villas with whitewashed patios encrusted with coloured glass and flagstone floors painted red; and it was to one of these houses that the family now moved. When Blanca qualified as a teacher and Juan got work travelling around the region selling such household products as 'Radical Soap' and 'La Rosa' floor wax, doña Juana gave up sewing for better things. There were no restaurants in this private and petit-bourgeois town, and doña Juana began to have 'guests' in her house.

Years later, when Evita was famous, it was said that at doña Juana's establishment there had been 'a great deal of flirtatious giggling, horseplay and some pretty little scenes of affection put on by the mother and the daughters for the benefit of the men'.[11] But this seems unlikely. Doña Juana had by now come to represent herself as 'the widow Duarte', and her 'guests', for it was thus that they liked to refer to the arrangement, were no less respectable bachelors: José Alvarez Rodríguez ('don Pepe'), the Principal of the Colegio Nacional, who was wholly above suspicion and was a frequent, magniloquent, contributor to the letter and editorial columns of the local paper; his younger brother Justo, who was a lawyer; and Major Arrieta, a little younger, sad-faced and silent. He was in charge of the division garrisoned in the town, and his offices and his lodgings were a few doors away. Don Pepe, his brother, and the Major would eat together at a table in the small front room off the street, while doña Juana cooked and her daughters washed up afterwards. The family ate separately in the cramped kitchen. Sometimes they would sit with the men after meals but their presence was always compatible with doña Juana's representations of gentility fallen on bad times; if she did indeed ever suggest that the girls should make themselves pleasant to the men, it was probably in the context of being polite and deferential to stolid middle-aged guests.

Eva María went to school just off the main square of the town. A school photograph shows a withdrawn but strong face, sad, staring eyes and tightened lips. She was a 'very beautiful little girl with dark hair and skin like porcelain,' one teacher said, 'a self-absorbed child with an intense inner life, great sensitivity and great vulnerability.'[12] With Elsa, her best friend when she was twelve, she was 'sweet, very loving', but there were many girls at school whose mothers had told them not to speak to Eva María, because of 'what her mother was', and Evita must have felt their rejection bitterly, though she would never speak about it. Elsa was an orphan brought up by her two aunts and they liked Eva María.

Weekdays were workdays or schooldays, but Sunday was the '*día de salida*' on which the people of Junín, smart or shoddy, respectable or not, would walk through the empty streets to the centre of town, stopping to look at what they had seen so many times before in the windows. 'I used to go early to church with my mother, who was very religious,' said one friend of Evita's. 'And that was one walk into the centre. Then, in the afternoon, I'd take the twenty or thirty centavos I was given as pocket money and walk up and down the three blocks of the Calle Rivadavia. The town boys were lined up in two rows and they used to whistle and say rude things to us as we passed. Chocolate was five centavos, an ice-cream sandwich a little more. We couldn't go to the movies on Sundays, because that was matinée day and seats were eighty centavos, and we weren't allowed into the bars anyway. So we just walked up and down, ate our candy in front of the boys and when it was dark we went home. . . .'[13]

Only once a year did the town offer more than this routine and that was at carnival time when there was music and dancing in the streets. The girls wore masks and decorated their disguises with the flowers the boys gave them. And on Tuesdays, when movie seats cost only thirty centavos, the little girls bought their sweets, stood in line at the Roxy or the Crystal Palace and waited in their wooden seats for the lights to dim. The sound would come up and they could forget that they were too big or too small, too skinny or too fat and that they lived in Junín, a small, lost town in the middle of the pampa. And there on the screen, instead of the drabness of weekdays and Sundays, were images of European or North American life, depictions of wealth and power, visions of great and glittering cities and most of all, *love*: love across class barriers, love and money, love and furs, love and destiny, love in 'spacious drawing rooms with black marble staircases and chrome banisters, white satin chairs, white satin drapes, fluffy white wool rugs, tables and chairs with chrome legs, where a beautiful New York blonde, a typist, seduces her handsome boss and by means of tricks forces him to divorce his elegant wife.' As Manuel Puig indicates in *Heartbreak Tango*,[14] his novel of small town life, it did not matter that American movies came to towns like Junín four or five years after they were released abroad, were execrably dubbed, and displayed fashions which had been worn and discarded long ago, even in Junín. They still worked. There were Argentine movies as well, some of them quite accomplished, but their budgets were low and they did not seem exotic. They could never compete with the imports from Hollywood.

The girls would buy *Sintonía*, the tabloid Argentine movie

magazine, cut it in pieces, exchange photographs and dream about Hollywood and Paris. Eva María's favourite star was Norma Shearer, who was born poor in Montreal but who came to Hollywood, met Irving Thalberg and starred in dozens of MGM films including *Marie Antoinette*. Eva María always offered to do the dishes for her sister Erminda in exchange for movie photographs. 'In the place where I spent my childhood,' Evita would say – she never named it –

> there were more poor people than rich, but I made myself believe that there were other places in my country and in the world where things could happen in some other way . . . I imagined, for instance, that large cities were marvellous places where only wealth existed; and everything I heard about them from other people confirmed this belief. They talked about the great city as if it were a wonderful paradise where everything was beautiful and outstanding and I seemed to feel, from what they said, that people there were *more really people* than those I saw around me in my town.

By 1934, with Blanca teaching in a local school, Elisa still working in the post office and Juan also employed, the family was much better off. Juan, a dice-player and ladies' man who wore white palm-beach suits, drove a Packard convertible. Eva María was fifteen and had a boy-friend named Ricardo who was in the garrison. She could expect the sort of life that her sisters had; dances with the music of *pasodobles*, *rancheras*, even ragtime, where the boys were well-behaved and touched the girls only in order to dance. Later, there would be a job of sorts and later still a marriage; someone as safe as Major Arrieta or Justo Rodríguez, who did indeed later marry Blanca and Elisa. It is not likely that she ever met such well-heeled citizens of Junín as the English from the railway company or the *gente bien* of the Spanish or Italian clubs, but this can have meant little to her, because the town itself meant so little to her.

Eva had always recited poetry, limp and sentimental lyrics, in school; she had appeared in a student production and one Saturday she went to the town's record shop and declaimed her poems through their amplifier. She told her mother she wanted to be an actress and when her mother paid no attention she persisted. Don Pepe was called in and he heard Eva acting in the house and said, in his pompous way, that parents should never stifle their children's incipient sense of vocation. 'If she fails,' he said, 'there is nothing to worry about and if she succeeds, so much the better for her.'[15]

It is commonly said that later that year the tango singer Agustín

Magaldi performed in the Crystal Palace theatre of Junín. Born in Rosario to a poor family, he had worked in a firework factory until one day he heard Caruso sing on the radio. Inspired, he began to train his own fine tenor voice. By the time he came to Junín he was thirty-seven years old and second in popularity only to the great tenor Carlos Gardel. Magaldi's latest record, *Vagabundo*, had sold more than a million copies. When he performed, he wore a boater and a blazer or a double-breasted suit and plastered his hair with brilliantine. His mournful features were held continually in the pose of stricken masculinity adopted by tango masters, though actually he was soft, even chubby, without much physical dignity. Yet from the darkness of the movie house, he was without doubt a real star.

Most accounts [16] of Evita's life say that she fell in love with the spotlit image of Magaldi or that she decided to seduce him and use him; but that, in either event, she was introduced to him, asked him to take her to Buenos Aires, and when he wavered, forced her way into his train compartment and rode with him to the city, thus leaving her family and becoming a married man's mistress. Yet there is no record of the tango singer's having come to Junín that year. Magaldi, a mild man who was devoted to his mother, used to bring his wife on tour, and it is hard to understand what he would have seen in small, skinny Eva María. If he did help her to leave Junín, it is likely that his assistance was of the most innocuous kind. Evita's sister insists that doña Juana, prodded by don Pepe, accompanied Evita to the city. According to her account, mother and daughter kept visiting the radio stations until they found a programme for which a young girl was needed. Eva María recited her poem about death and dissolution with such pathos that the station director offered her 'a little contract.'[17] Then she had to stay at the house of some friends, while doña Juana went home, 'enraged with don Pepe, enraged with the world'.

How Eva María left Junín is really of little importance beside the fact that she did so. Many girls possessed what she called a 'fundamental feeling . . . a sense of outrage at injustice' directed at their families, their dull villages and their poverty. Many of them wanted to be actresses, but most of them followed their parents' wishes, married safely and well, continued to live in the provinces and to go to the movies once a week. Eva María had no money, little education and no proven talents, but she wanted to conquer the city and be a star. Whether with her mother or with Magaldi, she took the train to Buenos Aires some time in the early months of 1935, came out of the iron-and-glasswork Retiro terminus and began to live on her own. She was fifteen years old.

2

Buenos Aires

In the 1930s Buenos Aires was still a city of immigrants and transients. At the turn of the century, when it was called *La Gran Aldea,* its population of half a million had lived in a series of villages: *barrios,* distinct neighbourhoods cherishing their separate identities, and *arrabales,* half-rural settlements where the *barrios* faded out and the plain began. But the city, like the country, experienced a remarkable transformation. By 1914 the population had increased to a million and a half, and by 1936, the year after Eva María came to the city, it was more than two and a half million. Buenos Aires had become *La Reina del Plata,* the largest city in South America and the third largest, after New York and Chicago, in the Americas as a whole.[1]

Buenos Aires was where the web of railways met. Here cattle were slaughtered and the meat was frozen and shipped to Europe. Here Congress debated, the President decided and the bureaucracy disposed. The banks, the stock market, the flourishing publishing industry were all located here, and the population – which had mostly come by boat up the muddy Rio de la Plata, which was too wide to see across – included Spaniards, Italians, English, Irish, Germans, Syrians, Greeks, Turks, and Polish and Russian Jews. Like New York, it could be called first a Babel then a melting-pot. Now, in the 1930s, the immigrants were no longer coming from abroad, but from the agricultural interior. Like Eva-María, they arrived not at the docks but at the railway stations.

The people of Buenos Aires called themselves *porteños,* the 'people of the port', and lived remote from the country behind them, choosing to believe that their city was all that mattered of Argentina.[2] It had been developed very quickly, but also in an expansive, turn-of-the-century spirit that would have appealed to Baron Haussmann, the creator of modern Paris. It was as cosmopolitan in its architecture as it was in population. The American writer Waldo Frank wrote in 1931: 'Houses are a chaos and a confusion; Spanish, Creole, Gothic, Baroque, Plateresque, Moorish, Neo-classical, Georgian, Victorian, French of all epochs, bungalows of Southern California, streets tenemented like the East End of London, others like Menilmontant . . . nowhere is Italian pastry-work more flamboyant, nowhere are hospitals, clubs, private and public mansions, more grandly expressive.'[3]

It was the English who had played the most substantial role in the development of modern Argentina, but for the inspiration of civilization the Argentines looked to France, or rather to Paris, which they identified with France in much the same way as they identified Buenos Aires with their own country. Frenchmen arriving in Buenos Aires were astonished and bemused; the city had the texture of a dream. For the purist Georges Clemenceau the imitation was not a success, containing every style of architecture but 'principally that which hurts the eye'.[4] But Anatole France felt at home, although he noticed that the city, unlike Paris, was not constructed of stone. It was the grey *pampa* cement which had given Buenos Aires its distinctive colour and tone. Buenos Aires was a city of *belle époque* solidity, sculptured cherubs and flowers, arches and mansards, but it had been made from impermanent material; a city with high plane trees that looked like Paris in the winter rains, but under the bright Argentine sun seemed oddly artificial.

The country's middle class was formed largely from the immigrants who had poured in during the last thirty years of the nineteenth century and the first thirty years of the twentieth, particularly from the Italians and the Basques. In Buenos Aires at least, most immigrants spoke Spanish and thought of themselves as Argentines. But alongside this new, immigrant Argentina, and still controlling it in many respects, was a different, older country. This other Argentina was based on landed wealth and its members were a colonial élite of landholders. This élite felt itself to be a landed aristocracy, although by the 1930s it was commonly and less flatteringly called the Oligarchy.

The Oligarchy's land-holdings were enormous. It has been estimated that in 1930 a mere 1,804 people owned land equivalent in area to Holland, Belgium and Switzerland combined.[5] This had been amassed by the Oligarchy during the civil wars or the Indian wars when military heroes had been recompensed with gifts of land. Some of it came from relatives who had been clever enough to buy huge tracts from the State in times of financial trouble. Sometimes these Oligarchs worked the land themselves, sometimes they rented it to tenants and sub-tenants, while the owners waited for the country to develop and sold pieces of land at vast profits at various times.

The style of life on which the Oligarchs spent their money was a cross between that of the English country gentleman and the French *boulevardier*. Tudor manors and formal gardens were created on the plains and French palaces or *petits hôtels* were built in Buenos Aires. Palermo, a landscaped *bois* with shaded walks surrounded by a suburb of mansions, was conceived in homage to the Bois de Boulogne. Calle Florida, the Argentine version of Bond Street or the Rue de Rivoli, was a long street of glittering windows stocked with tweeds, perfumes and European antiques. At the Hipódromo to the north of Palermo was an Ascot or Longchamps, and nearby were polo fields and croquet lawns. The city had great gentlemen's clubs, none greater than the Jockey Club, with its Turkish baths, leather and plush salons, its not inconsiderable collection of art and its excellent library, well stocked with English and French titles. Buenos Aires even had Harrods, the great London store, which sold much of what it did in London, everything required for a gentleman's life.

The Argentine social season began in May or June – that is to say, in the winter – when the wealthy opened their town houses and attended the Teatro Colon. This magnificent opera house boasted performances of all the celebrated works and visits from artists such as Caruso and Pavlova. By November Paris fashions from the preceding autumn would be worn on the streets, and sometimes it was possible to arrange for the coming spring's fashions to arrive in Buenos Aires before they had been shown, let alone worn, in Paris. During the hot, humid summers the Argentine rich would either retire to the country or embark on their European tours, taking with them their ladies' maids, butlers, laundresses and cooks – and, of course, the 'Misses' or 'Mademoiselles' for the children. The writer María Rosa Oliver remembers that in her family the question of whether to take a cow to Europe was seriously discussed and that they decided not to only because it would not look right.[6]

In the first decades of the century the peso was quoted higher than any European currency but the pound, and Argentines had a free choice of European countries in which to spend the summer. They went racing at Longchamps or Epsom, often running their own horses. They were to be seen on the Côte d'Azur, on the Italian lakes and, of course, in Paris where the expression 'rich as an Argentine' became common. These Argentines behaved as if they were European, and the older the family, the more European it had to appear. As for the more recent rich (who were in fact more European than the older Argentines), they were dubbed *rastaquouères* or *rastas* (literally, someone covered in leather), an expression later used in French about any flashy man whose origins were dubious or whose occupation was questionable. Many rich Argentines chose not to live in their country at all, and throughout the twenties and thirties there was a substantial number of Argentine 'exiles' in Paris.

As far as the Oligarchy was concerned, the most important aspect of Argentine history was the history of their own families. Buenos Aires was full of statues of heroes of the nineteenth-century wars, and the families honoured their dead in the Recoleta, a cemetery so large and solid that it seemed a city within a city. 'There is little difference,' wrote a French journalist called Jules Huret in 1911, 'between the pride of an *estanciero* who tells you that his grandfather planted the trees of his *estancia* fifty years ago, and the self-complacency of a descendant of the crusaders who says to you that his shield was present at the battle of Bouvines.'[7] To this genealogical view of the past, the Oligarchy added pride in the achievements of the present, which were, in their eyes, entirely their own. When an official historian surveyed the history of mankind on the occasion of the Republic's hundredth anniversary, he could proclaim confidently that the nation which had accumulated the most wealth and culture in the shortest time was Argentina.[8]

The Oligarchy's definition of who had the right to call himself an Argentine was restrictive. In their clubs and even in their newspapers they would bemoan the *chusma* – the riff-raff – who had invaded their country, although they allowed that the industrious and sober British working class compared favourably with the Italians and the Spanish. They were not much better disposed towards the middle classes, whom they suspected of wishing to take their place.

Liberalism still retained its nineteenth-century connotations. To be a liberal meant subscribing to the separation of Church and State, adhering to the principle of Free Trade (particularly with one's chief trading partner, Britain), and professing vague opinions as to the wisdom of encouraging European immigration. Progress was seen in terms of higher exports of beef and a greater influx of European culture and goods, not of increased political democracy. Although the country had a constitution modelled on the American, a President, two houses and a federal system, elections habitually took place in an atmosphere of violence or fraud and votes were either bought or delivered at gunpoint. The establishment of male universal suffrage and secret balloting in 1912 put an end to these abuses. In the next election the Radical Party, speaking for the Argentine middle class, won by a substantial margin. Some members of the Oligarchy experienced great regret over the reforms and the Radicals' popular triumph, and were to complain about the evils of popular sovereignty.

World War I was good for Argentina, so remote from the disasters of Europe, so happy to remain neutral and increase its exports of food and hides to the mobilised English and French. The affluence of the war lasted well into the 1920s, long after it was apparent that the great system of the British which had produced that wealth was under strain. Those years are still regarded in Argentina as a Golden Age, a period of growth and confidence, a time when the world came to the modern city of Buenos Aires and left satisfied that there was money to be made there and that it was indeed the city of the future. The Army, with no coups to make, no wars to fight, stayed on the ceremonial margins of national life, which seemed to support the Argentines' claims to superior Europeanness. Among the stream of immigrants were more important guests. The Prince of Wales, for instance, delighted the wealthy and fell off a number of polo ponies. The franc had collapsed and French intellectuals were happy to give lectures in Argentina on their superior culture.

The economic crash of 1929, the decline of the British pound and the collapse in the value of Argentina's exports, turned this Golden Age suddenly to lead. For a while it seemed as if the country would default on its loans and be unable to pay its civil service. The Radical president Hipólito Yrigoyen, now in his eighties, was serving his second term; he 'could not understand what he read, and nobody could understand what he said. He was painfully and publicly senile'.[9] In the early months of 1930, there were governmental crises, rumours, and· then on 6 September, after a squadron of planes had showered the city with leaflets, two small detachments of the Army left their barracks and marched on the Presidential Palace in the Plaza de Mayo. They had the tacit support of the other political parties, and the active encouragement of Conservatives in Congress. Yrigoyen resigned and was taken out of the city by the Army. There were riots and civilian deaths. The president's house was sacked, his library, his possessions, his iron cot were thrown into the streets.

Though there were elections in 1932 which did produce a Conservative government, they bore little resemblance to those in which the Radical Party had triumphed. The police confiscated ballot books, the dead arose and voted, and where, in spite of these measures, the Radicals were successful, the results were annulled and the Conservative candidates were imposed on the electorate. The 1930s would later be known as the *Decáda infame,* and from a political perspective it was an accurate characterization. Though the government presented itself to the world as a functioning democracy – and could indeed claim to be less totalitarian than some of that decade's regimes – it fell far short of real democracy. Behind the formal, orderly succession of governments was the pro-British and conservative Oligarchy, hostile not merely to new ideas, but to anything perceived as a threat to its interests. The civil service and the unions were purged of subversives, some of whom were deported to the prisons of antarctic Patagonia. The 'order' of which the government boasted to foreigners would lead to much accumulated bitterness, much anger.

Yet despite these setbacks, 1936 was a year in which the *porteños* could still feel proud of their city and lucky to be Argentines. The new Kavanagh building, the tallest building in South America, rose like the prow of a liner over the Plaza San Martín towards the river and the docks. A huge obelisk was erected at the intersection of Corrientes, the boulevard of theatres and movie houses, and the Avenida 9 de Julio, said to be the widest street in the world. 1936 also marked the death in a plane crash of Carlos Gardel, the man who had been not only the city's greatest singer but also the most prominent example of its distinctive social type, the 'man of Corrientes and Esmeralda', a lówer-middle-class dandy and *flâneur*.

Carlos Gardel had sung:

> *Buenos Aires, la reina del Plata*
> *Buenos Aires, mi tierra querida,*
> *escucha, mi canción,*
> *que con ella va mi vida.*
>
> *En mis horas de fiebre y orgía*
> *harto ya de placer y locura,*
> *en ti pienso patria mía*
> *para calmar mi amargura.*[10]

> Buenos Aires, Queen of the Plata,
> Buenos Aires, my beloved country,
> Listen to my song,
> For with it goes my life.
>
> In my hours of fever and orgies,
> Sated with pleasure and madness,
> I think of you, my fatherland,
> To soothe my bitterness.

The *porteños* came to his funeral by the hundreds of thousands.

They had loved him for his tuxedos, his carnations and brilliantine, his simple manners, his love for his mother and particularly because, despite his great fame, his North American movie career and his European tours, he always felt, or said he felt, that Buenos Aires was special. The coffin was placed in the Luna Park stadium: 'There were men and women camped in the Plaza and the surrounding streets as if this was a pilgrimage from all over the country,' an observer noted, 'and thus they said farewell to the last singer, the most beloved of them all.'[11]

There were *salas* throughout the city – dance-halls with raised daises for the orchestras – and there, as well as in tea-rooms or *boîtes,* the *porteños* listened to or danced to the tango. 'The youths have sallow eyes,' Waldo Frank observed.

Their clothes are cheap, their hair is too well glossed. The girls wear flimsy imitations of the styles of Paris, their heels are too high and their legs are scrawny. But as they pace within the tango, they are ennobled. The man leads in low, lithe style. His body is erect, it does not turn. The head is held in profile to the body and flat against the profiled face of the partner.[12]

After its beginnings in the brothels of the port of Buenos Aires, its sudden respectability in Paris and its cult status throughout Europe in the 1920s, the tango had become the most popular music in Buenos Aires, the only music that was genuinely Argentine. Its lyrics were about loss of a world or of a woman and its sadness and nostalgia had meaning to a city in which there were many uprooted people. The tango spoke in slang and with vivid cynicism:

> Que el mundo fue y será una porquería
> Ya lo sé, en el 510 y en el 2000 también
> Que siempre ha habido chorros, maquiavelos y estafaos,
> Contentos y amargaos, valores y doblez.
> Pero que el siglo XX es un despliegue de maldad insolente
> Ya no hay quien lo niegue.
>
> Vivimos revolcaos en un merengue
> y en un mismo lodo todos manoseaos . . .
>
> Hoy resulta que es lo mismo
> ser derecho que traidor!
> Ignorante, sabio, o chorro
> generoso o estafador . . .
> Todo es igual . . . nada es mejor!
> Lo mismo un burro

que un gran professor!
No hay aplazaos, ni escalafón,
Los inmorales nos han igualao.

Si uno vive en la impostura
Y otro roba en su ambición,
Da lo mismo que si es cura,
Colchonero, rey de bastos,
Caradura o polizón . . .

Qué falta de respeto, qué atropello a la razón!
Qualquiera es un señor! Qualquiera es un ladrón![13]

That the world was and will be a pigsty
I know; in 510 and in 2000, too;
That there have always been crooks, schemers and suckers,
The happy and the embittered, ideals and frauds.
But that the twentieth century is a display of insolent evil,
No one can deny.

We live wallowing in the mess
And we're all covered by the same mud.

Today it makes no difference
Whether you are honest or a traitor,
Ignorant, wise or a thief,
Generous or crooked;
All's the same, nothing is better.
A donkey is the same
as a great professor.
There are no failures, no hierarchies;
People without morals have brought us all to their level.

If one man lives in imposture
and another steals through ambition,
It's the same if you are priest,
Mattress-maker, King of Clubs,
Huckster or stowaway.

What lack of respect, what an assault on reason!
Anyone is a gentleman! Anyone is a thief!

An essayist of the thirties, Raúl Scalabrini Ortiz, would draw attention to the love of boasting, the cult of the hustler among lower-middle-class Argentines. Those who had come to Argentina from Europe had come to *hacer la América*, to make their fortunes; and in common with other immigrant cultures, they had no great sense of the immutability of class divisions. The men, no matter what they were paid, dressed up in the double-breasted suits of dandies. They thought of Buenos Aires as their city and for them it was a place of football stadiums, boxing matches, bars, men in groups, men without women. 'Tenderness destroys the man of the city.' Raúl Scalabrini Ortiz wrote. 'Perhaps he sees it as a dangerous threat to his virility. If he was convinced that tenderness defined a strong man he would make an end to these attitudes.'[14] The rage he found in Argentine men against families or against women was also a rage for significance, to be rich and not to be trapped, to be of consequence. The country had for long sustained itself through its illusions of fluidity and its very incoherence, but now in the thirties it was apparent that these had collapsed, leaving the huge and shabby city and the prototypical *porteño*, 'the man who is alone and waits'. What he was waiting for he could not say.

The centre city near Congress was honeycombed with *pensiones*, cheap lodging houses with exotic names, narrow streetfronts, cramped, tastelessly decorated lobbies and threadbare stair-carpets which led to airless corridors and small rooms with windows facing walls or stairwells. It was to one of these that Eva María came and in one such room that she spent much of the following weeks, short of money and food. She continued to seek work in the theatres on Corrientes until in April 1925 she got a part, the role of a maid with the Argentine Comedy company. A critic said she was 'very precise in her brief appearances'. She had two more parts with the same company and then she lost her job and was unemployed again. A month before her seventeenth birthday in 1936, she found work touring Argentina with another theatrical company. Those productions dealt with scenes from bourgeois life, *What . . . Me Work? Never, Lie and you'll be happy*. The plays were not drawing-room comedies, for they were not particularly witty, nor farces, because they were only mildly titillating. They were about familial misunderstandings – conflicts with mother-in-law, courtship when the elders were not looking, pompous paterfamilias, vain and brilliantined dandies. They were never really shocking, but simply a safe night out for the family filled with guffaws and belly-laughs. Part of the company's repertoire was *The Fatal Kiss,* a free adaptation of a high-minded play by the little-known French dramatist Louis de Gouraviec, that dealt in schematic form with the evils of social diseases. This was sponsored by the Prophylactic League of Argentina, and it was extraordinarily successful, playing to capacity four times a day and critically well received. As one provincial critic said: 'Works of this nature are as sane, as moral and as instructive as they are necessary.' Eva played the role of a nurse, ministering to a victim in the last stages of his awful illness.

Actors on such tours were, according to the critic Edmundo Guibourg, 'picked up, hustled around, treated like cannon fodder.'[15] Only actors in the lead parts stayed in real hotels, the rest were lodged in *pensiones*. When the tour was not a success, the actors were often left without pay; the producers simply abandoned them and returned to Buenos Aires. Eva became friends with Fina Bustamente, another actress, and was photographed with her and some Brazilian sailors in Rosario. Eva inscribed the photograph she gave to Fina 'to my friend and mother.' In Mendoza the company performed *The Fatal Kiss* no less than forty-three times. It was there, according to an actress on the tour, that José Franco, the leading actor and manager of the company, came into Eva's dressing room and told her that if she did not sleep with him she would have to find her own way back to Buenos Aires. Eva cried and asked the prompter what to do. She did stay with the company until it returned to Buenos Aires and was dissolved, when she moved into a *pension* with a friend and began to look for work.

There were a few genuine companies working in the Buenos Aires theatre, but they were rarely able to employ actors on any but the most casual basis. Most companies consisted of a group of actors assembled in great haste for a single production and instantly dismissed if the show was a failure. There was never more than a week of rehearsal, the prompter was in frequent demand, and the scenery – 'walls creased as though they had been packed in a trunk, doors simply nailed onto the walls and furniture clashing horribly with the rest of the set'[16] – was used over and over again. There was a Conservatory where acting was taught, but it had no effect on how the theatre functioned.

In the thirties there was a demand for revues, made up of short sketches, jokes and songs. To compete with them, more and more formula comedies were produced, with trite characters which demanded little or no acting. The backers of such productions could place anyone they wanted in the cast, and would often favour their mistresses and friends. Next, the principal actors would have their say, choosing their relations or friends, and right at the bottom came the *partiquinas,* the apprentices, such as Eva.

Girls from 'decent' families rarely went into the theatre unless the family was very poor, and when they did their mothers would sometimes wait for them backstage and escort them home after the show. Actresses often had a *punto fijo*, a steady man to look after them, or a *caballero blanco*, a sugar daddy, or sometimes they had many men friends. Their status was discussed with animation, not least by the many male predators surrounding them.

In the shoddy dressing rooms the small-part actors and actresses would gossip, play dice or knit. The most they could earn was sixty to one hundred pesos a month, the current industrial wage, and that was only if they did two shows a day and three on Sundays and holidays. They had to provide their own costumes, they were not paid for rehearsal-time, and they were not recompensed if the company went bankrupt, as it often did. They had no security and no unions, so it is not surprising that they sought other means of support. When one young actress complained to her impresario that she did not have enough money for clothes, he laughed and said: 'What kind of actress are you, if you haven't anyone to pay for your dresses?'[17]

The theatres were on Corrientes, and their business was conducted in the *confiterías* lining this avenue: high ceilinged, marble-floored cafés such as the Real or the Nobel which were open most of the twenty-four hours and were packed both before and after dinner. Nearby were such restaurants as Los Inmortales, El Tropezón and El Pasteur, where elegant young men took their mistresses or pick-ups. One of the habitués of the Confitería Real was Pablo Suero, a critic, tabloid journalist and director nicknamed "The Toad". Although he was grossly fat, with a wide face and round eyes, all the actresses looking for work courted him: 'In an hour half a dozen girls would come to his table and he would pinch their asses.' In December 1936 Suero gave Evita a part in his Spanish adaptation of *The Children's Hour*, Lillian Hellman's Broadway success about a girls' school. She played Catherine, a pupil who sews and reads from a textbook in the first five minutes of the play and does not appear again. Another member of the cast found her 'young and pretty, very pretty; with dark eyes, deep red lips and a skin the colour and texture of a magnolia, quite transparent. She seemed a personification of innocence and that is really what she was, very pure inside . . .'[18] She had to be on stage when the curtain rose and she was often late, half dressed, her make-up streaky. Once she fell as she came hurrying on at the last minute and the audience laughed. After one performance she told people in the cast that she had been given some jewellery by her boyfriend in Junín, a lieutenant, and had then been forced to sell it to pay for her lodgings; and they laughed at her, first at the thought of jewellery coming from Junín, then at the thought of selling it.

The play went to Montevideo, where Evita met the nephew of the impresario and some teenage friends of his from wealthy families, *niños bien*. In a photograph taken on the beach at Montevideo, she still has an adolescent's body, small breasts and skinny legs, and a frightened and unhappy expression. A friend of the impresario's nephew who was present thought she was attractive, but 'neither stupid nor intelligent, perfectly unremarkable and rather lower-class.'[19] When the play ended, back in Buenos Aires, Evita came to the Astral theatre, where Suero was rehearsing another production, to ask him for more work. She was wearing a white cotton dress with a green flower print, and a big, floppy hat. The lobby was full of people and when Suero was told she was there he came out of the theatre and began to insult her, regardless of the onlookers. He said he was married and asked her why she was bothering him. When she said she had only called to ask about her job, he said that his having slept with her meant nothing. 'She could barely reply,' said an actress who was present, 'and when she did speak her voice was very soft and she became whiter and whiter.'

In the next two years there were more *pensiones,* more bit parts, perhaps more Sueros and many stretches when Evita was not working. It is not clear how she lived. She had one small radio job on a science fiction programme called *White Gold,* entered and lost a beauty contest, and she presided over a tango contest, introducing the performers and talking to the audience between acts. She was an extra in a movie about boxing, and she was photographed spread-eagled astride a recumbent wrestler in a series of 'photo-features' for a tabloid. On stage she was given either non-speaking or otherwise minor parts, as a member of a crowd, a pregnant maid, and on one occasion, an odalisque.

For six months she lived with a young actor who wanted to marry her.[20] She had, according to a cousin of the actor, 'a real apartment, a home with furniture and everything, a real life, a decent life,' and then one day she came home to find the apartment entirely empty; the actor had found 'someone respectable' and now he was going to marry her. He had left, taking everything and Evita returned to her *pensión* rooms.

For a time afterwards she worked in a company where the leading actress, Pierina Dealessi, liked her, and it was she who taught Evita to speak on stage. She remembers that Evita was hungry, unhappy and careless about herself, her hands were cold and sweaty, and she came to the theatre early because it was warmer than her room and she had nowhere else to go. She was making less than before, only 180 pesos a month, and of that she sent some to her family in Junín.

At some point during her first few years in Buenos Aires Evita began to change in the way she dressed and presented herself to the world. It is unlikely that she did this knowingly, because she was never analytical about herself; but her bitterness and her desire to avoid humiliation had toughened her and improved her defences. The gossip about her which ran riot once she had become powerful dates from these years.[21] Since it was retailed mostly by men, there was an element of sexual hostility in it, but this does not mean that it was not at least partly true. In 1937 Evita was hardly an actress at all, merely a girl who wanted to act and who appeared on the stage just often enough to give her hope of becoming an actress. By 1939 she had become quite successful. She had not, as people still say, become a *putita* who slept around for parts, nor a courtesan who took presents and manipulated her admirers. These images of her belong in the category of fantasy. But she had learnt how things worked.

She began to frequent the offices of *Sintonía,* the movie magazine which she had read so avidly as an adolescent, seeking (according to a journalist who worked there) 'a mention in the gossip column, a feature or a photograph.'[22] The magazine's editor, Emilio Kartulowicz, was a good-looking man in his forties who drove in car races. Evita would sit waiting for him, polishing her nails and chatting with assistant editors, and her name became 'linked' with his, as they used to say at the time. It was also linked with those of Juan Llauro, a manufacturer of household products, and Hector Blomberg, an alcoholic middle-aged poet who wrote radio scripts for a living.

In April 1939 a new radio company was formed to broadcast a cycle of Blomberg's work. It was headed by Pascual Pelliciotta and 'Eva Duarte, the young and dynamic actress'. *The Jasmines of the Eighties,* a love-story set in *belle époque* Paris, went on the air a few days before Evita's twentieth birthday, and there were features about her in magazines, including a cover photograph by a well-known fashion photographer. As the company worked its way through several more confections, there were more puffs, romances within romances, soaps within soaps: Eva in a hat, Eva in a fur coat, Eva's cheeks beside the cheeks of soft-eyed, slick-haired actors. 'Eva Duarte wants to know why Marcos Zcuker isn't thinking of marriage,' a caption coyly enquired, "and the boy humours her with this reply, "I'll stay single as long as I retain my taste for the bachelor life, and I wouldn't think of marriage as long as you wear that tigress' skin." ' 'Truly,' the caption ended, 'there is something feline about that skin.'[23]

There had been a heroic period of broadcasting in the 1920s when artists were paid in the goods produced by the sponsors, ham or soap; but the Argentine radio was now the second largest commercial network in the world, after the United States, and the most lucrative source of employment for actors and singers. There were several radio stations in Buenos Aires. The largest of them, Radio El Mundo, had just moved into its new headquarters with a marble lobby, a formal staircase and seven studios. As radio took hold in Argentina, reaching out from Buenos Aires to the farthest provinces, the soap operas came to occupy a special role in the country's life. In the mornings there were tangos, boleros, housework music for the maids; in the evenings light music, news and sports. At 5.30 pm began programmes for women to listen to as they took their tea and waited for their men; the hour of love. *Chispazos de Tradición* (Old-time Gossip), an epic of rural inconsequentiality, was the first Argentine soap and it became an instant and extraordinary success. The radio manufacturers equipped special sound trucks and despatched them to remote villages that had no electricity or radios. The whole village would come to see the trucks and listen to the rural words from the city.

A half-hour instalment was a 'chapter', and a successful work might run to many chapters. A good writer was capable of turning out a script in two hours, so he could do his work on the day of transmission, delivering the script to the director at 11 am. Then the sound effects were written in: 'a door shutting, a door opening, a horse on asphalt, a horse on earth, the steps of a woman, the steps of a man.' In the afternoon the cast assembled with the sound man and his gramophone. A narrator with a sonorous, trembling voice set the different scenes, while music signalled changes of mood. At the rehearsal and later for the evening's live broadcast, the actors simply stood round the microphone and read from their scripts.[24]

These productions resembled recitals rather than dramas. They carried factitious but intense emotion to a high pitch and held it there, whatever the incidentals of time or place. Eva was pretty, photographed well for the publicity, and her soft, plaintive and monotonous voice had the timbre needed to project the moods of the soaps. Their formula was love frustrated, usually over a great number of episodes, then love fulfilled in the final one. As the vehicles of their provincial audience's fantasies, the heroines were always young, always poor and obscure, always hopelessly in love with men beyond their station, and always chaste – though there might be moments when they were led astray. They suffered endlessly and then they were rewarded. Eva was good at conveying suffering. When she found the soaps she found her acting career.

In 1940 she had two small parts in movies, an epic about Argentine Independence in which she wore a wig, and a rural comedy. Neither was successful, though the movie magazines, having printed their usual hyperbole about imminent stardom, went on sleazily to speculate on her relationship with the boss of Pampa Films. 'She was Paradise for him,' the omniscient copywriter of the radio magazine *Antena* declared. 'It is not for nothing that she is called Eva . . . Did this Romance come to pass? The reply is frankly yes; there was a Romance and there was a sad ending. It ended as all Romances end . . . .' Such 'features' simultaneously made the star and denigrated the person, glamour being equated with loose behaviour. Often the scribes of the movie world simply invented these entries – some of them were indeed formulaic, interchangeable except for the names – but often they were based at least on common knowledge, if not on fact. Their real function was not to tell the truth, but to say what might have happened, and Evita's presence in these columns meant that she had arrived, at least in the terms of the copywriters.

Only once since leaving Junín had she been back to see her family. That was when she was on tour and had learned that Erminda was ill with pleurisy. Then doña Juana had asked her to stay at home, but she refused. When Erminda later came to Buenos Aires to ask the same thing, Evita said she might return some time, but 'not as a failure', only when she had conquered Buenos Aires. Juan had come to Buenos Aires to work in the soap business and he was now the only member of the family at all close to her. He had met many of his actress friends through his sister, and it was he, according to Erminda, who arranged the next step of his sister's career. Until now it had been the producers and radio station proprietors who had been interested in her work, and it was they who encouraged her to form a radio-theatrical company. They paid her salary and contracted with several sponsors. Juan altered this situation by arranging for all of Evita's programmes for the next five years to be sponsored by Guerreno, the makers of 'Radical Soap', the company for whom he had first worked in Junín. This did not guarantee Evita an income, since it did not specify how often she would broadcast programmes, but it made it likely that she would become very successful since Guerreno advertised a great deal on the radio. A year later her company moved to Radio Argentina, and later in the same year it merged with another quite successful company and moved to Radio El Mundo, the most important station in the country.

By 1943, after two years' work with her own company, Evita was earning five or six thousand pesos a month, which made her one of the best-paid radio actresses of that time. She moved into a small apartment near the radio station in the Barrio Norte, the city's best residential district. Her smile was no longer sweet but hard and teasing, and her hair was up-swept and rolled in the elaborate style of the forties. The actor with whom she jointly ran the company, Pablo Raccioppi, did not like her, but he admitted that she was thoroughly dependable in a milieu where dependability was, after all, a primary asset. She took her role as head of the company seriously enough to rebuke Raccioppi for being over-lenient with a girl who lived outside the city, had a child to look after and was late for rehearsals. 'This isn't a charity,' she told him. 'If she can't arrive on time at 10 am, let her stay at home and find something else to do.'[25] She also had become aware of the value of appearances. There were two cafés on the block of the Radio El Mundo studios, and the actors would all go to the cheaper one together after rehearsals. Eva suggested to Raccioppi that this was a bad idea. 'As leading actors...we have to make our way,' she said. 'We can't go to the same café as everyone else. I suggest we go to the corner *confitería* and have our tea away from the herd.' She had been in Buenos Aires for six years, she was twenty-three and she felt, or wanted to feel, like a star.

3

The Colonel and the Actress

The nearest the Second World War had come to Buenos Aires was the pursuit and scuttling of the *Graf Spee* off Montevideo in the Rio de la Plata in December 1939. Yet the progress of the war, reported in detail in every newspaper, engrossed and divided Argentines. There were Argentines who supported Germany and Italy because they were of German or Italian origin, Argentines who called themselves fascists and Argentine nationalists who wished ill to the British. Set against them were Argentines who lamented the fall of civilized France, applauded the British resistance and the entry of Communist Russia into the conflict. The government maintained Argentine neutrality as it had done in the previous war and the policy was good for the country's business interests. The British themselves encouraged this position since for a while it enabled Argentina to send goods to Britain in safety. But the government was by this time so generally resented and despised that its neutrality seemed less a matter of good sense than evidence of national weakness. Few Argentines wanted to fight in the war, but it became the issue around which national passions about the future of Argentina developed. So deep were these passions that they led to a state of muted conflict defined by one historian as 'cold civil war'.[1]

By this time there were different faces in the government but they looked the same. The Conservatives had been fraudulently elected in 1932 and fraudulently re-elected in 1939, and though it has since become apparent that their policies had several important, if unforeseen, effects on the country, it seemed they had done little but keep their old ideas intact. They represented the landed class, which had always done business with the British, and it seemed that they would agree to whatever the British insisted on. They placed their relatives in positions of power and when there were scandals – over the purchase of land for army bases, the regulation of public utilities, the speculation in raw materials – they suppressed them *en famille*. The other parties were divided internally and their attempts to unite came to nothing; there seemed little point, in any case, since there was every indication that the government would resort to fraud in the next elections. By 1943 it seemed again that only the Army could resolve the impasse and restore democracy. Though there were a number of plots, none succeeded; either the government was too strong within the Army and could thus thwart the attempts, or the Army, divided like the country about the future, could not bring sufficient force to bear. Thus amid public attitudes of rage or cynicism, the 'Infamous Decade' of the Oligarchy came to its close.

Robustiano Patrón Costas[2] had been selected by the government to be the next President in June 1943. Patrón Costas was known to the public as the owner of Salta, a province of northern Argentina. His sugar plantation, El Tabacal, extolled by his supporters as a model of paternalist capitalism, was associated in the public mind with the evils of the sugar monopoly – company stores that kept labourers in their debt, and supported conditions of filth and disease. He was a very rich man and he had become richer still with the great increase in the price of sugar during the previous year. Although he was a senator, he had few expressed opinions, taking the Allied side but being on excellent terms with the German embassy. But he did adhere to the principle of electoral fraud. While the newspaper he financed let it be understood that he did not believe the *peons* of El Tabacal should vote in secret, the candidate defended fraudulent electoral practices by attacking 'a fraud far more pernicious than the other one: the demagogic actions of parties swindling the public with spurious promises'. The candidacy of Patrón Costas was certainly unacceptable to most educated Argentines; more important, it was also unacceptable to the Army.

On Friday 4 June 1943, a grey winter morning, the banks and business houses were shuttered. There were rumours of a revolution, but there were no troops, nothing on the radio or in the papers, and only police patrolling the streets. Later that day, however, six thousand troops marched on the city and after an error which led to an exchange of shots at the naval academy, they entered the Plaza de Mayo and captured the Casa Rosada at 2.30 pm. A crowd cheered the troops and smashed some buses belonging to the English transport monopoly. By Saturday there was a new President, General Arturo Rawson, who had led the coup, and a government that declared itself against 'fraud and venality' and 'usurious capital'. It was publicly announced that the former President, Ramón S. Castillo, had embarked on the minesweeper *Drummond* with all his ministers, one of them in such haste that he fell and cut his lip on the gangplank; that the

Drummond had sailed towards Uruguay and then sailed back again to La Plata, south-east of Buenos Aires, where a dishevelled and humiliated Castillo had disembarked and tendered his resignation. That Sunday, there was first silence, then the announcement that General Rawson, who had been President for a day, had resigned and that General Pedro Pablo Ramírez had taken his place. The banks and businesses opened again, the burnt-out vehicles were removed from the streets; and so ended the Revolution of 4 June and the era in which the landed interests ruled Argentina.

Evita was not interested in politics, but she could not long remain indifferent to the implications of the military government. One of its principles, vaguely expressed, was that the country should be modernized, managed and taken in hand where the previous regime had allowed it to run itself. The government's belief in regulation extended to radio,[3] which before the Revolution had thrived without it. Major Alberto Farías, a stern provincial and a patriot, was placed in charge of communications and ordered to eliminate abuses in advertising and programme content. As part of his programme to smarten up Argentine radio, the Major eliminated battle scenes, whistles, and bugle calls; forbade the adulteration of classical music; and prevented foreign musicians from speaking on the air in their own language. A memorandum went further, requesting 'the elimination of all theatrical expressions carrying sombre descriptions, sensational narratives or stories tending to undermine morale as well as all idioms adultering the language etc.'[4] Folk music was preferable to tangos, and scripts for soap operas, a form of entertainment of which the Major disapproved, were no longer to be improvised on a day-to-day basis but must be submitted to the new Inspector for Posts and Telecommunications for approval at least ten days before they were broadcast. A list of vulgar expressions and neologisms to be avoided was circulated to writers and station managers.

Evita was not working at the time of the coup, if the movie magazines are to be believed, because she 'had not been offered a role worthy of her'. Actors, writers and producers all complained about the 'dictatorship of entertainment' and then submitted to the regulations. If they wanted to work, they needed permits from the second floor of the Ministry of Posts. Before, the sponsors or the owners had determined what went on the air and it was to them that the actors addressed their pleas, but now the owners had as little power as the actors. But the military had no experience in running radio stations, only the vaguest prescriptions of moral tone, and the race to influence them began. The officer in charge of allocating air-time, Colonel Anibal Imbert, who wore his uniform at work and made his staff stand to attention in the corridors, was not easy to reach, let alone influence, so the actors went to his assistant, Oscar Nicolini. In explanation of Evita's success at reaching him it has been said, incorrectly, that Nicolini was a lover of doña Juana's in Junín, also that Evita had an affair with Imbert. What seems to have happened is that Nicolini simply liked Evita and that he was responsible for getting her project approved by Imbert. In any case, the project was likely to appeal to a colonel in charge of raising the quality of soap opera. There had been other series about famous lovers in history and this was substantially what Eva was proposing. Her project was entitled 'Heroines of History' and promised – this is probably what appealed to the Colonel – to deal with high moral and historical themes. Her scriptwriter was Francisco José Muñoz Azpiri, a lawyer and aspiring historian. In September 1943 the radio magazine *Antena* announced that 'the celebrated leading actress Evita Duarte, an artist who has acquired ample and justified renown in a long and varied acting career in important radio stations' would shortly begin this series. The first programme was about Madame Lynch, the wife of the Paraguayan *caudillo*, who became the leader of her husband's army after he died, and who killed herself rather than fall into enemy hands.

The army government, like the country as a whole, was divided over the question of neutrality, and was therefore obliged to maintain the neutral policy which had been followed by the previous government in spite of increasing pressures from the United States. It had made no commitment to hold elections and its officers envisaged the continuance of rule by decree. To those, therefore, who had hoped for a resolution of the question of neutrality or for free elections, it seemed as though the government was totalitarian. It had in fact, little in common with the European dictatorships, but the interpretation is easy to understand. There was an odd lack of connection between the government's ostensible aims and its practices and this gave the sense of a phony war, of a state of emergency that was unjustified. Sometimes vetoes on political activity were exercised, sometimes they were not; the same was true of restrictions on the press. There were people who spied on behalf of the government, but no one knew against whom they were acting; sometimes, measures would be taken against the fascists or nationalists, sometimes against the supporters of the Allies. The only perceptible economic sign of the war's effects were odd shortages of such consumer goods as tyres, and nickels for the trams. Otherwise, the economy was experiencing its most substantial boom since the twenties. To replace what could not be imported, whole industries had grown up, and with them housing shortages, particularly for workers coming in to the city.

The shortage of armaments was particularly vexing to a military government, and it was here that Argentine remoteness and unreality about the war had their most curious consequences.[5] In August the government, still resistant to the United States' demands that it abandon its position of neutrality, asked Washington for supplies. These were refused in somewhat humiliating terms; the US government made public the request and enquired why it should be supplying a neutral country with links to Germany. President Ramírez, acting through a German businessman who claimed to be a friend of Hitler's, then resolved to send a mission to Germany to enquire about arms. A naval officer was assigned this mission, given the post of Consul in Barcelona, and entrusted with a number of compromising documents. As soon as his ship arrived in Trinidad he was detained by the British and searched, and the documents were found. In January the Allies revealed that the documents were in their possession and US ships of the South Atlantic fleet sailed into the Río de la Plata. Argentine funds in US banks were frozen, while the Argentine government debated, unable to agree on the formula it would have to adopt to legitimize its surrender.

The hot summer evening of 16 January 1944 was interrupted by a mild tremor, just enough to shake a chandelier and cause people throughout the city to ask what was the matter. In fact it was a serious earthquake that completely destroyed the Andean town of San Juan. For some time there were no communications with the stricken area, but eventually the government launched a major campaign for the victims. In San Juan, the President examined the destruction; in Buenos Aires a nationwide collection on behalf of the families of the six thousand dead was begun.

The San Juan fund was raised by the Secretary of Labour in the military government, Colonel Juan Domingo Perón. It was he who had the idea of an 'artistic festival' – actors and actresses, escorted by members of the armed forces in dress uniform, would go through the streets of the capital with money-boxes. At the end of the week there would be a great subscription gala, with tangos, comedians, expensive tickets. Perón himself went through Calle Florida at the promenade hour with a group of theatrical, film and radio personalities. He wore a white tunic, a peaked cap and black boots and people stopped to put money in his box.

In Evita's memory, the occasion on which she met Perón was simply her 'marvellous day'. Perón in his memoirs, recalls that Evita came into his life 'as if brought by destiny . . . . It was a tragic earthquake that struck the province of San Juan and destroyed virtually the entire city that made me meet my wife.'[6] At the Secretariat of Labour, where the actors came to collect their money-boxes.

> there was a woman of fragile appearance, but with a strong voice, with long blonde hair falling loose to her back and fevered eyes. She said her name was Eva Duarte, that she acted on the radio and that she wanted to help the people of San Juan. I looked at her and felt overcome by her words; I was quite subdued by the force of her voice and her look. Eva was pale but when she spoke her face seemed to catch fire. Her hands were reddened with tension, her fingers knit tightly together, she was a mass of nerves.

Evita had been standing behind some other actresses, but she came forward to offer advice. Everything should be simple because extravagant charity occasions were old-fashioned, and the actors should remain in the better parts of town. 'We have to get money from those who have it,' she said. Perón was impressed: '"Good, very good," I said then, "since this is your idea, organize it!" And so it happened; she organized everything.'[7]

Perón's memoirs are not a reliable source for those seeking information about his career or his private life. His memory is in any case often hazy and where his actions have become the subject of controversy, he is almost invariably concerned with placing himself in the best possible light. This is the case wherever he speaks of Evita, his wife, his most important political follower and the person who more than anyone else and almost as much as he did, gave an identity to the movement which bore his name.

Evita was not a blonde at that time, nor did she organize the collection, but she did go through the streets with a collecting-box, and she went to the gala at Luna Park stadium with Rita Molina, a singer friend of hers. That night Evita wore a black dress, long gloves and a white feathery hat. After speeches by Perón and the President, Rita and Evita, like the other actresses, went over to Perón to say hello and congratulate him. They sat and talked with him and when the evening ended, around two in the morning, Perón and Evita left the stadium together.

Perón was taller than most Argentine men and muscular, with a wide face, black hair combed back and plastered down. He had a movie actor's smile, a wide mouth and white teeth, and a heavy, almost brutish appearance – a masculine man in a country where there was a cult of masculinity. He was a widower, aged forty-eight, but he looked much younger. A form of psoriasis, recurrent and incurable, had left a reddish rash around his cheeks and chin and required the application of a special cream. But this cream also functioned as make-up and with it Perón photographed well. This was fortunate because in the first months of 1944, he was frequently photographed. He was the only member of the government to have emerged as a figure of public interest. His middle-aged, soldier-bureaucrat colleagues evaded the press or addressed the public in curt military-style communiqués, but Perón was infinitely ready to talk, to explain. He gave the impression of a man who took pleasure in power and he could communicate this pleasure to others. His manner was direct and friendly, neither hectoring nor condescending.

At this time Perón held two distinct government portfolios simultaneously. Each morning he was Secretary of War, second in importance to the Minister of War, and each afternoon he was Secretary of Labour and Social Security, which was his own ministry, though it did not as yet confer cabinet rank. He rose at six and took a brief siesta at noon. In the evenings he held informal meetings with civilian politicians in his small apartment on Arenales and Coronel Díaz.

To some of these meetings and to some of the public functions which he attended, Perón brought a very young girl whom he called his daughter. A few days before Perón met Evita, he had taken the girl to the première of a radio series at the station where Evita worked. However, this girl was not Perón's daughter but his mistress. He had met her in Mendoza, where he commanded the Argentine Army's ski unit, and now that he had met Evita, it seemed that he was uncertain what to do with her. It is said that it was Evita who resolved the problem. One morning, after Perón had left for the War Ministry, she hired a truck, loaded it with her own possessions, took them to Perón's apartment and told the girl to go back to Mendoza.[8] When Perón returned for his siesta, he found that Evita had unpacked and settled in his apartment. 'He said absolutely nothing to her, he never questioned her at all,' a friend of Perón's said, 'and from that day Evita stayed with him.'

That week, Perón and Evita appeared in public together for the first time, when one of Evita's programmes was broadcast. The Colonel inspected the microphones and spoke to the other actors. Later he, Evita, his friend Domingo Mercante and the director of the station, Jaime Yankelevich, posed in a group photograph for a movie magazine,[9] an indication that times had changed and that it was time for the public to know.

Perón's personality, like Evita's, has been the subject of persistent controversy in Argentina. It is difficult to find convincingly disinterested judgments of him or of what he accomplished. To those who were *for* him, he was a generous, gregarious and sexually attractive man, a brilliant teacher and intellectual, a good judge of men and a political genius capable of holding together the loosest coalitions. To those *against* him he was at various times a coward, a nazi, a tyrant, a bungler, an embezzler and a child molester, a man who disgraced his caste and bankrupted his country. This sort of judgment is still repeated, even after Perón's death.

He was not young when he suddenly became important in Argentine politics in 1943, and he was an old man when he returned to Argentina to be elected President over thirty years later. The most persistent error of those who have written about him has been the tendency to see Perón consistently as a dictator. Even if there is such a thing as a 'quintessential Latin American dictator' – which is doubtful – his ambiguous record shows him not to conform to this type. For someone supposedly ruthless, his behaviour was often surprisingly mild. He did accumulate great power, but his use of it was erratic rather than consistently authoritarian and when the time came he was eager to renounce his position of power to avoid bloodshed. In this he can be contrasted with some of his succcessors. His own persistent misrepresentation of the past, the most striking thing about his memoirs, is likewise not the conclusive indictment of Perón that it is often made out to be. Perón did distort the past, but not always to misrepresent what he had stood for. As an old man in exile, he wished to seem better than he had been.

There is no one Perón, but a series of Peróns. The complexity of his career comes not from his character, which was at first straightforward enough, bluff and charming, but from his ability to reflect and interpret the mood of his supporters and also to shape it. He appeared to be mysterious – a word often applied to him – because his personal attitudes were never clear. He stood for many things, often contradictory. His evasions were great, but so, too, were the uncomfortable truths he conveyed to Argentines. But in 1944, when Evita first met him, he was still in the process of becoming Perón. For Argentines he was his matinée idol's smile, his deep, brown voice and his uniform. These came first, long before his policies were elaborated or it was clear what sort of a man he was.

He was born in Lobos, in the province of Buenos Aires, on 8 October 1895. There is some doubt as to whether his family originated in Sardinia or Italy, an ambiguity which Perón would sustain.[10] In the company of Spaniards, he would say that his ancestors had settled in Sardinia when that island was ruled by Spain, hence he was called Perón and not Peroni; and to an enquiring Italian journalist, he would insist that there were Perrons or Peronis all over Piedmont, and that was where his family most probably came from. His paternal grandfather was a distinguished doctor, but his father aspired to own land, so the family moved south when Perón was small to the desert of Patagonia at the southern end of Argentina. This was the outer frontier of a country that was still, in that decade, mostly frontiers. Mario Perón worked as a tenant farmer first in Santa Cruz, near Rio Gallegos, then at Puerto Camerones. He then acquired his own farm, which he called La Porteña in memory of Buenos Aires. He had not been married to Perón's mother when their son was born, but he had married by the time Perón went to military school at the age of sixteen. Perón seems not to have been as bothered by questions of legitimacy as Evita was, though he never made this fact public.

When Perón joined the Army in 1915 it was still profoundly influenced by its German connections. German officers came to teach in Argentina and Argentine officers completed their military education in Germany. The Argentine Army received its arms from Germany, wrote its manuals in the German style, wore spiked helmets and marched the goose-step. Perón claimed that his favourite books at the military school were Plutarch's *Lives* and Lord Chesterfield's letters to his son, but all his life he retained an admiration for formality and discipline, qualities that he would associate with his German training.

When he graduated, Perón was posted to a series of remote garrisons in the interior of Argentina. He had fenced at military school and he fenced and rode a lot in these years. He also devised plays and entertainments and made his fellow officers take part in them. Because of his contacts with recruits, his first-hand experience of garrison life and his close view of rural poverty, he was able to grasp the realities of Argentina. The early twenties were years of labour troubles, and the Army, in the absence of a sufficient police force, was frequently called in to maintain the peace. At the 'La Forestal' strike, when five thousand workers were picketing a *quebracho* processing plant, Lieutenant Perón compelled the owners to open the company stores and supply the strikers with the food and water they had withheld.

In 1926, Perón was promoted captain and returned to Buenos Aires. The military establishment was located in or around the capital, and Buenos Aires thus exercised the same sort of dominance in military affairs as it did in other matters. The Palermo barracks in the outskirts housed the First Division, the War Academy, and the palace which was the Círculo Militar, the officers' club. Farther out, to the north-west, lay the military academy, the large Campo de Mayo base and the El Palomar air base. The 1930 coup, in which Perón played a minor role, was a small-scale affair executed by only nine hundred men, but its success established the Army in a new relation to political power. The Army had often debated the future of Argentina through its publications or in lectures at the Círculo Militar. Now that the Army had intervened in national politics, such debates became more frequent. Perón spent four years at the Superior School of War as a pupil and in 1930 was appointed Professor of Military History. He was an admirable lecturer, and he acquired the reputation of being a scholar, but as yet he played little part in the elaboration of the Army's ideas. The Army debated whether or not it should intervene in politics, although it had already done so, and as the decade wore on, whether it should impose a corporate state on Argentina or whether liberal Argentine notions of society were still viable. If he had ideas on these questions, Perón did not make them public. But in his analysis of the 1930 coup he did describe General José F. Uriburu, the proponent of a fascist Argentina, as 'a perfect gentleman and a person of decency, even when conspiring'.[11] He did not, however, approve of the debilitating effects of conspiracy on Army morale and discipline. 'Every officer will have to be kept busy in professional tasks from reveille to retreat,' he wrote, 'otherwise this will go from bad to worse.'

Perón had married Aurelia Tizón, a teacher, when he was thirty-three years old. Aurelia played the piano, did the housework and waited for children that never came. She accompanied Perón to Chile when he was appointed military attaché to that country in 1936. Soon after Perón had returned to Buenos Aires in 1938 Aurelia died of cancer of the uterus.

In 1939, months before the outbreak of World War II, Perón was sent to Europe, ostensibly to study the methods of the Italian army's Alpine troops. He skied in the Alps and travelled in Hungary, Austria, Germany, Spain and Portugal. Years later it would be claimed that in Spain he had an affair with an Italian actress, and though he later discovered she had become pregnant, he was never able to find her or her child.[12] In Germany, he had the sense of 'an enormous piece of machinery functioning with marvellous perfection, where not even the smallest piece was missing'. He was to become a great exponent of the theatrical in politics, its ceremonies and spectacles, and he was attracted by the spectacle of Mussolini's pseudo-imperial Rome. 'I would never have forgiven myself in my old age,' he said later in life, 'if I had been to Italy and not known so great a man as Mussolini. He gave the impression of a colossus when he received me in the Palazzo Venezia. . . . I went straight into his office where he was writing; he lifted his face to me and came over to greet me. I said to him that I knew his great works and I would never have gone home without shaking his hand.' In reality, it appears that Perón never met Mussolini. Some twenty years earlier he told his official biographer that he had seen Mussolini only once, when war was declared on France and Britain and he, Perón, was standing 'a mute witness amidst a clamorous multitude'.

Perón returned to Buenos Aires in 1942, influenced by the apparent strength of wartime fascism. At this stage he seems to have been convinced, like many Europeans, that the European democracies, Britain and France, were in a state of irrevocable decline and that the real choice lay between communism and fascism. As a nationalist, of course, he welcomed the defeat of Britain, and he hoped the Axis powers would win the war. Yet he was not in the strictest sense a fascist, though he would frequently be called that; nor was the military lodge he helped to found shortly after returning to Buenos Aires, the GOU (Grupo de Oficiales Unidos), concerned with strict implementation of fascism in Argentina along German or Italian lines.[13] Its members, including Perón, at this stage were concerned with what they thought was a more practical question, namely what would happen after the war. Perón believed that Mussolini's Italy demonstrated that the interests of capital and labour could be reconciled by the state and it was this principle that he urged on his colleagues. But there were officers who did not subscribe to these ideas, 'cave-dwellers', as Perón referred to them, 'of whom there are a great number in any army'. Indeed these individuals seem to have been responsible for Perón's next posting, as director of the mountain training centre in Mendoza, where the Colonel spent a year teaching recruits how to ski.

After the June Fourth Revolution, in which he did not, once again, directly participate, Perón found himself in a strong position. The GOU gained considerable leverage over the government. He had influence over General Edelmiro J. Farrell, his boss at the War Ministry, and he was thus able to beat off numerous attempts to bring him down. President Ramírez, 'the little stick', as he was called, disliked Perón and was wary of his growing influence, but he was unable to mobilize sufficient support within his government to get rid of the 'colonels' Colonel'. He was frequently warned of the danger Perón represented; it was said that his wife found his dilatory behaviour so surprising that she had his coffee tested each morning to find if he was being drugged. By the time Ramírez finally attempted to curb Perón's power by securing the resignation of his supporters in the government, Perón was able to summon a meeting of garrison commanders and secure their support. The President decided not to arrest Perón – and could in fact no longer have done so, since his residence was surrounded by troops loyal to Perón. Next day, 24 February 1944, the President signed his own resignation, drafted by Perón. General Farrell, Perón's boss, became President, and Perón took his old job as War Minister. He was now in name as well as in fact the strongest man in the government.

'I knew,' Perón said in 1972, by way of explaining his obliquely executed assumption of power, 'that revolutions begin with these little things that come to nothing, these merely political things. . . . At the beginning one has to stay well outside the field of fire'.[14] On 27 October 1943, Perón had been given the apparently minor post of director of the Department of Labour, at that point a dependency of the Ministry of the Interior. The President had remarked of the post that it was 'a toy without interest, of which he will soon tire,' but there were others who came to see Perón in his small office and listened to his ideas about labour, who were not of the same opinion. 'If things take their course,' a Chilean journalist wrote, 'Colonel Perón within a brief space of time will have become the strong man, the great *caudillo*, of the Argentine republic, and who knows for how long.'[15] By November, Perón had already been promoted to the post of Secretary of Labour.

Perón was undoubtedly ambitious, a quality which accounts of his career have usually emphasized. But ambition alone does not account for what he did with the Secretariat of Labour, and beyond that, how he transformed the entire perspective in which labour was viewed in Argentina. He began from the position that unions were either powerless or dominated by 'extremists', socialists or communists. But instead of concluding, like previous governments and many of his own colleagues, that the answer was to repress further the 'political' unions and impose greater curbs on union power, Perón began to encourage the creation of new unions, as well as to purge the old ones of 'extremists'. He granted the workers considerable privileges while reassuring those who questioned this policy, that these privileges were strictly limited by the power of the State, which he proposed to increase in labour matters. In his speeches he could sound like a policeman or a social revolutionary, depending on who was listening, but he did believe in the coexistence of discipline and union privilege, justice and order. His policies distressed many people in the union movement as well as many conservatives, but there was little they could do about them; as sole spokesman for labour affairs in a government which was acquiring extraordinary power, Perón could do much what he liked.

Perón had assistants, most notably the lawyer José Figuerola, who had served in the government of the Spanish dictator Primo de Rivera. For the most part, however, the impulse behind these changes came from Perón and the demands of Argentine unionists. It was Perón who overturned tradition by personally receiving labour leaders and listening to their complaints. Retirement pay was granted in industries where there were unions, and in those where there were none unions were formed and comprehensive labour agreements signed. With the creation of work tribunals, labour disputes in principle ceased to be simple questions of public order to be dealt with by the police. With the Statute of the Peon, signed in November 1944, the government established a minimum wage, paid holidays and medical care for agricultural workers.[16] Though this may not appear revolutionary, it was deeply resented by the great landholders who regarded any intrusion of the State into their affairs as a trespass on private property.

Only twenty per cent of the work force was unionized before Perón's arrival, and that percentage was heavily concentrated in old industries, such as railways and food-processing plants. Some unions were led by communists or socialists, though they were never as powerful as Perón maintained. But the existing unions had not expanded to include the great number of workers who had come to Buenos Aires in the 1930s or more recently. No one before Perón had done anything for them, and it was they who became the first Peronists and remained the most persistently faithful ones. They made possible the odd paradox of a 'workers' colonel,' a working class brought into politics not by a President, but by a man who was merely a member of an authoritarian government which otherwise had little interest in such questions.

* * * *

When the funds for the earthquake had been collected, Perón says in his memoirs, he asked Evita to work with him at the Labour Secretariat. He wanted someone to develop a labour policy for women and beyond that, he 'wanted a woman to be the female leader of [his] movement', and he thought that Evita had the qualities of devotion and initiative which the task required.[17] He says that she told him she needed to organize her affairs at the radio station and then she came to work with him. But this was not in fact what happened. For the first year and a half of their life together Perón and Evita lived not as collaborators, but as Colonel and mistress.

Until they moved to Calle Posadas, where they rented two apartments on the same floor with adjoining doors, they shared an apartment and received visitors in such a way that there could be no doubt that they lived together. The dress designer Paco Jamandreu came to Perón's apartment at Evita's request. Evita was wearing 'silver-grey satin pants, a sky-blue blouse and white shoes with cork heels' and Perón was lying on the bed.[18] The apartment was small and badly furnished, 'like a middle-class home in the village I came from'. Evita showed the designer a cupboard full of furs: jackets and coats, silver and blue foxes, otters. She was 'going to be in the movies' and wanted some new clothes, she explained. Later, she went to a society photographer with Perón's chauffeur and took him with her again when she selected the prints. These show her in a conventionally feminine pose, but the face is hard; in one of them her head is supported by her wrist and there is a conspicuous ring on her finger.

In her radio work, Evita continued her cycle of lives, playing Queen Elizabeth I, Sarah Bernhardt and the last Tsarina. Radio Belgrano increased the publicity for these programmes and broke her current contract to offer her a new one, for 35,000 pesos, the 'biggest contract to date in radio broadcasting', as Evita explained in an interview.[19] At a special lunch in Evita's honour, attended by Perón, Radio Belgrano gratuitously announced that this new contract would be renewed next year. Film stock was in short supply during the war, as it was imported from the United States, and restrictions had been placed on its export to Argentina as part of US foreign policy. Mexico, which supported US policy but had a far smaller movie industry than Argentina, was allocated substantially more stock. What did arrive in Argentina came through the government and it was after first Perón, then Evita, had procured some of the available stock that the San Miguel studios announced her new contract and her coming role in a movie that was about to go into production.

It was for this first starring role that Evita bleached her hair. She arrived at the studios driven by a uniformed chauffeur in the Minister of War's limousine. On the set she was, according to the director, 'quite direct and undiplomatic', making her relationship with the Colonel clear and attempting to enlist the cast and the director, a maker of social-realist exposés, in Perón's support. The film, *La Cabalgata del Circo,* was a pot-boiler about a theatrical troupe in nineteenth-century Argentina – braids and bustled costumes – and the other star, Evita's rival in love according to the plot, was Libertad Lamarque. She had come from the same sort of background as Evita, and after a great success as 'the queen of the Tango' had been successful first on the stage in musical comedies, then on the screen as both singer and actress. She always played sweet girlish parts for which her high-pitched, squeaky voice, curly hair and chubby appearance suited her, and she was not a good actress, but certainly behaved as if she was. She supported the Allies, and she now found her dislike of Evita fortified by her opposition to Perón. At some point a trivial argument began between the two actresses, which developed into a shouting-match and ended with Libertad Lamarque supposedly slapping Evita across the face. For those who hated Evita, this slap and its aftermath became a *cause célèbre.* [20]

In May 1944 it was announced that the performers of the broadcasting industry had formed themselves into a union, and that, in line with government policy in other industries, this would be the only organization permitted to operate within the industry. It was further announced that Evita had been elected president. What had probably happened is that Perón had suggested the union be formed and the other actors found it prudent to elect his mistress president. Perón brought the appearance of procedural normality to the event by receiving Evita in his office, where he formally accepted her petition. Soon afterwards, Evita added to her daily schedule at Radio Belgrano another programme entitled 'Towards a Better Future'. Those tuned in to the national network at 10.30 pm on 14 August 1944 heard a half-hour programme entitled 'The Soldier's Revolution will be the Revolution of the Argentine People'. Over the sound of a military march, came a commentator's voice:

Here, in the confusion of the streets, where a new sense of purpose is coming to be born . . . here, among the anonymous mass of working, suffering, thinking, silent people . . . here, in the midst of exhaustion and hope, justice and mockery . . . here in this shapeless mass, the driving force of a capital city, nerve centre and engine of a great American country . . . here she is, THE WOMAN . . .[21]

Evita was THE WOMAN and she spoke of the recent Revolution as a 'torrent nothing can withstand'. In soap-opera form, the programme then dramatized, through the inspection by a doctor of a number of recruits, the statistics of TB, illiteracy, and undernourishment in the provinces. Rich women grumbled about their maids, *estancieros* about their difficult labourers, war-profiteers about government interference. THE WOMAN spoke again at the end of the programme:

> The Revolution did not come without reason. It came because something painful and hard had grown in the country, deep down, where there is hate and passion and the sense of injustice that makes the blood rush to one's hands and head . . . The Revolution was made for exploited workers . . . It was made because of the fraud of dishonest politicians and because the country was bankrupt of feeling, at the verge of suicide . . . There was a man who could bring dignity to the notion of work, a soldier of the people who could feel the flame of social justice . . . it was he who decisively helped the people's Revolution.

Then followed a recording of a speech of Perón's written by Evita's own scriptwriter, Francisco Muñoz Azpiri.

These nightly programmes were ostensibly in favour of the government's official versions of commonly proffered truths; actually, they dealt almost solely with Perón, and distorted events to such a degree as to make it appear that the Revolution belonged to him alone. They were electoral programmes, though the government had not as yet announced its intention of holding elections. They represented what Perón would stand for when the elections came, and they were directed towards those he hoped would be his supporters, the masses to whom no propaganda had been directed before, and who did not read newspapers. Evita had no previous knowledge of politics, but the ideas of these programmes became her own. She spoke in the most ordinary language, as a woman who wanted other people to believe what she believed about Perón.

There were always people around Perón in these months, assistants from the Labour Secretariat, officers from the Army, civilian politicians from the Radicals with whom the Colonel had contacts. In the evenings Perón's apartment became a meeting place for his supporters. The visitors were taken in to the small living-room with its windows on the street by Perón's maid, but if Evita was back from her broadcasts, Perón would first introduce her to the visitors. She would stay throughout the meeting, making the coffee, emptying the ashtrays or watching the guests in silence. Her presence among these educated men – graduates of the War College, doctors from the university or lawyer politicians – would not have been entirely acceptable if she had been married to Perón; as it was, it was quite incomprehensible. Evita had little education, and the sort of work she did on the radio was not considered respectable. It would have been permissible for Perón to say, as he had previously done, that she was his daughter and hide her in the back room, or to keep her in a *bulín*, a small apartment, from which she could periodically be taken to dinner and displayed. But to allow her to be part of his life in this way was damaging for him as a soldier and as a politician. As a soldier his prospects for promotion would be curtailed; as a politician he would be involved in scandal. When guests asked those who were close to Perón about Evita, they were told in characteristic *macho* manner that she was someone of limited importance and intelligence, 'one of those tiresome girls who screw all over the place in the hope that someone will give them a part', a folly of the Colonel's.[22]

Evita said so little in these first months that she seemed to bear out this judgment. She knew nothing about politics and there were consequently no grounds for argument, none even for discussion between herself and Perón. She simply absorbed what he thought or knew, becoming his first and greatest supporter. In the light of the conventions of the day, it is inconceivable that she would have entered the world of politics independently. Perón would later maintain that he had selected Evita and trained her consciously and carefully to take his ideas and 'create in them a second I'.[23] In his memoirs he says, 'She followed me like a shadow, listened to me attentively, assimilated my ideas and worked them out in her own extremely quick mind; and she followed my directives with great precision.' But he cannot then have guessed how useful she might become, particularly in the light of the criticisms made of her presence. Did he let her do what she wished because she loved him? Or did he deliberately thrust her on those around him as he would deliberately do so many other unexpected and therefore uncongenial things? Perhaps the explanation is even simpler than this. Perón had come to politics late and he was remarkably free from received notions of how things should be done. It is quite possible that he could merely see no harm in what Evita wished to do, and therefore let her get on with it.

1944 and 1945 were the years of Perón's increasing power within the government, but they were also years of growing hostility to him inside and outside the Army. Even when he became Vice-President in January 1945, his position was not assured and there were incessant plots and counter-plots as the struggle for power within the government continued. In political life, as Perón's importance grew, the question increasingly became: was one for Perón or was one against him?

Night after night Evita scrutinized their visitors to see which camp they were from. This was the first thing she learned about politics; to be perpetually on guard on Perón's behalf, ready to attack before any threat had materialized. She also came to hold a quite distinctive view of Perón's significance. She would say later that she had been 'continuously intimidated' by the injustices of the thirties in her first years in the city, but that she had not had the courage to confront them. 'I wanted not to look, not to feel, not to deal with these misfortunes, disasters, this unhappiness, but the more I tried not to, the more I found myself surrounded by them,' she says.[24] Though her case was different, in that she was an actress and had been successful, it was not wholly dissimilar to that of the masses on whose behalf Perón spoke. They too had come from the interior and been exploited, had been hungry. Evita came to think of herself as one of them, a *grasita,* a 'greaser' as she would later call herself. Who else had helped her but Perón? Who else had loved her?

With Evita's continued presence at these meetings, gossip about the couple began. A political revue of 1944 contained a sketch of two colonels, Perón and Imbert, a rumoured ex-lover of Evita's. A cross Imbert would not speak to Perón. 'I don't know what it is,' Perón said. 'We've both served the same body.' It was well known that Evita had got her movie role by providing film stock. *Sintonía,* the movie magazine, published a cartoon in which a suitor was turned away from the front door by a maid who said, 'The girl says she doesn't need you any more. She has some celluloid and she'll become a star.' As early as spring 1945 there were demonstrations outside the apartment in Calle Posadas, Perón's supporters shouting: 'Get married, get married.' Among those who were familiar with the couple, the arrangement was considered sufficiently unusual to require explanation in terms of some oddity in Perón's or Evita's character. Thus Arturo Jauretche, a politician who came to the apartment, would suggest that neither Perón nor Evita were sexual beings and that they were not in love, simply 'two joined wills, two commonly expressed passions for power'.[25] A more prurient version of this fantasy concerned Perón's childlessness, the pomade he applied to his chin, and his previous 'daughter'. It was suggested that he had been impotent, that his cure demanded the application of this cream, but that he was only able to perform sexually with very young girls.[26]

It was around this time that the fantasy that Evita was a prostitute took hold. It was based on assumptions about her 'obscure past', and it also reflected contemporary sexual myths. The idea that prostitutes, far from being exploited, possessed some mysterious power over men, was widely adhered to. Because they were not emotionally engaged in their sexual activities, prostitutes were supposed to be able to enthral their victims and hold them powerless. Wives were restrained by the marriage vows from such behaviour, and anyhow no decent woman would use such wiles and devices – the predatory prostitute was, of course, taken to be lower-class. This set of assumptions was readily applied to Evita, the more so because it seemed to validate the contempt and fear Perón inspired, particularly among the Argentine wealthy.

Evita was doing three radio programmes a day, and at one point she was also making a film. She went, with or without Perón, to galas, award ceremonies, trade union meetings. In September 1944, her never very robust health broke and her doctor forced her to take a rest. Yet in her interviews with the press, which were now frequent, she would portray herself as 'a quiet woman, homeloving, fond of the family', who shopped, took tea, went to romantic movies (particularly when they starred Greer Garson or Laurence Olivier). In the evenings, she said, 'I study, do my artistic work, have a light supper and if there are no friends I go to bed early.'[27] Once, anticipating some criticism, she said, 'You see, I am only a woman. . . without any of the merits or defects ascribed to me,' and then when the reporter coyly suggested she was 'quite indifferent to rumour', she replied in the approved code, 'My life is clear as the day. My career is an ordinary one.' She then lent herself to the formulaic falsehoods of the movie business: that she spoke French, that she liked to ride horses and sail, that she had been to acting school, and that she was a reader of 'classics and contemporaries' – she was even photographed in a library before a stack of books. In an interview about the characters she represented on the radio she once said: 'Almost all of them are tortured souls, exhausted by pain and despair. . .with a great capacity to love and suffer, quite authentic, of course, and one hundred per cent human, but I could not live with them. I understand them, I live them, but away from the microphone, they do not exist for me. . . .'

Lies about movie stars were so habitual that these interviews were often concocted by journalists. But for Evita, these conventional untruths became part of an entire structure of lies about herself. She told no one, not even Perón, that she was illegitimate, and she had by now completely buried her unhappy past in Junín and her years of unsuccess. The lies about her relationship with Perón were simply political additions to those she had previously told. A woman did not say that she was the mistress of a politician and that she was doing political work on his behalf.

Evita's next movie was supposed to be *Dawn Over the Ruins,* an epic about the San Juan earthquake, in which she would play a part similar to the woman in her propaganda programmes. Then in February 1945, she acquired some more film stock through Perón, took it to the studios and asked for a part in a new movie called *The Prodigal.* This had already been promised to another actress, Mecha Ortiz, but the studio boss owned the major casino in Mar del Plata which the government was about to nationalize, and in his efforts to secure better compensation for his property the part was given to Evita. The role was an odd choice for a twenty-four year old actress who because of her relationship with the most important man in the government could have whatever part she wished. The film was set in nineteenth-century Spain and dealt with an affair between an ageing society beauty and a young engineer constructing a dam. The woman was called *The Prodigal* because of her great and reckless generosity. From her large and secluded house, she helped and protected the villagers, spending her considerable fortune on good works. She had a melancholy and passionate personality, she was known as 'the mother of the poor', 'the sister of the sad', and she was thought to be a 'sacred person'. At the end of the movie, the young engineer leaves her and she discovers that her land and house have been mortgaged to pay for her good works. She then kills herself.[28]

There was no shooting schedule for the movie. It was filmed whenever Evita was free from her other work and it consequently took several months to make. Perón came to Mendoza while the exteriors were being shot, and drove around the hills with his mistress. Evita had miscast herself in the part of a woman far older than herself and her performance was quite without dramatic impact; her voice was monotonous, her gestures stiff, her face, though beautiful, was quite devoid of expression. Once, with *The Prodigal* in mind, Evita told her confessor, Father Hernán Benítez, that her performances had been 'bad in the cinema, mediocre on the stage, and passable on the radio'.[29] But there was no one working in the Argentine cinema of the 1940s who would now be called a good actress. 'The actors and actresses,' wrote Waldo Frank of the Argentine cinema, 'have not learned a film technique. They behave before the camera like human beings. That is, they express emotion, thought, struggle, like human beings, but since they do so with no capacity of translation to the film medium...they appear on the screen to be trained animals going through human motions.'[30] Evita never had the sexiness of Tilda Thamar, 'the Argentine atom bomb', but she was no worse an actress than many more successful than she.

By September 1944, a rough cut of *The Prodigal* was made. Evita liked the film and also the stereotype of suffering, sacrifice, and destruction she had portrayed. But it was the last film she ever appeared in, for before it could be premiered, her acting career – since 1935 she had appeared in twenty plays, five movies and at least twenty-six soap operas – was swallowed up in her other life, her political life with Perón.

4

17 October 1945

1945,[1] the year of the fall of Berlin and the end of the war in the East, was also the year when the ladies and gentlemen of the Sociedad Rural, gathered at their annual agricultural show in their best winter tweeds, demonstrated with whistles and jeers at the Argentine Army's traditional display, a huge and antiquated caisson pulled by a team of gleaming horses and led by two bemused conscripts.[2] Trivial as it was, the incident received attention and rightly so; it signalled one of those strange but characteristic shifts in Argentine politics. As the winter became spring, the military government, hailed only two years previously as the only force capable of restoring morality to political life, would come under such ferocious attack from every direction that it seemed it would either collapse under the pressure, or if it were determined to retain power, bring the country to a state of civil war. The feelings aroused by events of that spring were intense and long-lasting; not only the shape of politics in Argentina would be altered, but the way Argentines thought about themselves, and particularly the way they thought about the two people at the centre of the crisis, Perón and Evita, who had not anticipated it and who, like the other actors in the drama, possessed only the slightest understanding, let alone control, of the events that engulfed them.

The sense of drift that afflicted the military government by the beginning of 1945 was quite special. With the belated declaration of war on the Axis Powers in March 1945, made under great pressure from the Allies, it had forfeited its claim to uphold the principle of neutrality. The nationalists inside the Army and out who supported the principle felt betrayed, and the opposition, the vast majority of the country's upper-middle class and politically active citizens, felt vindicated. This was the 'terrible year' for the Argentine Army; each advance of the Allies was celebrated as a defeat for the 'Nazi-fascist' government, as it was called. The July 1945 declaration that elections would be held before the end of the year, a concession to circumstances on the part of the government, increased the intensity of such propaganda attacks.

Much of the hatred was directed not at the government but at Perón. All of the political parties – Communists, Socialists, Radicals and Conservatives – had good, if conflicting reasons to dislike Perón and his policies, but it was not over these issues that arguments developed. There was a great hatred and fear of Perón, and this was expressed, through the preoccupations of the rest of the world that year, in the assertion that he was a Nazi. This was not a figure of speech, it was widely believed. It was in these months that one of the most quaint but most durable fantasies of Argentine politics first appeared; the suggestion that in the closing months of the war, a 'Fourth Reich' was established in Argentina in a clandestine series of episodes involving Perón, Martin Bormann and Evita.[3] This began as a rumour, but documents were later faked and made public. The story was repeatedly discredited, but it nonetheless survived, even into the second period of Peronism in the 1970s.

It was easy to be an Argentine democrat that spring, for all one had to be was against the government. All the multiple rifts in Argentine politics combined to make a single huge division, Nazi or democrat, government or opposition, pro-Perón or anti-Perón. For a while the most prominent democrat in the country was not Argentine at all, but North American. Spruille Braden, the US ambassador, had no sooner presented his credentials than he found himself a principal actor in Argentine politics.[4] It is not clear whether this was his doing or whether, to begin with at least, he was manipulated by those Argentines who found his presence useful. A blunt, massively built man, he was an heir to the Braden copper industries in Chile. He met Perón several times and found him 'incredibly brutal and ignorant'. Braden's speeches, delivered at luncheons at places like the Plaza Hotel, became important events in the opposition's campaign, and they were reprinted in full in the opposition newspapers. The opposition political parties had formed a Junta de Coordinación Democrática, and Braden lent himself to this organization. He had few doubts that the government was fascist, and since this was what his audience wished to hear, he received ovations everywhere he went. In July Braden went on a tour of the provinces which, judged solely in terms of the audiences he attracted, was a remarkable success. Yet Braden's background was bound to prejudice his campaign. When a mine in Chile collapsed in the midst of his tour of the interior, the streets were filled with leaflets denouncing the Braden interest and 'cowboy diplomacy'. The suggestion that the 'democrats' were controlled from abroad would be one of Perón's electoral points, but it was the United States ambassador who first created this issue.

As early as June, political groups had taken to the streets. Perón would address rallies organized by the unions outside the city, in the industrial suburbs such as Avellaneda or Berisso, reiterating his own reforms and evoking the community of interest that united the Army and the workingclass. He would usually describe the opposition as 'an obscure combination of foreign elements, reactionaries, bankrupt politicians and egotistical plutocrats'.[5] His speeches were raucous and combative; they were meant to incite rage, and they did. The city itself remained the preserve of the opposition and there were frequent rallies and student demonstrations, particularly after dusk. Stones were thrown and machine guns fired from passing cars. Sometimes it seemed as though these nightly affrays had no function beyond the simple, theatrical statement of hatred, group against group, class against class. 'It is a sad commentary on the present state of Argentina,' wrote the correspondent of *The Times,* 'that in a city where rioting occurs almost punctually an hour after nightfall, withdrawal of the police gives the public confidence. The citizens of Buenos Aires take rioting playfully and laugh as they run for cover from revolver bullets, but the laughter changes quickly into panic when the screeching of sirens and the clatter of hoofs heralds the arrival of the police.' For the students, the police were 'fascists' or 'assassins'; the attitude of the police would later prove of some importance.

19 September 1945, a beautiful early spring day with a pale blue sky framing the city's avenues so that they seemed to lead in each direction into the purest air, was the high mark of the opposition's attempts to bring the government down by popular demonstrations. The 'March of the Constitution and Liberty' began early in front of the shuttered Congress building. A strike of buses and trams arranged by the pro-Perón unions had sealed off the outlying parts of the city, but the demonstrators arrived nonetheless, with banners bearing phrases from the Argentine constitution or likenesses of the great men of the nineteenth-century Argentine history – San Martín, Belgrano, Sarmiento and Roque Saenz Peña. They represented every political party and they were all opposed to Perón. The city's shops, the stock exchange, and most of the factories were shut, and many employers had given their workers the day off. Escorted by trucks equipped with loudspeakers and by hundreds of officials, the column made its way down Avenida Callao towards the river, gathering people at each intersection until it came to Plaza

Francia, which contained a statue given to the Argentines by the French community of Argentina. Partly to mark their delight in the liberation of France and partly to identify their own democratic values with those of the European country to which they had always felt closest in politics and architecture, the crowd stopped there. Speeches were made and the phonetic versions of the French Marseillaise printed in the newspapers made it possible for everyone to sing that national anthem before dispersing in peace. Perón retired for a siesta while the crowd passed his office, but Braden later declared that he had marched in the demonstration and that he had asked embassy personnel to make a correct estimate of the number of people present.

It was agreed that this was by far the largest demonstration ever mounted in Buenos Aires, though there was some disagreement over how many people had been there. Most newspapers put the number between 250,000 and 500,000, while the police somewhat cautiously gave a figure of 65,000. Yet in the excitement created by the conviction that the city had, briefly, been taken from the government by a well-organised and peaceful mass movement, one important fact about the march was overlooked. Most of the city's working class and most of its unions did not take part in the march. The rhetoric used to describe the march stressed that the marchers represented the people and that the government could not resist the will of the people so forcibly expressed. Only a few observers cast doubt on such assertions, and fewer still were as sceptical as *The Times* of the real aims of the political organization behind the march: 'Many contradictory reports are emerging from Buenos Aires, some of them to the effect that the movement has been organized by "moneyed interests" who are using the popular front for the effect which this produces.'

At the time the march seemed to destroy the government's claim to represent anyone at all. There was a hasty, ill-organized and unsuccessful military coup, in response to which the government, panicking, reimposed the state of siege lifted five months earlier, muzzled the newspapers and reimprisoned all the recently liberated politicians. The students of Buenos Aires summarily occupied the university and were ejected only after the most savage police assault on the buildings. 1,600 arrests were made and one student was killed by a group of *Aljancistas,* right-wing vigilantes. Once again the city was filled with demonstrations and processions, but this time they were angry and bitter and were brutally dispersed by the police. By the first week in October, the city's jails were again filled with politicians and students, although there was little in the papers about this. Far from restoring order, the reimposition of censorship encouraged the wildest rumours. It was apparent that the military government would not survive, at least in its present shape, yet it was far from clear just how the situation would change as long as the government's main source of support, the Army, was faithful to it. The *porteños* were reduced to reading the newspapers as if they were encoded information. Yet it is unlikely that many of them could have foreseen the implications of the announcement on Tuesday 9 October that Oscar L. Nicolini had been appointed Secretary of Communications.

Nicolini was a friend of Evita's. He had some real claim to the appointment, having worked for twenty-five years in the same department and having been a supporter of Perón's labour policies from the beginning. It is unlikely that Evita did not encourage the appointment, but it is just possible that Perón, who had enough problems in those days, was not aware that the announcement of his mistress's friend's promotion had been made; the decree effecting it was signed and issued by the Minister of the Interior. In ordinary circumstances the appointment might have been considered routine, but circumstances were no longer ordinary. The post had been promised to a Lieutenant Francisco Rocco of the Campo de Mayo garrison, a powerful group thirty miles outside the city. What annoyed the officers of the garrison was not so much the fact that one of them had been passed over as the implication that at this critical stage in the affairs of the Army, the government and the country, decisions were being improperly made. They now took violent objection to Perón's private life.

'It was something that annoyed us very much, to an extent that perhaps few can understand today,' explained General Eduardo Avalos, Commandant of the Campo de Mayo, many years later.[6] Perón's open cohabitation, though certainly not compatible with 'the pure tradition of the Army', had been tolerated, but there had been many small episodes which had bothered or vexed the Army. Thus, at the formal swearing-in of a minister, one general had been shocked to see Evita attending a ceremony that was none of her business and leaning irreverently over the back of the presidential chair. On another occasion, Perón had come to the President's antechamber carrying a record player, and said to the generals assembled for a cabinet meeting, 'Boys, come and listen to a poem about the Revolution.' The recording consisted of a stirring march and a florid ode. 'What do you think?' Perón asked. 'Do you know who did that? . . . My friend Evita.'

Episodes like these, set in the chaos in which the Army now found itself, came to seem a coherent indictment of the Colonel.

He was one of the officers who had been trusted with the task of saving the country from the corruption of civilian politicians, but through weakness or personal ambition he had surrounded himself with undesirable people, chief of whom were Evita, her friends and her family with its 'obscure antecedents'. Many of the officers were probably more concerned with the 'subversiveness' of Perón's organizing activities, but they perceived this issue, too, in exclusively moral terms and it merged into the general perception that Perón had let them down. 'As a result of Perón's attitudes,' explained General Gerardo Demetro, head of one of the regiments stationed at the Campo de Mayo, 'the Revolution had lost all sense of hierarchy . . . We were convinced that it was our duty to stop the nation from falling into the hands of that woman, as in fact ultimately happened.'[7] Because of the reimposition of the state of siege, all regiments were confined to barracks and the fate of Perón was thus discussed and determined in a military-democratic fashion. The pressure to present Perón with an ultimatum came from the younger officers, and it was agreed that General Avalos, as Commander of the Campo de Mayo garrison and a personal friend of Perón's, should be sent to deliver it. When Perón refused to cancel Nicolini's appointment, Avalos went to the President and when the President was unsympathetic he went to see Perón again; who since it was Saturday, was sitting in his apartment with Evita.

While a few hundred yards away the student recently killed in a street clash was being buried amidst vivid expressions of public grief and hatred, Perón told Avalos that he was sick of the garrison's interference and accused the General of trying to separate him from those on whom he could depend. Evita several times interrupted the argument to tell Perón not to give way, and when Avalos insisted that Perón would do well to listen to the officers, she said. 'What you should do is just leave the whole mess, retire from the Army and get some rest . . . let them work it out themselves.'[8] Avalos left the apartment without securing Perón's assent to the proposal with which he had come and returned to the garrison, where his report of Evita's part in the discussion can only have increased the feelings of aversion towards her. Perón was exhausted and depressed and spoke of retirement to those who came to his apartment that evening and the following day. Out at the base that Sunday, the troops were placed on alert ready to march in to the city. On Monday 8 October there was another meeting between Perón, Avalos and some of the officers opposed to Perón. It was Perón's fiftieth birthday, and after receiving a gold cigarette holder from his colleagues at the War

Ministry, he told Avalos he would not resign. The next day, a delegation went to the President and informed him that unless Perón resigned instantly, the troops would march on the city and put an end to the government. The President rang Perón, who was in his office at the War Ministry surrounded by his supporters, and Perón wrote out his resignation from his three government posts and also drafted a petition to resign from the Army.

On the day Perón resigned, Evita received notice from Radio Belgrano that her employment was to be terminated, even though she was in the middle of her role as an astronaut in a science-fiction fantasy about the world after the third world war. She had been with Perón throughout the meetings of the previous days in Calle Posadas, and each day when Perón left she stayed by the telephone waiting for further news. Yet whatever hopes she had had that Perón's resignation would put an end to the uncertainties of the last week, they were not fulfilled.

The next day Evita stood in a pro Perón crowd of fifteen thousand while Perón, under pretext of saying farewell to the employees of the Secretariat of Labour, took the opportunity to defend his policies and ask 'for peace, to carry on our triumphal march'.[9] He also announced a general wage increase and the institution of a system of indexation throughout the country, making wages and salaries proof against inflation. He received a great ovation and the speech was broadcast nationally. This infuriated the officers who had hoped that the Colonel would depart quietly according to military etiquette, much as the previous President had departed following Perón's urgings. That afternoon, there were the first threats against Perón's life and the Campo de Mayo called for his arrest and internment. In the evening Perón, dressed in his boots, breeches and undervest without a jacket or shirt, and with Evita at his side, received the expressions of sympathy of his disappointed supporters.[10] He spoke dispiritedly of the end of his career and to those who pointed to the success of his speech that morning, he could only reply that one must wait and see. There was desultory talk of leaving the city, leaving the country; perhaps they should hire a boat and go across the river to Uruguay. Present were Domingo Mercante, Perón's collaborator at the department of Labour; Roberto Petinato, an official of the propaganda section of the Secretariat of Labour; and also a German-Argentine, Rodolfo Freude, an early Perón supporter, whose industrialist–rancher father had prominently supported the Germans during the war. At 9 pm a captain friendly to Perón arrived with the news that the authorities, under pressure from the Campo de Mayo, had decided to arrest Perón and would shortly be at the apartment. Perón stirred from his lethargy, pulled out his pistols and said that no one would take him and that he would kill the first soldier who came through the door. At Perón's behest, the party set about fortifying the apartment, clearing the furniture and pulling the shutters closed. Evita, who was in the kitchen, asked Petinato what was going on and when he told her, she gave him 300 pesos and sent him down to the corner store to purchase enough cans of food for several days. The civil servant did as he was told, and when the storekeeper asked him why he needed so much food, said he was going on vacation on his yacht. He returned to find Perón washing out the bathtub to keep the salads fresh, and an air-force brigadier who had an apartment in the same building, and three soldiers armed with machine-guns, guarding the door and windows. Thus embattled and ready for the worst, the party spent the night.

It is hard to imagine that Perón would have offered any resistance had the Army come for him then, since he had avoided the possibility of violence two days earlier by leaving when asked. On the other hand, his fears of violence were real enough. In 1930, in the course of another crisis, a crowd had broken into the President's apartment and sacked it. Perón, symbol of 'Nazi-fascism' to much of the country, was as hated as President Yrigoyen had ever been. However, that night passed without incident and in the very early morning a messenger arrived with the news that the decision to arrest Perón had now been reversed. Everyone relaxed and Perón and Eva discussed what they should do. They decided to leave the city and began throwing their clothes into suitcases. At 5 am, Evita's brother Juan arrived at the apartment with Román Subiza, a rancher friend of Perón's. It was decided that Perón and Evita would first rest at Evita's sister Blanca's apartment and then drive to Subiza's later that day. Perón gave to Mercante a piece of paper explaining where he was; if the police approached him, Mercante was to hand the card over, thus absolving himself of any responsibility for Perón's actions.

That afternoon all of them – Perón, Evita, Mercante, Subiza, Freude and Juan – got into Freude's Chevrolet, but before they had left the city, they made another change of plan at Freude's suggestion. Instead of going to the ranch, they decided to go to Tres Bocas, an island eighteen miles outside Buenos Aires in the Tigre delta, a profusion of small, willow-covered islands, holiday or weekend places accessible only by launch.[11] It seems that Perón was still uncertain whether to leave the country or not, though there were those around him, like Mercante, who were pressing him hard not to leave. In the context of doubt and indecision, the island was perfect; if Perón suddenly decided to leave, he could hire a launch and cross the river to Uruguay.

Freude's father owned the only house on the small island. It was a wood cabin that he used as a summer home, whose sole resident was Otto, a German caretaker who spoke no Spanish. Perón and Evita spent that night and the next day alone with him on Tres Bocas, walking around the island and trying to decide what they should do next. Freude and Juan Duarte had remained on the mainland, where they were picked up by a detachment of local police and detained for questioning. Once it was ascertained that Perón and Eva had left their apartment, the order to find them had immediately been issued to all local police units. When Mercante arrived in Tigre that afternoon, on his way to see Perón, the police detained him also; and Mercante, who thought it would be better if Perón's political future was kept out of the hands of ordinary policemen, called Colonel Aristóbulo Mittelbach, the head of the Buenos Aires police, and offered to take him to where Perón was hiding. Mittelbach then drove out to Tigre with a detachment of his own men. He was met there by the local police, Duarte, Freude and Mercante. All of them embarked in two police launches and made their way out to Tres Bocas.

As the two launches crossed the narrow stretch of brown water in the late afternoon, the figures of Perón and Evita could be distinguished near the landing dock. They were strolling like lovers, Perón's arm around Evita. The man who until two days previously had been the most powerful man in the country was dressed in sports clothes, his mistress in trousers, her long blond hair unpinned. The Chief of Police spoke briefly to Perón. He said that the President had ordered Perón's detention on the grounds that his life would be endangered by the political situation. He would be taken either to a Navy vessel or to a fortress operated by the Navy on the island of Martín García in the midst of the Rio de la Plata. Perón was furious; as an army officer he demanded to be placed in the hands of the Army. He had little support among naval officers and feared it would be harder to secure his release if he fell into their hands. Mittelbach agreed to speak to the President, and Perón, appeased for the moment, agreed to be taken back to Buenos Aires. With Perón and Evita aboard, the two launches returned to Tigre, and thence the party made its way to the city. Perón, Evita, Mercante and the Chief of Police rode in Mercante's car; Evita cried most of the way back.

It was raining heavily by the time they returned to the city and there were a dozen black police cars parked on the block where

Perón and Evita lived, sealing it off from both directions. Perón packed another set of bags, while Mercante explained to him that he still had support among the unions, that all was not lost. An hour later another police official arrived and informed Perón that the President was adamant he should be detained by the Navy and that it was time to go. At that precise moment, Evita came into the apartment and asked what was happening. When Perón told her she began to cry again and asked him not to go. Mercante, Perón and the policeman left the apartment, Evita holding on to Perón's arm, until the policeman pushed her hand away from the elevator door, leaving her behind. At the docks, the rain had turned into a damp, heavy mist. Mercante escorted Perón to the gangway of the gunboat *Independencia* and Perón, just before walking up the steps, told his friend to look after Evita.

In most treatments of the events of the next few days, whether hostile or favourable to Perón, Evita's actions are clearly depicted. It is one of the rare occasions of her life when almost everyone is in agreement about what she did. Perón was in prison, politically defeated; she was in Buenos Aires, organizing his return and triumph, working effectively in his stead as surrogate or kingmaker. It is thus that she has been represented, depending on political preferences, as a power behind the throne or a political militant, but either way she has admirably fulfilled, in Perón's absence, the role of agent in history, orchestrator of events. Only after her actions have been described is there controversy and then it has been characteristically intense. For those who have loved her, there has been a faithful, suffering Evita who by her example inspired people to rise up on Perón's behalf; and for those who have hated her, a liar, a scheming woman who drags Perón back to fulfil her desires for power and revenge. But Perón in either case has been considered of little importance; it is Evita who has saved him in the hour of defeat.[13]

Neither of these billboard images have much connection with what actually happened. October 1945 was quite without precedent in Argentine history, and its implications would dominate the events of the next thirty years. Evita and Perón became different people. In a political context they ceased simply to be characters and became representatives of the forces that had altered politics, and perception of the events in exclusively personal terms followed naturally from what they had become. Because Peronism arose out of these events without the presence of Perón, the role of bringing it to birth, with all the reverence or

odium which that action implied, fell to Evita. She did not actually
do many of the things that were later attributed to her; and what
she did do was rather less sensational.

As the mistress of a fallen politician, Evita no longer had any
claims to consideration. She was hated almost as much as Perón.
She no longer enjoyed the benefits of police protection and was
lonely and frightened. Ten years of radio work had come to
nothing since Radio Belgrano had closed its doors to her. A small
incident, almost a 'demonstration', occurred outside her apartment in the course of which a lady from a 'good family' (with three
names) spat on her doorstep. The newspapers, controlled by the
opposition, had previously displayed some caution in mentioning
Evita by name. (The socialist newspaper *La Vanguardia* the
previous month had referred to 'a leading actress who has recently
achieved great popularity, not precisely by being an actress. We
will not mention her name so as to avoid giving you satisfaction' –
the last phrase reading in Spanish *evita darte satisfacciones.*[14]) Now
they referred to her as 'the actress Duarte'. Evita might well have
chosen this moment to desert Perón – such a decision would have
been in line with the selfishness attributed to her by many of her
enemies. Instead, she was loyal to him because she loved him, and
she attempted to get him out of the damp, windy, island prison
because she was afraid that his life was endangered.

Years later she wrote, 'Those eight days still cause me pain –
greater, far greater than anything I would have experienced had I
spent them in his company, sharing his pain.... I went out in the
streets, looking for friends who might still accomplish something
on his behalf.... I never felt – and I mean this – quite so small, so
utterly unimportant as I did during those eight memorable days. I
went through all the *barrios* of the great city. Ever since, I have felt
that I know everything about the hearts that beat beneath my
country's sky.'[15]

There were a number of friends who were still prepared to assist
her – Mercante, Román Subiza, her brother – but since she did not
want to remain in Perón's apartment or to compromise them by
staying at their apartments, she sought out Pierina Dealessi, an old
friend with whom she had begun her acting career. Evita told
Pierina that she had no idea what would happen to her or Perón,
and she wondered whether he had been killed.

In Perón's confusion on the night of his arrest, he had wavered
between abandoning his career then and there, and postponing
decision in the hope that his allies in the Army or the unions might
effect some favourable change in the situation. Before his
detainment in Martín García, Evita had wanted to leave the

country with him, and that is what he suggested she should arrange. The conventional means of being released from gaol was to apply for a writ of *habeas corpus* from a federal judge. In most cases, if no charges had yet been pressed by the government, the judge would issue the writ on the simple condition that the applicant had first sent a registered telegram to the Ministry of the Interior containing his intention of being out of the country within twenty-four hours. The application procedure was simple, an easily-obtainable palliative for the uncertainties of Argentine political life which many of Perón's opponents had had occasion to use.

The day after Perón had been taken away, Evita accordingly went to the office of Atilio Bramuglia, a labour lawyer who was also a personal friend and supporter of Perón. When she asked him to file a writ on Perón's behalf, Bramuglia was not sympathetic. He told her that if Perón left the country he would probably never be able to return. When Evita pleaded with him, he told her she was an egoist with no sense of what the country needed; all that interested her was saving her man and going off with him.[16] Evita returned to see him twice, and it is said that the last time Bramuglia lost his temper, throwing her out of the room and slamming the door in her face so that she fell over, an incident which Evita never forgot. She was thinking of Perón's personal future; Bramuglia was concerned with Perón's political career.

On 14 October Evita received news of Perón through Colonel Miguel Angel Mazza, an army doctor who had got to the prison island by telling the authorities that Perón was suffering from pleurisy and needed treatment.[17] On the island there was a fort, and around it a number of separate huts that served as cells; it was to one of these, furnished with a cupboard, a bed, a table and a chair, that Perón had been taken. During the day he sat disconsolately at the table writing a justification of his actions 'distorted by my former colleagues in the cabinet and the opposition'. He proposed to call it 'Where Was I?'. He was angered by the insultingly close surveillance and confused because he had no idea what was going on in the city. To Mazza all he could say was that he would do anything to avoid civil war and if that was going to happen he was prepared to leave the country. He sent Evita this letter via the doctor:

My adored treasure,
    Only when we are separated from those we love can we know how much we love them. Since the day I left you there with the greatest pain you can imagine, I have not been able to calm my unhappy heart. Now I know how much I love you and that I cannot live without you.

This immense solitude is full of your memory.

Today I wrote to Farrell [the President] asking him to hurry through my retirement and as soon as I get out we'll get married and go somewhere and live peacefully . . .

They took me here from home, to Martín García and I don't know why I'm here and they aren't telling me anything. What do you think of Farrell and Avalos? A couple of bastards, doing that to their friend. Such is life. The first thing I did when I got here was write to you . . .

You should keep calm and take care of your health while I am away for when I shall return. I would be more calm if I knew you were not in danger and that you were well. Please tell Mercante to speak with Farrell to see if they will leave and we can both go to Chubut [a southern province of Argentina. Perón seems to have been thinking of retiring there]. I also thought you should start some legal paperwork . . .

Be very calm. Mazza will tell you how everything stands. I will do all I can to get to Buenos Aires . . . If my retirement is approved we'll get married the next day and if it isn't I'll arrange things one way or another; but either way we'll put an end to your vulnerable situation.

My sweetheart, I have those little pictures of you in my room and I look at them every day with tears in my eyes. Nothing must happen to you or my life will end. Take good care of yourself and don't worry about me, but love me very much because I need your love more than ever . . .

I'll write a book about all this . . . and then we'll see who was right.

The evil of this time and especially of this country is the existence of all these idiots, and you know that an idiot is worse than a villain.

Well, my soul, I'd like to write all day but Mazza will tell you more than I can. The boat will be here in half an hour.

My last words in this letter will be to tell you to keep calm. Many, but many kisses to my dearest *chinita*. Perón.[18]

Perón's whereabouts during these days had been kept secret by the government. His future only became a matter of public interest on 14 October, when Mazza handed to the newspapers a letter Perón had written to the President demanding his release. There was no cabinet by this stage, as the old one had resigned during the crisis. The President had instructed the Attorney-General to form a new cabinet. Perón's future seemed of small consequence, as his career seemed at an end, and the President's brief communiqué denying that Perón was in prison was not challenged or remarked on, at least not in the press. Many newspapers were in fact well aware of what was going on, but they chose to ignore it. Their reporting was highly selective, excluding anything that did not suit their preconceived notion that 'nazi-fascism' had ended and this was the hour of the democrats.

But even before the President's denial there were brief, well-organised walkouts at the meat plants of Berisso and Avellaneda in support of Perón. Both the rank and file and many union leaders were afraid that the gains they had made in the past two years would be cancelled, and they were not reassured by the new Secretary of Labour's assertions to the contrary. What they had gained came from Perón.

Perón's staff at the Secretariat of Labour was still intact and working on his behalf. Against a background of stoppages in the capital and a general strike on 15 October declared by the sugar-workers of Tucumán, the central committee of the CGT met on 15 October in Buenos Aires. The committee was composed of long-established labour leaders. There was a heated dispute between those who hesitated to associate their future with the political fortunes of the Colonel and those in favour of prompt and unconditional action on his behalf. A third group took the position that the strike was a fait accompli. After labouring for ten hours, the committee delivered a compromise; there would be a twenty-four-hour general strike on 18 October, but no mention of the Colonel would be made in the communiqué declaring the strike. By the time this decision had been made, the situation had already passed out of the union bureaucracy's control; strikes had broken out in factories all over the capital and no one knew who had ordered them, whether they were intended to free Perón or, more vaguely, simply to alert the government to the existence of labour dissatisfaction.

In later explanations of this rash of strikes Evita was later assigned a major role by many people, including Perón himself, who said unrealistically that since the government ignored her merely because she was little-known, she was able to move around the city in freedom: 'She could be seen with [union] people, sometimes in a little bar, sometimes in the houses of union leaders or in the homes of workers sympathetic to our cause.'[19] Evita herself frequently told the story of how, on the evening of the 15th, when she was on her way to a meeting, her taxi passed through an anti-Peronist demonstration and she was stopped, recognized and attacked, her face so badly bruised that she was able to make her way back into the city unrecognized by the police.[20] But this, as well as Perón's account, is a hagiographic improvement on the truth. Even if she did attend one or two meetings, this would not have had much effect, since at this stage she did not know any union leaders, nor did they know her. It is far more probable that when her attempts to secure a writ to free Perón failed, she did nothing, as he had suggested, and hoped that Perón would be released from prison and would marry her, as he had promised.

On the evening of 16 October, Mazza, the military doctor, again made the boat journey to Martín García. He had tried to see Perón before, but the naval authorities had refused to believe that Perón was really ill, and it was only after Mazza had procured some out-of-date X-rays of Perón's chest showing patches on the lungs that he was allowed to go. But this time a Navy doctor who was not a supporter of Perón's was sent along to make sure Mazza was telling the truth. The two doctors arrived at the fortress around midnight, and Mazza went first into Perón's cell and embraced him warmly, whispering in Perón's ear as he did so that he must under no circumstances allow the other doctor to examine him. Perón did as he was told, insisted he was ill and demanded a proper examination by military doctors in the military hospital in Buenos Aires. The night was spent in argument and telex messages, until at 3 am this issue of military punctilio was resolved and the two doctors, this time accompanied by Perón, returned to Buenos Aires. The night was damp and cold, and on arrival at 6 am Peron was immediately placed in a special room of the hospital, under guard. When Mazza came out of the hospital, he found Evita and her brother Juan in a car parked on the street. Evita said to him, 'He's still a prisoner', and although Mazza replied that he was not, but that she could not see him because he was being guarded for his protection, she was furious with him. Mazza made a bargain with her: he would arrange for her to speak to Perón if she then did exactly what Perón told her to. When they spoke, Perón told Evita that she must be calm and keep out of danger. Thus on 17 October she remained obediently at home.

Very early the next morning the first workers arrived at their factory gates, coming to work from the tenements or from the small houses on the long, straight streets that constituted the outer suburbs to the south. But this morning many workers did not enter their work places. At some gates there were pickets but not in sufficient numbers to explain by themselves what now happened. At each gate were groups who said they were going to the city to find out what was happening, and they set off, collecting other groups they met on their way, until there were enough workers heading for the city to constitute first a crowd, then a mass of people, sustaining each other in their will and momentum and filling the outer avenues with their shouts, their improvised banners and signs. In Avellaneda, the union leader Cipriano Reyes watched the crowd cross the huge articulated iron bridge linking the suburbs with the city over the Riachuelo, until the police came and raised the bridge. Then the crowd, as if enacting some prearranged spectacle, began to cross the river by crowding onto boats, or by standing on half-submerged rafts made of planks lashed together with rope.[21]

These people were smaller and darker than those who anxiously watched them come. Most of them had come to the city in the great migration of the previous decade and some of them, living and working in the *cinturón obrero*, the 'workers' belt', had never before ventured into its centre. But they were not violent, at the very worst they shouted insults at those who incredulously watched from their windows.

That day, which seems so hard to forget [the writer Delfina Bunge de Galvez would recall] the streets of Buenos Aires witnessed an unusual phenomenon. From all points outside the city groups of workers could be seen arriving, the poorest of the working class, and they passed by under our balconies. It was the mob we had always feared so much . . . and with that old fear still within us, our first impulse was to close our shutters, yet when we looked out we were amazed . . . because the mob before our eyes seemed as if touched by a miraculous transformation. These visitors to the city were gay and calm. There were none of the hostile faces or raised fists of previous years. More than anything we were surprised by the slogans, the shouts; *nobody's head was demanded.*[22]

The city's transportation system, debilitated by the walk-outs of the preceding days, was now overwhelmed. Buses were stopped and taken over by the crowds and people hung on the backs and sides of them or sat on the roofs. People grabbed the wires attaching the poles of trams to their overhead conductors, disconnected them, swung them around and reconnected them, thus forcing the drivers to go in the direction of the city. 'There was a noise of many thousands shouting and singing,' said the novelist Leopoldo Marechal, 'and the noise grew and seemed less of a continuous roar, until I could distinguish first the music of what was then a popular tune and then these lyrics:

> I'll give you,
> I'll give you, my beautiful country,
> I'll give you something,
> Something beginning with P,
> Perón . . .

and each *Perón*, coming at regular intervals, echoed through the streets like a cannonade . . .'[23]

People coming to their offices in the centre of the city had found the shutters up and had gone home, so the centre had become empty and still. Now it slowly began to fill up with this crowd. The pickets at the factory gates had suggested to union members that they go to the Plaza de Mayo and, though there was no organization capable of directing a crowd of these proportions, it was to this square that people now went. Some went on from there to the military hospital, where they stood shouting Perón's name. It was one of the first hot days of early summer, so the crowds splashed in the fountains, and though more and more people arrived from the suburbs, swelling the first 20,000 who arrived at noon until the plaza was quite full, the gathering retained its oddly gentle character, more of a holiday or *kermesse* than an organized demonstration.

Sir David Kelly, the British ambassador, had been alarmed at the prospect that the British-owned tramways would suffer, and he now drove over from the embassy in his limousine. His chauffeur wished to turn back, but the ambassador insisted on driving through the crowds. The mounted police in the square had ceased to keep the crowds back and were chatting with them. As the crowds parted around Sir David's limousine, they mistook the ambassador for a *yanqui,* but they were not offensive, 'simply shouting in a friendly fashion; *Abajo Braden! Viva Perón!'*[24] There were only two remaining government ministers, since the rest had resigned, and the one which Sir David was able to see in the Casa Rosada promised to do all he could, but added that he was not sure what could be done; indeed the government was not sure what was going on. General Avalos was responsible for calling in the troops, but it seems that in the morning he had been misled by conservative police reports of the march. Once its true size had become apparent, he had hesitated in the face of the likely bloodshed that a clash with the army would bring about. He was now unable to get troops into the city from the Campo de Mayo, thirty miles away, before nightfall. The police had evidently sided with the marchers, many of them having even joined them, wearing civilian clothes; and it was thus, against all expectations, that the unarmed and unorganized crowd temporarily found itself in control of the capital.

While the crowds waited and cried out for Perón, the Attorney-General, unaware like the rest of the city of precisely what had happened, came at last to the Casa Rosada, bearing a list of the prominent Argentines who had finally agreed to form a government. But it was too late for such measures – the President no longer commanded the means to enforce them.

Perón had spent the day in his room at the military hospital, at first in a state of informal confinement and then, as the situation became clearer, in the happy position of being the key figure in a drama which had developed in his absence. A number of messengers from the presidency came to see him, last of all Avalos, his successor, who was unhappily constrained to say he now had no idea what to do. Perón told him it was all his fault and represented himself as the only person standing between the country and chaos. 'It has happened because you are all idiots,' he told Avalos, 'the people have gone into the streets because you wanted to get rid of me. What did that accomplish? An upheaval of the entire country . . .'[25]

Perón was able to ask what he wanted, an entire new cabinet of his choosing. That evening, dressed in civilian clothes, he went to the Casa Rosada and spoke to President Farrell, the man who had once been his friend but had recently put him in gaol. Shortly after eleven, Perón walked out on to the balcony to address the crowd.

As he stood there in the glare of the lights which were trained on him, all he can have been aware of was the almost invisible presence of the enormous crowd, its size exaggerated by the night, its contours that of the square outside the Casa Rosada. This plaza, with its banks, its cathedral, its offices, its palm trees, fountains and the pink colonial building at one end, is the prototype of all Argentine city plazas. That night it was quite altered by the presence of the 200,000 people who had taken possession of it. Some of them had waited for more than ten hours and, at nightfall, they had rolled up newspapers and banners, turning them into torches. When Perón appeared, the flames swayed and flickered in the roar that began with his name and was then indistinctly drawn out, a cry to mark the apparition of a champion, the fulfilment of a miracle. There began what has been described by Felix Luna, an Argentine historian, as 'a curious pantomine, something quite unique in the history of any country'.[26] The crowd seemed not to want to hear what had happened, which was still quite without explanation, or even to hear what Perón had to say. It simply wanted to take possession of him. 'People seemed to have lost their minds; they cried out, they jumped up and down, they wept and shouted their slogans, getting hoarser and hoarser. Here was the man on whose behalf they had acted and he was safe and sound and triumphant.'

After fifteen minutes of cheering, after the national anthem had been sung again, after Perón and President Farrell had repeatedly embraced before the crowd, it was at last possible for Perón to speak. He said he had retired from the Army and he desired to serve 'the great mass' of Argentines. He seemed exhausted and his voice was rasping. The crowd interrupted him many times: 'Where were you?' someone said, 'Where were you?', and Perón did not answer directly, but said: 'I want to mix with this sweating mass as a simple citizen, I want to hug it close to my heart as I would my mother.' This was the signal for another long roar of gratification and, as this at last died down, more questions. 'Gentlemen,' Perón replied, 'since you insist so strongly, I must ask you not to remind me of what I have already forgotten. Men who are not able to forget do not deserve the love or respect of their equals and it is my ambition to be loved by you . . .' Again he was cheered, again there were pledges of love and fraternity. At last Perón told the crowd they must go, but that they should spend the next day, which had been scheduled three days previously as a general strike, not actively demonstrating, but celebrating their victory. The crowd at once made this suggestion into the slogan of the Perón years:

> *Mañana es San Perón*
> *Que trabaja el patrón*
>
> Tomorrow is Saint Perón's day
> Let the boss work . . .

The next day, the factories were indeed closed down and in a number of small and harmless occupations of plazas and city centres, the country celebrated 17 October, just as it would for many years afterwards.

As the first, most important *jornada* – big day – of Peronism, 17 October aroused bitter controversy for as long as it was celebrated. Until that date the only successful extra-legal irruptions in Argentine politics had been made by the Army. Now it seemed that in spite of the lack of organization by the unions, the country's working classes had made a non-violent and effective entry on to the national stage. This was not a coup or a general strike, since it seemed that the masses had been demanding no more than the liberation of Perón. Yet because of the exceptional circumstances of that day, including the powerlessness of the Army and the opposition, they had ended by unconsciously applying enough pressure to bend the shape of Argentine political life so that never would it be quite the same again. At its simplest this meant that the country's working classes could never again quite be disregarded, that 'those who were alone and waiting', as Scalabrini Ortíz said, 'had begun to demand things.'

The opposition would never accept what had happened, because it did not fit with their preconceptions. In no other country had the first act of an aware working class been to restore a Colonel to power. So the opposition responded by depicting the events of 17

October as a huge conspiracy on the part of Perón's followers, or else by treating those who had marched as political innocents, as 'the lumpen' or 'groups of street musicians'.

In the following days Perón's supporters became known as *los descamisados,* the shirtless ones. To start with this was a derogatory label bestowed by the opposition, but it was soon adopted in proletarian pride as a handy variant of the French *sans-culottes.* In the Peronist reading of the events of that October *los descamisados* meant the country's entire working class. Perón had been lost, and they had ensured his return; he had been a soldier and they had made him one of themselves. The relationship consummated on the balcony that night – the charismatic, mystical bond between the leader and *los descamisados* – would dominate Argentine politics for thirty years. The other person in this relationship was Evita, though this was not immediately apparent.

5
Wife of the President

Perón returned to Calle Posadas late that night to have dinner with
Evita. Afterwards they drove to Ramón Subiza's house at San
Nicolas, the place where they had planned to hide before they
changed their minds and went to the Tigre. Four days later, at the
most private of civil ceremonies and with Mercante and Evita's
brother as witnesses, they were married. Five weeks later (they
had been obliged to cancel one church wedding after a threat had
been made against Perón's life) a very private religious ceremony
took place in the Church of San Ponciano in La Plata. Doña Juana
came to the religious ceremony, and there were a few of Perón's
friends, but they supposed that they had managed to avoid any
publicity, and were amazed when the crush of supporters outside
the church forced them to leave by the side door.

The marriage contract bears witness to haste, which is
understandable, given the circumstances.[1] Neither Evita nor Juan
were 'residents of Junín', as was stated, nor was Perón a bachelor,
nor could the couple possibly have undergone a medical
examination at Junín the day before, as they were some two
hundred miles away in San Nicolas. And there were other, more
serious distortions of fact, particularly the statement, made here
on a legal document for the first time, that Evita had been born on
7 May 1922 and that her name was Eva Duarte.

It was the name that was important to Evita, not her age. She
claimed to be twenty-three instead of her real age of twenty-six so
that she could also claim the name of Duarte, under which Perón
knew her.

The original record of her birth had still existed in 1944 when a
local radical politician named Daniel Dilagosto examined the
registry of births at Los Toldos and noted with interest that the
Duartes were registered under the name Ibarguren. 'Out of simple
curiosity' he made a copy of Eva María's entry.[2] Then, early in
1945, Evita's sister Elisa came to the registrar's office to ask for
her own birth certificate and that of Eva María. The clerk made a
show of looking under Duarte, then explained that no such entries
existed. Elisa asked him to do her a favour and find them after all,

since 'Eva María would soon marry Perón and he would become President.' The clerk, intrigued but cautious, sought advice from his brother who was a lawyer in Buenos Aires, and together they asked for further advice from the Director General of the Civil Registry. It was finally agreed that the clerk at Los Toldos should not be responsible for altering the public record, but that if Elisa or Evita applied again they should be advised to submit their case in writing to the Director.[3]

Some time in the following months someone tore Evita's real birth certificate out of the Los Toldos registry and destroyed it. The records in Junín were then examined in search of a child born at about the same time as Evita, who had died, so that Evita's false birth date and false name could be substituted for that child's entry. This involved removing a set of four pages relating to 1922, dismantling the registry, rewriting the entries, forging the seals and signatures, reconstituting the volume, and destroying a duplicate volume which was stored in La Plata. The only slip in this series of precautions was the failure to create a believable marriage certificate for Evita's mother and Juan Duarte. Where reference to it was required by law on any of the other documents, the forgers simply gave a page and certificate number which had never existed but which, if they had existed, would have come at the end of a volume – a position from which the document could credibly have slipped out and got lost.[4]

It is not known who remade the Duarte family history, but it was not the clerk of Los Toldos. Many years later, in the course of a vivid argument about Evita's real age in the Social Club of Los Toldos, he had occasion to examine his books, discovered that a fraud had been committed and informed the authorities. Evita was no longer alive, but Perón was in power and the clerk was immediately removed from his job.

Since the forgery was evidently carefully conceived and set in motion some time before Evita's marriage took place, it is clear that for some time she must not only have hoped, but expected to marry Perón. Perón has said, as explanation, that they were both too busy to be married earlier, and this was probably the case. Although the letter he wrote her from prison suggests that the crisis, and her vulnerability, had precipitated his determination to marry her, it does not sound as though he was approaching the matter for the first time. But 17 October, made it essential anyway that they should marry quickly, for no Argentine politician, at that time or since, could run for the Presidency while living with a woman who was not his wife.

In the next few days much of the evidence of Evita's acting

career was quietly removed. She sent for and received all the publicity stills in the possession of the radio stations where she had worked, and all the negatives from the photographers who had taken pictures of her. Her last film, *La Prodiga,* still in its rough cut, was shown privately to Perón and Evita at Subiza's house by the boss of Pampa films and then given as a present to Evita;[5] it would never be shown publicly. Evita's own deep reserve about her past, of which she did not speak publicly, inhibited awkward questions. Her early life was never mentioned in official circles, or else it was romanticized in the vaguest terms. 'Eva Perón was born on 17 October 1945,' a characteristic work of hagiography declared: 'Like Venus, who emerged from the sea, achieving in contact with the light the immortal synthesis of art and beauty, Eva Perón was born from the sea. . . .'[6]

Many Argentines, sometimes because it was all they knew about Evita and sometimes because it represented what they wished to know about her, gave credence to this miraculous version of events, at least to the degree of frequently repeating it; and often it seemed as if Evita believed it too. Her marriage was like a fairy tale or the climax of a movie. Quite against all rational expectations, after much initial suffering and a surprising dénouement, she now found herself made new, the wife of a presidential candidate. She was of course grateful to Perón, since it was he who had married her. Later she became aware that throughout the country there had been many hundreds of thousands of people whom she did not know and who had been prepared to march on Perón's behalf; and her gratitude went to them too. 17 October marked 'a debt of honour contracted with the *descamisados'* in the romantic legalism of her political vocabulary. Most of the rest of her life would be devoted to the task of repaying that debt.

Perón entered the presidential campaign with no party, no electoral organization and little in the way of campaign funds. Within a few weeks, however, he found himself at the head of a coalition. He was supported by the Labour Party, which had been founded by union leaders from the CGT and those radicals and conservatives who had taken his side earlier that year. The opposition, largely composed of those who had sponsored and participated in the 'March of the Constitution and Liberty' – Conservatives, Progressive Democrats, Radicals, Socialists and Communists – was, by contrast, efficient and well-funded. It had adopted the Phrygian cap as its emblem and the slogan 'For freedom, against Nazism'. Its candidates accused Perón of being a demagogue, a Nazi, and a thief who had made off with the money raised for the reconstruction of San Juan. Perón's rhetoric was softer in tone; he wanted to increase his middle-class support, so he expressed his belief in capitalism and democracy. After meetings and speeches in Buenos Aires, the candidates travelled through the interior in specially equipped trains. The atmosphere was violent. The 'train of victory' of the opposition was subjected to attempted derailments, bomb threats and attacks by Perón's supporters. By the time it returned to Buenos Aires it was dented by stones, marked with bullet holes and under police escort. At the station there was a riot in which three people were killed. After this Perón's train, the *Descamisado,* was surrounded by the strictest security, Perón and his party being obliged to leave it before it arrived at each station.

The first trip coincided with the public announcement in the pages of *La Epoca,* the Peronist newspaper, of Eva's marriage to Perón. Evita joined the train in Santiago del Estero, spent the New Year with Perón, and later, on different trips, accompanied him to Junín, Córdoba, Rosario and Mendoza, all places she had passed through in her penurious actress days. Perón and his party travelled in shirt-sleeves, a badge of membership of the new movement and a conscious proletarianization of the formal manners of Argentine politics. Evita made no campaign speeches, but stood by Perón's side as he repeatedly made the same speech, his voice hoarser and hoarser, about breaking the power of the oligarchy through land reform. No candidate's wife had ever stood beside her husband during an electoral campaign before, and Evita was conspicuous both for this reason and because she was known to the provincial crowds as a radio actress. Her pale complexion, her blond hair, and the fairy tale of her marriage made her an arresting figure.

After the tour Perón and Evita moved into apartment B on their floor in Calle Posadas, leaving Evita's old apartment A free to serve as a conference room and electoral headquarters. Perón rose early and worked alone until 10 am when Evita would come in, often in a dressing gown or nightdress, comb her hair and spend the rest of the day with Perón and the other campaign workers. Evita's habit of calling everyone by the familiar *vos,* an Argentinism expressing great lack of formality, offended some of Perón's supporters. On some occasions she seems to have used the term on purpose. There was one campaign worker who made particular efforts to maintain a dignified distance from her until the day he had to ask her a favour on behalf of a friend, whereupon he said, still using the polite third person, 'You are the good fairy of the Peronist Movement.' Evita replied familiarly: 'Cut it out, you won't get around me with that sort of thing.'[7]

Since much of Perón's time was taken up with writing his own speeches, occasionally small details of campaign work were taken care of by Evita. Perón had no objection to this and therefore the other campaign workers were unable to object. Some of the labour leaders had rough manners and were in any case not used to women doing this kind of work. Their antipathy towards Evita soon became evident. Once it was clear that they disliked her she treated them in similar fashion. She particularly disliked Cipriano Reyes, the aggressive autodidact who had organized the meat-packers' union and was a founding member of the Labour Party. When Perón's supporters were still squabbling over the candidates for the province of Buenos Aires, Reyes was summoned by telegram to the apartment and told by Evita, in Perón's presence, that there 'had to be more Radical candidates' in the province. Reyes was furious and complained to Perón about what he considered to be interference on Evita's part, but Perón said he quite agreed with Evita.[8]

Evita attended only one rally without Perón, a function organized by the women's groups in support of the movement. She arrived two hours late to tell the assembled and by now very impatient women that her husband was ill, but the women, not interested in her, cried 'Perón, Perón' and would not let her finish her speech. In the streets outside the stadium there was rioting and the women had to be dispersed with tear gas.[9] The next day Perón and Evita boarded the *Descamisado* and again the crowds were enormous, bringing the carriages to a halt to see and touch Perón and Evita. Perón, both prudent and exhausted, had by this stage acquired a 'double', a railway official who looked like him and could sit at the window and wave on his behalf, but Evita sat at the back of the train, leaning out of the window to touch the people milling around it. By the end of the campaign her presence was a sufficiently familiar feature of political events for the Buenos Aires women's committee of the movement to wish to designate their centre 'Eva Maria Duarte de Perón'.

Both the issues of the campaign and its climate of violence had come from the political events of the previous months and, beyond that, from the central issue in Argentine politics in the previous years, the War. It was therefore appropriate that this issue should dominate its climax. Only nine days before the elections, newspapers opposed to Perón began to print excerpts from a document published in Washington entitled 'Consultation among the American Republics with respect to the Argentine Situation', or more familiarly, 'The Blue Book'. This had been compiled at the direction of former Ambassador Spruille Braden, now Under-Secretary of State for Latin American Affairs, and while it was presented as a reminder to other American states of pro-Nazism in Argentina during World War II, it was in effect little but an attempt to discredit Perón in the crucial last days of an election that was perceived as being close. As a work of investigation, the document was poor, prolix and lacking in revelations; as propaganda, it was disastrous, since it enabled Perón to raise once more the spectre of an oligarchy at the beck of foreign interests. He finished the campaign in the raucous and aggressive style he had first adopted in the early months of 1945. On 12 February 1946, in a nationally broadcast speech, he said, 'In our country, we are not discussing the issue of freedom or tyranny . . . democracy or totalitarianism. Ultimately at the heart of this national drama, we are witnessing a championship match between social justice and social injustice.' He attacked Braden as the real leader of the opposition, concluding, 'Those who are about to vote for the oligarchic–communist ticket should know that they are really giving their votes to Mr Braden. The real choice is this: Braden or Perón.' The election, held on 24 February 1946, the first truly open election since 1928, was clean by any standards, let alone those which had prevailed in the 1930s, and when the first results came in, there was unanimous agreement that the voting procedure had been proper. Perón's opposition was certain of victory, and it was only when victory became less certain that claims of fraud were made. Perón had received fifty-two per cent of the vote, his candidates had won all but one of the provincial governorships, twenty-eight out of the thirty seats in the Senate, and they held a majority of two-thirds in the chamber of deputies. Thus it was that the country now decisively entrusted its future to Perón.

In the months between the election and his inauguration, Perón drafted a program and formed a cabinet reflecting all the various groups that supported him. It was a good cabinet composed of able people. But he would still to a great extent rely on those closest to him and they tended to be those who had assisted him on 17 October. There was his personal friend, Domingo Mercante, and there was Rudi Freude, the German-Argentine who had made his house available to Perón. He was rewarded with a post in Perón's secretariat. Perón's opponents had been supported by the traditional Argentine business interests, the Sociedad Rural and the Unión Industrial; what Perón received came from isolated businessmen with their own reasons for backing him. One of these was Alberto Dodero, one of the richest men in South America, to whom Perón later awarded a contract to operate the first private airline out of Buenos Aires. Dodero became an adviser, though in what context would never be clear. His wife Betty Sundmark, an American ex-chorus girl from Chicago, was for a time friendly with Evita.

Perón's most astonishing appointment was his choice of Evita's brother Juan as Private Presidential Secretary. Juan had been faithful to Perón and his sister through October, but he had no experience of politics, having worked as a soap salesman for the previous decade, and there were rumours that he had worked the black market in imported commodities in 1945. He was not married, had a number of mistresses, and frequented nightclubs. Juan Duarte would never have been appointed had it not been for his sister, and once he was in, the importance of his post increased his sister's power. It was he who decided who saw Perón and this, in effect, allowed Evita to influence decisions.

Some political business took place during the weekends in San Vicente, at Perón's *quinta,* a low stucco building with a covered porch, outhouses for Perón's guns and fencing equipment, and stables for the horses that he and Evita rode. It was no more than the weekend place someone of Perón's rank in the Army would own, and arrangements for guests remained rudimentary. Ricardo Guardo, a dentist with a successful practice in the Barrio Norte, who had joined Perón prior to the campaign and would soon find himself President of the Chamber of Deputies and in charge of operating Perón's parliamentary majority, was astonished by the simplicity of Perón's private life.[10] Evita had little respect for the duties conventionally imposed by marriage. No matter who was present she dressed informally; when Guardo brought his wife to see Perón and Evita for the first time, she was wearing Perón's pyjamas with the waistband pulled up to her breasts and the sleeves and trouser-legs rolled up. Her hair was in two plaits. There was a political conversation that evening during which Perón suggested she should cook dinner. This she refused to do, so they all ate from cans which she opened. 'The Evita of those days was extraordinary,' Guardo said.

She was still almost a girl and much of the time she behaved like one. In the context of what was expected of women at that time, what she did might have been a calculated gesture with the intention of provoking or shocking, but it was not. She was like that and that is how she behaved. One would have thought that she would be worried by the responsibility of being Perón's wife, but if she was, she never showed it.

Guardo was still talking politics with Perón while Evita was in the kitchen opening her cans, when she called him, first softly and then, when he did not reply, shouting his name. She said she had spoken to Betty Dodero about what she should wear at the inauguration and Betty had offered her a choice of all the furs and dresses in her own wardrobe; but Evita thought that Betty, a *norteamericana,* would not know what was correct in Argentina, so she asked Guardo to help her buy a dress. Guardo went to the fashionable dressmaker, Bernarda, and though he was told that Evita was 'the sort of client one doesn't need', he did succeed in arranging a private fitting for her. Guardo did not think he should be there, as men in those days did not go to dress-shops with women who were not their wives, but Evita was not concerned about that. She could not make up her mind and tried on many dresses. One that she liked had epaulettes, but Guardo told her not to buy it lest she be confused with the numerous generals present.

Evita wore the dress she finally chose at the pre-inaugural banquet on 4 June 1946, held in the white salon of the Casa Rosada. As the President's wife, she was seated at the head of the table and by her side was the Cardinal, Monsignor Santiago Luis Coppello. Evita's grey silk dress left the shoulder nearest the Cardinal entirely bare, which was considered scandalous among the oligarchy, but the rest of the country was, on the whole, less censorious. A photograph of the Cardinal and Evita's bare shoulder was reproduced in *El Hogar,* a magazine for housewives, and at the Maipu theatre, the actress Sofía Bozán appeared in a revue wearing an identical, shoulderless dress with a small bird called a cardinal perched on it.

On the next day, after the inaugural address in Congress, Perón and Evita went for the first time with Guardo and his wife to the Presidential residence, the Unzue Palace. This was a turn-of-the-century palace of 283 rooms in Palermo, the great suburb of the oligarchy. It stood in the midst of a park and had been sold to the government by its owners in the 1930s because of the excessive cost of maintaining it. Perón, Evita and the Guardos walked around the salons and went upstairs where Perón stopped at the top of the wrought-iron and marble grand staircase, shaped like an inverted Y and ending in the marble and moulded-plaster cavern of the great hall, and made Guardo race him to the bottom by sliding down the banisters. Then all four of them went to the bedrooms where Evita unpinned and plaited her hair, changed from her dress into Perón's pyjamas and sat quietly on a bed eating an orange.

The Argentina which had chosen Perón was not only the richest country in South America, it was also one of the richest countries in the world. The war had left it a creditor nation; it was owed almost two billion dollars by Britain alone. The derelict state of the European economies gave Argentina an assured market for its exports, while making it difficult to import much from Europe, thus enabling the country to protect its own recently created industries. After the neglect of the thirties there was money for public spending and the country was once again absorbing a flow of immigrants. This time, however, they were not illiterate and unskilled, but scientists, skilled workers, intellectuals. Many of the recurrent problems of the country, therefore, seemed to have vanished, and for a short time all but the most bitter opponents of Perón felt that his election had at the very least resolved the long political crisis of the war years and given the country a democratic regime. Perón has been blamed for failing to make use of this favourable political and economic climate, but this seems an unduly harsh judgment. Notwithstanding some questionable decisions, he made as much use as possible of the country's favourable economic situation; what he could not do much about, for it had not in essence changed, was its political structure. The forces that assured his election, the Army and the unions, had historically few interests in common, yet Perón had little choice but to rely on their support by the implementation of mutually acceptable reforms. In 1946, this was still possible. There was widespread support for a number of reforms and there seemed to be ample funds to carry them out. It was only when these basic reforms were accomplished and there was no longer any money that Perón began to encounter difficulties.

If any single place was associated with pre-Perón Argentina, it was the Colon Opera House, with its red plush tiers, candelabra and cherubs. It had been built in the first years of the century and covered an entire block of the Avenida 9 de Julio, and its galas were important events in the social season of Buenos Aires. The city was proud of it, since it could compare with any of the great European houses, and it had been used to impress and entertain visitors such as the Prince of Wales. It was here on 27 November 1946 that Perón, wearing shirt-sleeves, and before a full house of trade-union officials wearing shirt-sleeves, chose to rally support for his five-year plan for the 'New Argentina'. What he offered was not so innovative in a European context, the year after the 1945 Labour government had been elected in Britain, or in a North American one many years after the New Deal, but in Argentine terms it was quite astonishing. Apart from such measures as the nationalisation of British-owned railways and utilities, Perón promised the creation of a number of other nationalized industries and a rapid programme of industrialization, to be effected by means of State intervention. The unions were promised more unionization, which is what Perón had already given them, a full programme of legislation in connection with arbitration procedures, and – more important – a series of comprehensive pension schemes amounting to the creation of a welfare state in Argentina. The change in the position of labour was extraordinary and aptly indicated by the circumstances in which Perón delivered his speech. No previous government, in its legislation or its ceremonies, had acknowledged the existence of an Argentine working class, yet now the President, who had been a soldier, called himself a worker.

There was an officially-sponsored cult of work which went with the self-conscious dynamism and labour-mindedness of the government. Early on, Perón began to tell visiting journalists that he worked harder than any previous President, most of whom had 'come to the office for only four hours each day,' and this was probably a correct statement. Evita, too, began to work. She started by visiting factories, first with Perón and then by herself, but in mid-July, only four months after the inauguration, she began to work three days a week on the fourth floor of the Department of Posts where her friend Oscar Nicolini, now Minister of Communications, had made an office available to her. Then on 23 September, the presidential Cadillac in which she habitually went to work drove past the Department of Posts to the newly created Ministry of Labour. From then on Evita worked in a suite in that building and would be publicly associated with the place from which Perón had first made contact with the *descamisados,* and effected his own rise to power.

At first, people came to Evita because of their union connections, in order to ask her for individual favours or financial assistance. A child might be ill in a town where there were no available hospital beds, or a group of mothers may have been living in shacks in the midst of marshland. Evita would listen and then act: the next day the child would be in hospital, five days later the families would be assigned homes in a new project under construction in another suburb of Buenos Aires. Evita liked bestowing this sort of favour and she realized that as the wife of the President she could make prior claim on the meagre resources of the bureaucracy for the problems she wished to solve.

In the past, apart from her mainly ceremonial role in the radio performers' union, she had taken little interest in the political concerns of the unions, or in their demands. Shortly before the elections, Hernán Salowicz, head of the Buenos Aires taxi-drivers' union, was present at a meeting in Perón' apartment when someone told Perón that the municipal firemen were about to strike. 'Why do they make all this fuss with their strikes?' Evita said. 'Why don't they organize themselves into a union like everyone else?' Both the union people and Perón laughed at her; she did not know that, as members of the Federal police force, the firemen were not permitted to organize themselves.[11]

Evita now became aware of the issues concerning unions. In the beginning, she was assisted by those who had worked with Perón in the Ministry and in particular by Isabel Ernst, a woman who had worked as the secretary of Domingo Mercante since 1943, and had excellent contacts with union leaders. Isabel Ernst would be present at each of Evita's meetings with union representatives, standing behind Evita, taking notes and making suggestions. Eventually Evita became resentful of this form of tutelage and sometimes even chided her assistant in public for not having executed her orders.

At these first meetings, Evita was 'wary, formal of speech, quiet', according to a union leader from the meat industry.

I had the feeling she was still shy of speaking in public. She would say the same thing in two or three different ways, using different terms and from time to time she would ask: 'Do you understand what I am trying to say?' . . . We had gone to her with a difficult problem concerning our struggles with the communists in the industry and she asked us to tell her all about it, even to the degree of repeating the same thing several times over. Then she finally understood what it was all about and gave us a solution none of us had thought of.[12]

Some of Evita's work was purely formal, a question of receiving delegations of union members when they came to the Ministry, or going to factories in order to make speeches, but she began increasingly to deal with the sort of issues that Perón had dealt with when he was at the Ministry. In many industries there were as yet no unions, and strikes took place to gain recognition. Evita was asked for support in the organization of unions. In other industries where there were still unions of which the government disapproved on the grounds of their being hostile, 'communist' or otherwise, Evita assisted members who sought to defect and create new unions. In the eventuality of union elections in which pro-Peronists were pitted against anti-Peronists, she might speak on behalf of the new union or, through Salowicz, provide a fleet of cabs so that the group she favoured could get its supporters out to vote.

Liliane Guardo, Evita's companion, was living the traditional married Argentine woman's life when Evita first met her. Though educated and intelligent, she spent her days looking after her four children. So unobtrusive was her presence that when her husband Ricardo, who was majority leader in Congress, first brought her to see Perón and Evita, Perón expressed astonishment at the fact that Guardo was married. Since Liliane had been told that Evita was 'interested in politics' she said little, and was astonished when Evita called her some months later and asked her to come to her office. Liliane liked Evita – she was 'charming, young and beautiful' – but it was soon apparent that this was irrelevant. Evita required Liliane to sit quietly in her office while the union delegations came in, and though she never consulted Liliane on political questions, Evita would periodically interrupt her work to talk with her. When Liliane announced that she had to leave, Evita would try to make her stay, often in the most disingenuous way, with such childish protestations as 'It gives me so much peace to see you sitting there.'[13] For a while, the two spoke by phone each morning, and then the telephoning became unnecessary. Evita's car would arrive at Guardo's house as a matter of daily routine to collect Liliane. Liliane, who knew nothing of such things, went to pasta factories and slaughter-houses, diplomatic functions and galas at the Colon, and rode in the truck from which Evita distributed packets of clothing and food. But it became too much for Liliane, who complained to Perón; and the President, when Evita had told him that she could not work without Liliane, said she must stop working three days out of the week so that Liliane could spend those days with her children. But Evita soon got bored with the days of not working, and her car was sent out for Liliane once more. That summer, arrangements had to be made to allow Liliane to work with Evita and yet also be with her family by the sea at the weekends. A special sleeping car was set up on the train that took señora Guardo to her family. She would board it on Friday night and wake up in the siding of the small station near her summer house.

Liliane was required to combine the unassuming function of a lady-in-waiting with the tact and acumen of a tutor in manners. It had always been a custom for those who visited the President, or who sought favours from him, whether they were foreigners or Argentines – to give presents to his wife. When the parcels arrived the gifts were inspected with Liliane's assistance. Liliane was able to distinguish for Evita between the Dresden and the Sèvres, the good emerald and the fake. When Evita went to Ricciardi, the best jeweller in Buenos Aires, Liliane would come and help her, sometimes accompanied by doña Juana, Evita's mother. On such occasions the store would be emptied of customers by Evita's bodyguards, and doña Juana would often overtly make use of her daughter's presence and position to secure good prices for her purchases. Of course, Evita would also receive special prices; nor was her account always punctually settled. Eventually, Ricciardi took to hiding his best stones whenever it was announced that Evita intended to visit his shop.

To Liliane, Evita seemed absorbed in her work, preoccupied with the numerous small ceremonies of politics, the patterns of favour and disfavour within the government. But with her she could also be childishly insecure, eager to please and afraid of failing. The pleasure taken in the presents, particularly the jewels, was simple satisfaction with material possessions, but it was also the pleasure in being approved of, valued, and Evita's desire to display these possessions could take oddly excessive forms. Thus one afternoon when she had been given a large emerald necklace, she insisted on driving with Liliane to the Casa Rosada, to show it to Perón while he was still at work. Liliane told her that the necklace didn't go with her clothes and that Perón would soon be home in any case, but Evita insisted on going all the the same so that their limousine crossed with Perón's which was returning to the Residence.

Having been an actress, Evita treated her clothes as disguises, not as an expression of her personality. She would order them sight unseen and when she had to go somewhere, she would ask Liliane if what she had selected was appropriate; if not, she would change her hat, skirt or shoes until Liliane was happy. When Evita dressed without Liliane's assistance, her clothes could seem loud or cheap, and for this she was much criticized. There were no rules for what women should wear in a political context, since there were no precedents for what Evita was doing. She still dressed, not as a politician, but as a film star – her hair piled up, her heels high, her hats enormous and floppy. But she was already aware of the function of clothing in political life and there were occasions when she would assert herself in this area. When Liliane's husband suggested that Evita might dress more quietly when she next visited Congress, instead of wearing her dressy jewellery, Evita said, 'Look, they want to see me beautiful. Poor people don't want someone to protect them who is old and dowdy. They all have their dreams about me and I don't want to let them down.' Paco Jamandreu, who made her clothes when she was a movie star, continued to make some of her clothes now. Evita would ask him 'for something that would shock all those women who came decorated like Christmas trees' and Jamandreu would devise giant pieces of jewellery with false stones and paste.[14]

In early 1947 Evita became the proprietor of *Democracia,* a newspaper which had formerly been unimportant and mediocre. The government lacked press support, as all of the Buenos Aires press had been hostile to Perón during the elections. Since Evita had no money of her own to make the purchase, the newly nationalized Central Bank was encouraged to lend her the funds. She did not play a great part in running *Democracia;* once a new staff had been recruited and the paper's general policy had been defined, it functioned of its own accord, presenting in tabloid form and with many photographs a simple, highly partial account of the incessant ceremonies of the Peronist regime. Perón's speeches were always prominently reprinted, and when Evita made a series of broadcasts telling housewives how to deal with inflation, these too found their places in *Democracia.* Only one of Evita's whims was actually expressed and thereafter became immutable editorial policy, and that concerned the depiction of Atilio Bramuglia, Foreign Minister and the man who had refused to secure a *habeas corpus* writ on Evita's behalf. Bramuglia was never mentioned by name in the newspaper. If he had to be referred to, only his title was used. Photographs in which Bramuglia appeared were doctored, either by removing him completely if he was on the edge of a group, or by airbrushing his face if he was standing in the middle. Sometimes the Foreign Minister seemed headless, sometimes ghostly, never was he allowed to appear as an entire person.

There were many photographs of Evita in her newspaper. According to the editor, Valentin Thiebaut, she had given no such instructions and the staff simply assumed this was what she wanted. Then, as the paper's circulation climbed from 6,000 to 20,000 and then 40,000, it became apparent that the reproduction of Evita's image was good for business. On gala nights, when she wore an evening dress at the Colon, the demand for *Democracia* would be such that the paper was sold out and its offices visited the next day by many disappointed admirers, mostly housewives.

Within only a few months of Evita's purchase of the newspaper, special Colon night issues had to be printed, with runs of 400,000, almost entirely devoted to photos of Evita and copy about her dress. 'People came to regard Evita as the daughter of the family who had wanted to go to a dance and had then gone without food so that she would have enough money for it,' the editor recalled. 'There was a vast, though always implicit, identification with her and it came from affection or empathy; those who bought the paper wished they were her.'[15]

In every culture with mass communications there are figures around whom such collective fantasies develop. In societies with notions of inherited social class, members of the aristocracy or of royalty play such roles, but in Argentina, outside the society pages of magazines like *El Hogar, La Prensa* and *La Nación* in which the doings of the oligarchy were set down for its own benefit, no such tradition existed. The fantasies of ordinary people revolved around the meteor-stereotypes of movie star, tango singer, boxer or soccer player – people who had come to great fame from obscurity. It is not surprising that Evita should have been aware of this, since as a child she had experienced these fantasies, and as an actress she had assisted in their creation. What is extraordinary is the speed and sureness with which she now applied these principles to political life.

There were criticisms of her by the Parliamentary opposition as early as June 1946, when the Radical Deputy Ernesto Sammartino presented a Bill to the effect that the 'wives of public servants, politicians or military men' should neither share their husband's prerogatives nor represent them at public functions, a measure that could only be interpreted as applying to Evita. That same month *Newsweek* called her *La Presidenta* and suggested that she was becoming 'the most important "woman behind the throne" in Latin America'.[16] It was in response to these criticisms that the government, in December 1946, issued one of its only definitions of what Evita was supposed to be doing. She had no secretaries and only one collaborator, and without actually being part of the government, she was 'an active contributor' to its social policies, serving as the government's ambassador to the people, the *descamisados*. But this official announcement of her unofficial role satisfied no one except those who benefited from it.

Neither Perón nor Evita ever adequately explained how it was that she came to occupy this position. Perón's earlier decision to let her work with him is startling enough, but it is less important than the one he made now, which in reality involved giving her considerable responsibility at the age of twenty-six. She was his sole liaison with the *descamisados*. He described her as 'a genuinely passionate woman, driven by a will and a faith comparable to that of the early Christians',[17] but this is no real explanation of why, as he said, he 'decided [she] should go to the Ministry.' Nor are the many personal reasons Perón may have had, adequate explanations in themselves. He was not, contrary to what has been suggested, in the habit of letting Evita do exactly what she wished, despite the unorthodox circumstances of their marriage. Certainly this was not the sort of decision he would have taken lightly.

Perón's real reasons for allowing his wife this sort of freedom were political rather than personal and they arose out of weaknesses of his position. He had risen because of what he had accomplished on Labour's behalf, but he was far from controlling the labour movement. Strikes continued through 1946. After his inauguration Perón dissolved the Labour Party thus reducing the political power of the CGT. But this action did not give him enough control over his most significant group of supporters. He was careful never to appoint potential rivals to important posts in which union contacts were necessary. His own choice for the Ministry of Labour was José María Freire, an anodyne former glassmaker. Evita could thus continue Perón's work unobstructed, in his own style; and she alone could do it in a way that could not threaten Perón, for she was a woman and, more than that, she was his wife, his 'shadow' as she would call herself.

In one important respect, she could do more than he could. Although the tolerance of rhetorical excess was high in Argentine politics, there were things which a President could not say about himself without appearing ridiculous. His wife, by contrast could say what she liked and in her excesses she would be sinning only out of loyalty. In Evita, Perón thus possessed a permanent source of propaganda.

Her influence was exercised independently of ministerial or administrative rank and depended on what Perón wished her to do, what she herself wished to do and what it seemed useful for her to be doing. There was a great thirst for rituals and symbols in the New Argentina – great 'days', emblems, conspicuously paraded shirtsleeves, opera houses turned into people's theatres. Perón had enjoyed symbolic life as the 'Workers' Colonel' and now it was to be his wife's turn. To begin with at least this was little more than a title and a series of gestures. Perón must have been aware of this, but there were others who were not and his wife's symbolic presence in the government was immediately confused with real influence.

For the opposition, whether Radicals, Socialists or Communists, anything Evita did was suspect (no sooner had she gone to her office than a Radical deputy, Silvano Santander, suggested a public inquiry be conducted into her activities), but for the Argentine upper class, it was Evita herself, regardless of what she did, who was unthinkable. Only one 'artiste' had ever been married to a President and that was Regina Pacini de Alvear – and she had been an opera singer, not a soap-opera actress, and in any case, she had kept out of politics. The oligarchy thought they understood Perón (he was an Army officer and they had seen plenty of those) but women like Evita they had only seen in domestic service.

So immediate criticism came from all sides. As early as 14 August 1946 a report from the US Ambassador pointed to the 'certainty' that Evita was doing Perón 'a good deal of injury in public opinion and not only among those who are opposed to him . . . but also among some of those who are his closest friends and supporters. . . .'[18] Evita's arrival in the Ministry of Labour, the ambassador said, had been widely resented and her hand was now seen in a number of appointments or firings of people opposed to Perón before the election; it was thought that, without Evita, Perón would have been less ruthless. A newsreel of the inauguration ceremonies shown at the Naval Academy had prompted a fit of 'coughing, reaching a crescendo when Mrs Perón appeared on the screen'.[19] The authorities had conducted an inquisition to determine who had coughed, had expelled three cadets, stripped three others of their honours, and given the entire class guardroom duty.

According to 'some hostile sources', which the US Ambassador wisely counselled must be 'taken with a grain of salt', Evita had marched into a closed session of the Senate, interrupting the senators while they were discussing diplomatic appointments. When criticized, she left the room 'sobbing audibly'. Perón was furious at the way she had been treated and summoned the senators to lecture them on matters of etiquette. Evita was present throughout, and stood leaning on the presidential desk. A May 1947 report from the British Labour attaché more vaguely credited her with 'interference in affairs of state . . . daily more conspicuous'. 'Among the members of the oligarchy,' an American visitor noted the next year, 'the relating of juicy items (especially juicy when it comes to the señora) has become almost an obsession. Many of them spend their evenings whipping themselves into hysteria by exchanging gossip about the regime.'[20] The oligarchs, now that they were out of power, knew nothing of what was really going on, and these stories 'from a man who knew a man who had a friend who worked in the President's office' were invariably fictions.

When the women were out of the room, jokes were told, unfunny and mildly obscene: for example, Perón the *caudillo,* Evita his bejewelled wife who was really a tart, both of them before St Peter at the seat of judgment. While they wait for judgment, Perón steps on St Peter's toe, St Peter exclaims *'Puta!'* [whore] and Evita steps forward. Or the one (often told) that Spruille Braden includes in his memoirs as a prelude to his judgment of her character. Evita is in an elevator with a retired general. The operator is saying under his breath, *'la Gran P',* a common abbreviation of *puta.* As they leave the elevator Evita, enraged, says: 'That man must be punished. Did you hear what he said?' 'Think nothing of it, Excellency,' the general replies. 'I've been retired from the Army for five years, and people still call me "General".'[21] In the first months of the Perón government, a great number of postcards depicting a plump and very lightly draped Evita reclining on a plush couch found their way through the salons of Buenos Aires. Evita had never done this sort of modelling, and in fact only the face was hers; the photos were the work of an Italian printer who was apprehended by the police and deported.

Whatever Evita was said to have done, it was interpreted by her enemies as an attempt to imitate her social superiors or as an attempt to take vengeance on those whom she had tried unsuccessfully to emulate. There was little that could not be inserted into this scheme – Evita's illegitimacy, for instance, nicely explained her motivations. Her presence could thus be reduced to a simple cycle of wound and revenge, envy turned to vindictiveness. This explanation was easily understood (hence easily transmitted to visiting journalists) and it made sense of the present without needless excursions into the complexity of Argentine history. There was a woman who was where she should not be. She was there because she was hard and vindictive. With her background what else could one expect? One of the attractions of this view of Evita's importance was that it reflected so well on those who held it. They could take consolation in the thought that being displaced because of Evita proved that they still mattered.

In 1947, Evita looked at first sight like someone aware of the implications and satisfactions of power, but in reality she still had no very clear sense of what to do with it. At no time would she quite fulfil the fantasies of her critics, but it would not be long before she gained this sense. It would come to her after a far more spectacular play of symbols, her regal tour of Europe.

6

Europe

The suggestion that Evita might soon visit Europe was first put forward in the Argentine press in February 1947, at that stage simply as a possibility. A few days later a group of working-class housewives came to the offices of *Democracia* demanding to see her. When the editor told them that she did not actually work there, they left her a message: when she went to Spain, she should wear her hair piled up in the style that suited her so well.

A month later, the Argentine government formally acknowledged, and accepted, an invitation from the Spanish government for Evita's visit, indicating at the same time that she would also go to Italy in a non-official capacity. A month after that, France was added to her itinerary. Persistent rumours of a British visit were neither confirmed nor denied, though the British Foreign office announced, on 2 June, that she was expected to come to Britain and would be welcome.

The purpose of Evita's growing itinerary was never explained by the Argentine government except in the most general terms: she was usually said to be bringing 'a message of peace' to Europe, or 'stretching a rainbow of beauty' between the new continent and the old. In fact, the voyage had been first suggested by Generalissimo Francisco Franco, and the invitation had been addressed not to Evita, but to Perón. Franco had many excellent reasons to encourage a state visit of the new Argentine President. The defeat of fascism in Europe had isolated Spain diplomatically and excluded it from the various plans financed by the United States for the reconstruction of Europe. Argentina was the only country with which Spain still maintained excellent diplomatic relations. Only the previous year, Spain had signed an agreement with Argentina by which Spain received a substantial loan with which to buy Argentine grain and meat. But there were also excellent reasons why Perón should not visit Spain. 1947 was the year in which Argentina finally emerged from its wartime quarantine, resuming its diplomatic relations with the USSR, taking its place at the UN, and improving its relations with the United States; and it was thought that a visit to Spain by Perón might place in jeopardy all these substantial improvements in the country's position. It was at this point that Evita seems to have decided that if Perón was not going, she certainly was. Once she had made this decision and Perón had accepted it, it became necessary that she should go to other European countries as well, lest her journey seem excessively linked to the question of Spain. The more places she went to, the less this would appear to be the case. In the confusing, often contradictory, style of pragmatism displayed by Perón's government, a difficult question of political principle was thus transformed into a grand spectacle with hazy implications but rich promotional possibilities.

Evita had always wanted to go to Europe. She was the first wife of an Argentine president to be invited on an offical visit by a foreign government, and she was flattered by the prospect. It was probably in a spirit of defiance that she decided to show the ladies of the oligarchy what she could do. The idea that she should go to countries other than Spain of course appealed to her. The more places visited, the more her trip would resemble the peregrinations of the oligarchy, or the rituals on which these were modelled, the leisurely tours of nineteenth-century royalty, part state visits, part pleasure trips.

Evita went to see her friend Liliane Guardo to propose that she accompany her on the trip. Liliane at first refused to leave her children, whereupon Evita called Guardo to ask him to persuade his wife, which he refused to do. She then had Perón act on her behalf. The Guardos came to dinner and Perón approached Liliane. He told her that Evita would cancel her trip if she did not go with her, and finally Liliane consented. Together, they bought Evita's evening dresses, hats, shoes and suits. Evita would have arranged a substantial 'allowance' for Liliane from the foreign office, had not Guardo refused the offer.

In Evita's party were her brother Juan, ostensibly accompanying her as a member of Perón's secretariat; her hairdresser, Julio Alcaraz, who devised her most elaborate pompadour styles (he was also give responsibility for Evita's jewels, kept in a special leather box lent by Perón, more of a strong box than a casket); two journalists, both employed by the government: Francisco Muñoz Azpiri, to write Evita's speeches (it was he who had written her radio series, 'Heroines in History'), and a photographer from the lavishly-illustrated *Democracia;* two Spanish diplomats, the Marquis of Chinchilla and Count Foxa, sent by Franco to accompany Evita to Madrid; and of course, maids to attend her personally.

The only important participant in the spectacle who did not

leave Buenos Aires with Evita was Father Hernán Benítez, who had been sent ahead to Rome. He was a Jesuit priest, an old friend of Perón's who had given the last rites to his first wife. He had met Evita when she was still an actress and they had become close friends.

According to Perón, when the ship-owner, Alberto Dodero, heard that Evita was going, he said, 'Alright *patrona*, I will be your secretary, but I will pay for everything.' [1]Dodero owned houses in Biarritz and the Côte d'Azur to which he proposed to take the party. It is not clear how much of the trip he paid for, though his contribution was undoubtedly substantial.

There were receptions and rallies, rich and empty tributes to Evita. At a farewell party held in the Ministry of Labour, the Minister referred to Evita in the course of his address as 'the archetype of Argentine womanhood, who displays her personality not with the vanity of a peacock but as an incarnation of exquisite feminity,' and at the end of it even Evita was embarrassed and said, 'So what do you want me to bring back for you?' The day before she left a political meeting was held, followed by a reception in the Sociedad Rural. At the reception Evita said, 'I am going as the representative of the working-people, of my dear *descamisados*. I leave my heart behind with them.' Next day, 6 June 1947, the entire government and a substantial crowd gathered at the airport to see her take off in a specially equipped DC4, lent for the occasion by the Spanish government. They gave her a warm Latin farewell as they would a member of the family. Evita waved goodbye, and kissed Perón as the crowd cheered. Following her plane, another Spanish aircraft took off, bearing the first lady's costumes, and the group's luggage.

She had only been outside Argentina once before, had never travelled by plane before and had rarely, except when Perón was in prison in Martín García, been away from him. She was afraid of flying but she was now also afraid and angry about something concerning her past that had emerged in the previous few days. Evita wrote few letters and hardly any of them have survived, but this is the one she wrote to Perón that night in one of the DC4's sitting rooms:[2]

Dear Juan,

I am very sad to be leaving because I am unable to live away from you, I love you so much that what I feel for you is a kind of idolatry, perhaps I don't know how to show what I feel for you, but I assure you that I fought very hard in my life with the ambition to be someone and I suffered a great deal, but then you came and made me so happy that I thought it was a dream and since I had nothing else to offer you but my heart and my soul I gave it [*sic*] to you wholly but in all these three years of happiness, greater each day, I never ceased to adore you for a single hour or thank heaven for the goodness of God in giving me this reward of your love, and I tried at all times to deserve it by making you happy, I don't know if I achieved that, but I can assure you that nobody has ever loved you or respected you more than I have. I am so faithful to you that if God wished me not to have you in this happiness and took me away I would still be faithful to you in my death and adore you from the skies; Juancito, darling, forgive me for these confessions but you have to know this now I am leaving and I am in the hands of God and do not know if something may happen to me . . . you have purified me, your wife with all her faults, because I live in you, feel for you and think through you; take care of the government, you're right it's unrewarding, if God lets us and we finish all this alright we'll retire and live our own lives and I'll try to make you as happy as I can because your happiness is mine. Juan if I die *take care of mother please* she is alone and has suffered a lot give her 100,000 pesos; to Isabelita [Isabel Ernst, Evita's collaborator at the Department of Labour] who has been loyal and still is give 20 and pay her better and J'll look after you from above. My jewellery I want you to keep and San Vicente and Teodoro García so that you can remember your *chinita* who loved you so much. I ask you this for doña Juana because I know you love her as I do, what has happened [is that] because you and I are living in this endless honeymoon we don't show our love for the family though we do love them. Juan, always keep Mercante as a friend because he adores you and he's so loyal to you he will always work with you. Be careful of Rudi, he likes deals, Castro told me that and he may do you a lot of harm and all I seek is your own name clean as you are. Besides, it hurts me to say this, but you should know it, what he arranged to be done in Junín, Castro knows well, I swear to you it is an infamy (my past belongs to me that is why in the hour of my death you must know it, it is a lie), everything is so painful, to love friends and to be thus rewarded. I left Junín when I was thirteen years old, what a horrible thing to think that vileness of a girl. I couldn't leave you thus deceived. I didn't tell you when I left because I was sad enough as it was and didn't want to add to all of that. But you can be proud of your wife because I looked after your good name and adored you. Many kisses, but many kisses . . .

Evita June 6, 1947

At that time Raúl Castro was in Perón's cabinet, and Rudi Freude, the German who had made his house in the Tigre available to Perón and Eva, was a member of Perón's private secretariat. But what were the 'deals' and what did he 'arrange to be done' in Junín? It was around this time the details of Eva's illegitimate birth were first published, not in Argentina, but in *Time* magazine.[3]

Evita is probably referring to this. On the other hand, the 'vileness' may refer to something more personal. She actually left Junín when she was fifteen, not thirteen, and if Freude's sin was merely to have gossiped about the tango singer or her other putative small-town loves, it would explain this small lie. Whatever it was, she felt disgraced at the very moment she needed to feel worthy of representing Perón.

Evita, much like a director before a performance, assembled those who were with her and told them that they should be on their best behaviour because they were going to be carefully scrutinized by the world, the press at home, and the opposition. 'There are those who are waiting for us to make mistakes so that they can jump on us,' she said, 'so let's have nothing stupid . . . .' The aircraft landed first at Cisneros, in the Spanish Sahara, and then flew on to Madrid the next day, escorted by a squadron of forty-one planes from the Spanish Air Force. The airport had been decked with tapestries, flowers and flags, and a crowd of 3,000,000 Madrileños awaited Evita's arrival. Franco, his wife, his daughter, and his cabinet were standing on the tarmac. Franco kissed Evita's hand, introduced her to the small crowd around him, and then, as a twenty-one-gun salute was fired, walked past a guard of honour to an open limousine. Evita rode with Franco into Madrid, through Calle Alcalá, where the balconies were decorated and crowded with people who shouted her name, to the Puerta de Alcalá, and then to the El Pardo palace, where she was to stay. There the servants brought her the first of many gifts she would receive from the Spanish government: a tapestry depicting a work of El Greco, a gold and ivory fan, an eighteenth-century mantilla, bottles of perfume, Moroccan artefacts, and a travelling case embossed with the arms of Argentina and Spain.

That evening, as her party prepared to retire for the night, Evita asked Liliane if she would sleep in her room. Though there were servants and a police guard, she said she was afraid someone might come. The two women pushed some of the furniture against the door and thus shut themselves in. Evita never explained what she was afraid of, whether it was out of an exaggerated sense of her honour or whether she was simply homesick, but she slept in the same room as Liliane every night of the three months she was in Europe. In fact, she slept little, but talked instead about the events of the day, about her work and Perón's, about friends and enemies. In particular she spoke of those enemies who might benefit from her absence, and from whom she must save Perón – as though her husband and his political house were in her charge.

In spite of the heat of the Madrid summer, the next day Evita wore a mink cape to the Royal Palace where she received from Franco the Grand Cross of Isabella the Catholic. On that occasion Franco made a brief speech in praise of the ideals of Peronism, and Evita replied with an odd sequence of turgid, scripted tributes to Isabella of Castile, and impromptu propaganda on Perón's behalf. Argentina, she said, had known how to choose between 'false democracy and the genuine, distributive democracy where the great ideas have simple names, like better bread, better housing, better food, a better life.'[4] The Spanish government had declared a school holiday and given the city's workers the day off. The square was full of people shouting 'Franco and Perón'. Evita took the microphone: 'General Franco,' she said, 'feels at this moment exactly as Perón does when he's acclaimed by the *descamisados*'; and it was then that she raised her hand in what was described throughout the world press as a fascist salute, but which was not that at all, but only her habitual gesture of putting her hand high above her head and waving it.

In the fifteen days that Evita spent in Spain, banquets, firework displays, performances of plays, and displays of folk dancing were given in her honour. Everywhere there were crowds, gifts, speeches. Evita had already worn most of her substantial wardrobe and was given a new one – a traditional dress from each of the Spanish provinces. She arrived half an hour late for a bullfight and the crowd was so anxious to see her that there were no catcalls; afterwards, the bullfighter complained that everyone had come to see Evita and not him. In Granada she saw the tombs of Ferdinand and Isabella, stone effigies lying side by side, and when someone said to her that Isabella's head sank lower into her cushion than Ferdinand's because it had been thought that her brain was larger than her husband's, she said, 'That is always the case.' In Saragossa she left her gold earrings at the shrine of the Virgen del Pilar, and everywhere she went she carried handfuls of 100-peseta notes which she gave to the children who crowded around her car. On the road to Toledo, a child stopped the car, but when she handed him the 100-peseta note, he explained he did not want the money but the insignia on the hood of the car; Evita gave it to him.

The Spanish press, which was censored, neither discussed the cost of the visit nor speculated as to its purpose; a *New York Times* reporter improbably placed its cost at $4 million, and in the absence of any convincing reason for the trip weakly termed it, 'the most original diplomatic mission in recent times'. Though there was an acute shortage of electricity in Franco's Spain, the fountains had been activated and illuminated the day Evita arrived, and remained so throughout her visit. She would have been cordially received had the Spanish people felt no particular enthusiasm for her, but there is every indication that their enthusiasm was quite genuine. In city after city, there were huge crowds and strong expressions of feeling. Many Spaniards had relatives who had emigrated to Argentina and prospered there, and the country was well-liked. After the many drab years of Franco's regime, her presence in a Spain long-isolated was an odd, startling and welcome political event.

Evita behaved like a queen, as if she had received such expressions of affection and respect all her life. One night she asked Liliane what she wanted from life and when Liliane said she would be happy if she could be a good mother to her children, Evita replied that that was all very well, but that she wanted to be 'something in history'. Yet a sense of displacement was often strong, and sometimes her mask slipped. At the Palace of Pedralba, after she had taken communion from Father Benítez, she experienced some sort of collapse. She told her confessor she could no longer deal with the strict protocol or the receptions. She asked him who was she, an illegitimate whom everyone had simply called 'China', and what had she done to deserve all this.[5]

Franco, who had not gone to Granada or Seville, joined Evita with his family once more in Barcelona, where an elaborate leave-taking was staged. The visit had produced only one measurable result: the gift by Evita of a boat-load of Argentine wheat. It was related in *Time* magazine[6] that Franco, who had hoped for a loan, not a gift of this kind, said to Evita, 'Señora, we need nothing. We have so much flour that we no longer know what to do with it'; to which Evita replied, 'Then why don't you use it to make bread?' But the good feelings between Fascist Spain and Peronist Argentina were now quite apparent, and Franco could feel content; in the following year he would sign the trade agreement which he had sought. On 25 June, after another twenty-one-gun salute, Evita boarded her plane and flew to Rome.

Reports of Evita's stay in Spain preceded her, spreading her fame throughout Europe. In this period of postwar poverty the display of wealth that her apparently purposeless journey represented seemed at first outrageous and then, when it became apparent that she had aroused genuine feelings of interest and sympathy, perplexing. There were protests about Evita's visit from Socialist and Communist groups in Italy and France, but discussion about her was most intense in Britain, where a Labour government held office. There was still some doubt as to whether she would come to England at all. After parliamentary questions from Labour Members of the House of Commons, on 15 July, the left-wing *Sunday Pictorial* published an editorial to the effect that she would 'not be welcome'. Though the predominantly conservative business community was in favour of her visit, controversy now began inside the Labour party. The 'moderates' felt obliged to tolerate her presence because Argentina was an important trading partner, and the left wing of the party, remembering the Spanish Civil War, felt she should not be admitted to Britain. Even after the Foreign Office had issued another communiqué stating that she would be welcome, the arguments continued.

Evita found a defender in Lord Strabolgi, a Socialist peer who had visited Argentina the previous year and now described her as 'the South American Eleanor Roosevelt'. As evidence of Evita's seriousness, Strabolgi adduced the numerous conversations she had had with his wife about the social reforms of the Labour government. Perón had given him a signed photograph inscribed 'to Lord Strabolgi of the old Labour Party of England, with affectionate greetings from the new Labour Party of the Argentine.' In fact, however, Perón had dissolved the Labour Party since Strabolgi's visit to Argentina. In the pages of the *Sunday Pictorial*[7] Strabolgi asked himself, 'How true is it that the present government in the Argentine is fascist?' He answered, 'Of course certain phases of the government are dictatorial, but we must remember that this is South America where democracy is comparatively young.' Aside from ideological hostility to Evita and Peronism, there was another basis for the aversion shown her. The Argentines were rich, there seemed no reason why they should not become richer and they were resented as parvenus.

Buckingham Palace had from the first emphasized the unofficial nature of Evita's visit. This was not to be interpreted as a sign of disfavour but meant that, according to protocol, she was considered of less importance than Eleanor Roosevelt, the only wife of a head of state whose visit had been accorded official status. When Evita's visit had first been planned, the British Foreign Office assured the Argentine government that she would have tea with the Queen of England. This had appeared to satisfy Argentina, but now, Evita having decided that she would come to Britain two weeks later than planned, the tea party was put in jeopardy. The Royal family were in the habit of spending their summers in Scotland, at their Balmoral estate. A counsellor from the Argentine Embassy in London went to Madrid to explain that, as things stood, the Queen would be picnicking, grouse-shooting, and entertaining locally at the time when Eva proposed to come.

Evita and her party, having become accustomed to the full welcome they had received from Franco, were perhaps understandably unable to see the sense of social priorities that underlay the Palace's point of view. Because the Queen was unable to see Evita when Evita wished to see her, it was thought that she did not wish to see Evita at all, and for the next two weeks, while the visits to cribs and shipyards were rescheduled, while the Palace waited, and telegrams passed between London and Evita's party, no decision was made on the question of whether she would go to London.

The entrance way to the Argentine Embassy in Rome had been repaved in marble, and a urinal removed from the sidewalk outside, by the time Evita was met at the airport by Count Sforza, the Minister for Foreign Affairs, and eighty children from the Opera Nazionale d'Infanzia, dressed in white and waving the Italian and Argentine flags. On 27 June, two days after she had arrived, Evita was granted an audience with the Pope, for which she dressed in a heavy silk dress and a black mantilla, with the cross of Isabella pinned to her chest. She was allotted twenty-minutes, the time accorded by Vatican protocol to queens. Afterwards, she walked around the palace escorted by six elderly members of the Vatican nobility dressed in gaiters, cloaks and ruffs, and by five Swiss guards with halberds and helmets. Evita, looking devout, was photographed with her hand on the arm of an Italian dignitary with a beard and an eyepatch. 'Coming into St Peter's Square,' she told Perón that night, 'I had the sense of being on a different planet. Rome seemed thousands of kilometres away, and not even the slightest whisper could be heard. That small state around the Basilica is like a continent. The Pope was like a vision, with a low and distant voice, as if out of a dream. He said he was following your work, that he considered you a favoured son, and that your policies had laudably implemented the fundamental policies of Christianity.'[8]

Evita's presence in Rome caused several demonstrations to erupt; twenty-seven arrests were made one night outside her window, amidst Communist chants and cries of 'fascist'. The Communists were at that time attempting to dislodge the coalition of Socialists and Christian Democrats ruling Italy, and these demonstrations had been planned to jeopardize what Evita's visit was supposed to accomplish: loans, and an increase in the quota of immigrants allowed into Argentina. The Communists were confronted by another group of workers who demonstrated on

Evita's behalf by shouting her name in rhythms which Italians associated with chants of the Mussolini era. According to an American broadcasting reporter, these workers said they were Socialists, but they thought Evita was beautiful and that 'Italy must be nice to her because Argentine had been nice to Italy'.

Evita held a press conference in the Argentine embassy, at which she gave her views on divorce (of which she did not approve) and on Chopin (of whom she did approve). She said she was 'not political,' but that her favourite colour was red; when a journalist asked whether this did not express some political preference, she said no and appeared to be embarrassed. When asked what she thought of the disturbances of the past night, she said 'that is my reply,' pointing to the window behind her, outside which a crowd had gathered to chant her name. By now Evita was exhausted, and after briefly visiting Milan, took the advice of her doctor and went to rest at a villa in Rapallo provided for her by Alberto Dodero. Here, Ricardo Labougle, the Argentine Ambassador in London, attempted to persuade her that the British Royal family had meant no discourtesy, but neither Evita nor her brother was convinced. Publicly, Evita's decision not to go to London was justified on grounds of ill-health, but in reality it had to do with feelings of wounded vanity: 'Tell the Queen that if she isn't capable of inviting me officially, I don't want to see her,' the Ambassador reported her to have said.[9] When the Ambassador insisted that it could all be explained in terms of protocol, her answer was, 'When I say I won't go, I won't go.'

Evita's next stop was in Lisbon, where she paid a visit to Don Juan de Borbón, despite the advice of a counsellor at the Argentine Embassy, who had warned that this might seem discourteous to Franco. "I'll go where I like,' she is reported to have said, 'and if fatty doesn't like it, that's too bad.' From Portugal, the party flew to Paris, where they were met by the Foreign Minister, Georges Bidault. As he watched her descend the steps of the aircraft, he exclaimed, *'Qu'elle est jeune et jolie.'* The curiosity of the French was muted by the fact that the Argentines arrived during the Tour de France. Evita stayed at the Ritz, and was driven around the city in a car that had belonged to de Gaulle and had been used by Churchill on his visits to Paris. Her presence had been scheduled to coincide with the signing of a commercial treaty between Argentina and France, the ceremony of which she attended at the Quai d'Orsay. Afterwards she received the Légion d'Honneur from Bidault.

She had been anxious to see clothes from great fashion houses, but the Ambassador's wife advised that she have a private showing at her hotel, rather than attend one put on for the public. A private display was organized for her, but shortly before its scheduled beginning, she had doubts and called in Father Benítez. He said it would be viewed as 'an unacceptable frivolity'.[10] She immediately cancelled the show, a tactless error that offended many people. Nonetheless, before Evita left Paris, she left her measurements at Christian Dior and Marcel Rochas, who would thereafter make many of her clothes, either submitting sketches to her through the Argentine Embassy, or designing what they felt would be acceptable and sending it directly to Buenos Aires.

A reception was given at the Cercle d'Amérique Latine, in a large hall with a grand marble staircase. The entire diplomatic corps from Latin America filed before her, the women curtseying and walking back three paces when they greeted her. Evita was dressed extravagantly in a golden dress, skintight and décolleté, with a long fish-tail train. She wore a gold veil over her blond hair, and an 'enormous jewelled necklace, long earrings to match, and three jewelled bracelets'.[11] When she turned away from those to whom she had been presented and, holding her train, made her way up the marble stairs, the diplomats could see the jewelled heels of her gold sandals. After the reception she went with Dodero to dine at the Pré-Catalan, in the Bois de Boulogne, where other patrons stood on their tables to get a better view of her.

In Madrid and Rome Evita had been able to make herself understood in Spanish, but in France she was obliged to rely on Liliane Guardo's translations. After one reception Dodero offered to take them all to a cabaret, but Evita supposed it would be disreputable, like those of Buenos Aires, and refused to go. She did visit the circus, but was offended by one of the clowns who finished his act by presenting a bunch of flowers to a woman in the audience, then making it disappear as she reached out for it. Evita disliked this joke when it was played on her, and proceeded to walk out.

From Paris she went with Dodero to Monte Carlo where she stayed at the Hôtel de Paris. Years later, after she was dead, Aristotle Onassis would say that he slept with her there, and afterwards gave a cheque to 'one her favourite charities.' He may have met her, since he was a citizen of Argentina and a friend of Dodero's, but the rest of the story is probably an invention, revealing the extent to which she was still regarded as a sex-object.

The last place she visited was Switzerland, and it was never made clear why she went there. The opposition in Buenos Aires assumed that the genuine purpose of the whole European visit was for Evita and her brother to deposit money in Swiss bank accounts, and that the rest had been devised to conceal this. Many wealthy Argentines did this, but there are many more convenient and less conspicuous ways of depositing money in Swiss accounts than meeting the Swiss Foreign Minister and being shown around a watch factory. In Berne Evita and the Foreign Minister were pelted with tomatoes, and in Lucerne the windscreen of her car was broken by a flying rock. The aggressor was a Swiss citizen, brought up in Argentina and recently released from a lunatic asylum.

On 10 August Evita flew from Geneva via Lisbon to Dakar, where she boarded the *Buenos Aires,* an Argentine ship which was also carrying three hundred Italian immigrants. During the crossing to Rio de Janeiro she made speeches to the immigrants, explaining the principles of Peronism. In Rio she disembarked to attend the Inter-American Conference for Peace and Security. Ricardo Guardo, accompanied by cabinet ministers and members of Perón's press secretariat, had come from Buenos Aires equipped with 50,000 badges embossed with likenesses of Perón and Evita, and enough posters bearing Evita's likeness to plaster the walls of the city. Posters were inscribed in Portuguese with: 'To the Brazilian woman, who like the Argentine woman, is fighting for justice, work and peace. 'Evita attended a number of banquets, listened to the speech of the United States Secretary of State, George Marshall, and was mobbed outside the Copacabana Palace Hotel. Her press conference was better than the one she had given in Rome. As one commentator explained,[12] she was better at 'being brilliant with short evasive phrases, [and] circling the question without actually answering it'. Thus: 'Have you returned with additional ideas on how to give aid to Europe?' 'In my country all I do is aid the working class . . .' 'Did the *descamisados* of Europe impress you favourably?' 'The *descamisados* of the world, all of them, impress me favourably.' 'What did you think of Franco?' 'Exactly what I thought of all the chiefs of state I met.' 'How did you begin your artistic career? In films, in radio or in the theatre?' one reporter asked Evita. The smile left her lips. She looked at him, and with some asperity answered, 'That is of no conceivable interest to the public.'

Evita flew to Montevideo the next day and after attending more receptions and meeting the two hundred labour leaders and Peronist officials who had crossed the Rio de la Plata to welcome her home, she boarded the steamer *Ciudad de Montevideo,* bound for Buenos Aires. As the ship came into port, it was surrounded by smaller craft blowing their sirens, while a plane flew overhead in the sunlight, the word 'welcome' stencilled on its wings. A large crowd lined the red carpet on the quayside and overflowed on to the docks. In her hurry to leave the ship Evita ran past Perón, and then, when she found him, burst into tears. Perón smiled as he always did, while Evita made a brief speech about 'my three loves: my country, my *descamisados* and my dear General Perón.' She promised she would see everyone next Monday at the Secretariat of Labour, and was driven away from the dockside to the presidential residence in a state of exhaustion.

As a means of covincing the rest of the world of the acceptability of the 'New Argentina', Evita's visit to Europe was less than successful. The European Left had not been impressed by the image of Argentina which she had projected, and where the press had been favourable, it had managed to be so only by making some distinction between Evita and the regime she represented. This reflected a serious attempt on the part of journalists to reconcile the attraction they felt towards the idea of Evita, with what they presumed to be the sordid aspects of Perón's rule. It was inevitable that Evita be viewed in a fascist context. Therefore, both Evita and Perón were seen to represent an ideology which had run its course in Europe, only to re-emerge in an exotic, theatrical, even farcical form in a faraway country. Thus the correspondent of the London *Observer* would characterize the regime as 'glamour demogogy' and the trip as one of a series of extravagant gestures in a country that could afford them' at the sole cost of annoying a few millionaires and, of course, nauseating the civilized and sincere democrats among the intelligentsia.'[13] As for Evita, she could be excused 'for making herself the darling of the world . . . to us, the fascist salute means a nightmare that happened. To señora Perón, it evidently seems just a gesture in a great show, the theme of which is: Poor girl makes good and is beloved by one and all for ever and ever.'

In Argentina, the opposition had understandably been very critical of the great cost of the trip. The government threatened those newspapers which continued with their defamatory campaigns with closure, and in two cases carried out its threat. In the first instance they shut a newspaper for reprinting a hostile report from the British press, and in the second, they shut one for having dared to print a cartoon of Evita visiting Switzerland beneath a hail of tomatoes. Yet the criticism was for the most part restrained, and many Argentines were astounded and pleased that Evita had represented them in Europe to such acclaim. Evita in particular looked with satisfaction on what she had done. She had prepared for the trip much as an actress would prepare for her

Eva Maria Ibarguren at school in Junín, taken *(right)* when she was in the second grade, and *(below)* when she was in the sixth grade.

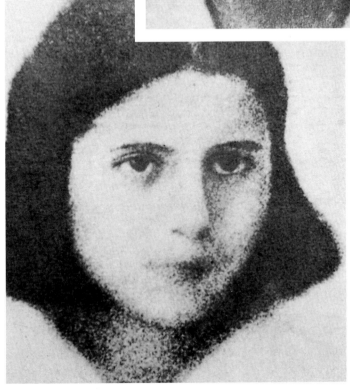

Evita as actress: a publicity photograph.

Perón and Evita with the British Ambassador in 1949. Evita's brother Juan Duarte is the moustached man behind her right shoulder;
(bottom) Campaigning with Perón.

President Juan Perón.

After her European journey, Evita began to order dresses from the
great French couture houses.

Evita at work.

The image of herself Evita chose to present on posters, stamps, postcards –
this picture was used everywhere.

In August 1952 Evita was put forward by the Newspaper Vendors' Union
as a candidate for canonisation.

most momentous performance, and by her own standards, she had been successful. She would later distinguish between her ceremonial Eva Perón role of receiving honours and attending state functions and her role as Evita, doing her social and political work. After the trip to Europe, her role as Evita became prominent. The change was gradual. To begin with it was merely a question of dressing less elaborately and abandoning her pompadour hairstyle. But in the next three years she worked full time with the unions, with women and with the poor, and though she seems never precisely to have aimed for it, she ended by having in her own hands a large and efficient political organization.

Because Evita's power was personally exercised, it has usually been assumed that it was motivated by personal characteristics, whim or vindictiveness; and that its effects were little other than her own aggrandizement. Yet this was not the case. Evita always worked within the context of what Perón was accomplishing and the period in which she began to be powerful – from 1947 to 1950 – was also the period in which Perón first increased his own power and then began to change Argentina. To understand the development of 'Evita' it is necessary to turn first to Perón's own creation, the 'New Argentina'.

7
The New Argentina

'One does not encounter in Buenos Aires today the orthodox trappings of a dictatorship,' a perplexed American observer remarked in 1948[1]. 'There are no restrictions on travel; people move about freely. Opponents of the regime have no fear of speaking to foreigners, meeting them at their hotels, or inviting them to their homes. There are no concentration camps, and, as far as a stranger can make out, no political prisoners.' Yet among intellectuals or opposition politicians a 'heavy air of dejection and depression' could be felt. This reflected the widely held view that under Perón the country was becoming a dictatorship, in spite of appearances. Indeed it was this absence of any marked sense of abnormality that most bothered these opponents of Perón. People spoke vaguely, in terms of dreams or presages. It was in this year that Hitler and Eva Braun were repeatedly sighted on remote *estancias* in the South. Although these apparitions were not really taken seriously, they seemed to show that Argentina was the sort of place to which the Führer might have wished to come. There were Argentines who bemoaned what they saw as the novelty of Perón's methods of rule. 'He is subtle, devious, charming,' an opposition lawyer remarked. 'He does not come out into the open and crack skulls . . .. He does his work silently and cynically. You see, there is so little we can put our hands on these days – everything he does is in the name of "democracy" and "social betterment" – and yet we sense the smell of evil in the air, and the thin ledge on which we walk.'

By 1955, when he was finally ejected by the armed forces, Perón had indeed imposed a dictatorship on Argentina. Yet this does not seem to have been his aim when he came to power in 1946, nor was the Peronist police state instituted either quickly or systematically. If Perón did ultimately fulfil the prophecies of his opponents, it was after he had brought to Argentina the first working democracy since 1927 and after he had significantly increased the participation of Argentines in national politics. Perón is remembered as a dictator, but he was popularly elected and he imposed his form of authoritarianism with overwhelming popular support. His real interest lay in the accumulation of power and the main source of his power came to lie with this 'New Argentina' – the crowds which had liberated him and whose acclaim he had enjoyed. Yet he never attempted to destroy the old Argentina, just as he left his most frequently reviled enemy, the Oligarchy, intact and prosperous. Perón had a majority in Congress, and Congress continued to sit and to pass laws. This was what one observer astutely called 'the fiction of democratic legality'[2]; Congress was allowed to sit because it had become innocuous. The real power of the regime lay elsewhere, in its new institutions, in its mass support, and in the relationship between Perón, Evita and their supporters.

Perón's need to control his wayward supporters found expression in a variety of measures. In 1946, the Labour party was dissolved. In the next two years what would become Perón's own, Peronist party, went under a variety of names; first it was merely 'an organic mass', then it was the 'Only Party of the Revolution'.

Some Labour party members accepted Perón's decision, but there were others, most notably Cipriano Reyes, one of the founders of the party, who did not. Reyes, who was a deputy, denounced the 'totalitarian *junta*' which now controlled the party. He sat by himself in Congress, he continued to produce the party's newspaper, and when he was repeatedly attacked in the street, he appeared in Congress with a bandaged head.

On 20 September 1948, the State radio network announced the discovery of a vast plot to assassinate Péron and Evita, naming among the twenty-odd conspirators the former cultural attaché of the US government in Buenos Aires, John Griffiths (then resigned from his post and in business in Montevideo), Reyes and his brothers. There was a government-inspired strike in support of Perón and much indignation about the 'plot'. Reyes and his supposed associates were jailed, but never tried; they were briefly released in 1949, but jailed again. Reyes remained in prison until 1955, learning English and writing a novel. It is said that he was tortured, but he would never speak about this.[3]

Perón next moved to increase his control over his supporters in the CGT. When Luis Gay was elected secretary general of the CGT in November 1946 against Perón's candidate, Perón summoned Gay and told him that all the important press releases of the CGT should in future be drawn up by a 'special team' in the Presidential secretariat. When Gay refused the services of this team, Péron first gave him a series of lucrative appointments and, after these had failed to influence him, moved to expel him.

In January 1947 a group of American labour organizers and

members of the ILO came to Buenos Aires at the invitation of the CGT. Perón was opposed to their visit and, when the Americans arrived, he denied them contact with the CGT and accused Gay of selling the organization to the US. Gay met privately with the Americans in their hotel suite, which Perón had had bugged; and he was thus, in his own words, able to summon Gay and say, 'Look, you resign or tomorrow I'll break your head.' There was a series of meetings in which Perón asserted he had evidence of Gay's 'treason' but refused to show it (it was, he said, 'in a safe at Army headquarters') and in the end Gay did resign. After a series of threats against his life, he left Buenos Aires, unable to find work or rejoin his old union.[4]

Where the law made the strategy of legal coercion possible, Perón made use of it; otherwise he resorted to dire threats and petty intimidation. Of the strongholds of anti-Peronism in Argentina, the Supreme Court offered him least resistance. As in the US, the provision of impeachment existed in the Constitution, though it had rarely been used. Perón unearthed a variety of impeachable offences committed by the court, the most piquant of which was its illegal ratification of many decrees of the military government of which he had himself been a member. On 1 August 1946, the four impeached Justices of the Court tendered their resignation and four new Justices, including Eva's brother-in-law, Justo Rodríguez, were sworn in.

By 1948 most of the CGT leadership had been replaced. Not only was the union leadership no longer controlled by the anarchists and socialists who had been in positions of power in 1943, it had also passed out of the hands of people such as Gay who had helped Perón to power. In selecting José Espejo as Gay's successor, Perón could not have made his intentions clearer. Espejo had never, as has been alleged, been the doorman of Perón's apartment, but he drove a truck for a biscuit manufacturing concern, he was a committed Peronist and he was devoted to Evita and Perón.

Newspapers of which the regime had cause to disapprove could be dealt with in a number of ways. When *La Razón,* a highly conservative evening paper, published a number of critical editorials, it received a series of visits from municipal inspectors complaining about its lack of workers' amenities. Fans and new washrooms were installed, but the visits and fines continued until the paper's editorial page disappeared, replaced with advertising. *La Vanguardia,* the newspaper of the Socialist party, had criticized Perón's social reforms as window-dressing and launched some attacks on Evita. In August 1947, the newspaper was shut down on the grounds that its printing-presses violated municipal anti-noise ordinances, that its trucks kept people awake at night and that its pressroom lacked proper first-aid equipment. In August 1947 the paper ceased publication and the Socialist party was forced to reach its members by means of clandestine publications.[5]

In 1948, the government acquired a monopoly of printing ink, which further intimidated the remaining independent newspapers. It had meanwhile, through various intermediaries, begun to acquire its own chain of newspapers and radio stations. By the early 1950s, ALEA S.A., of which the chairman was Carlos Aloé, the governor of Buenos Aires, had acquired thirteen publishing houses, seventeen newspapers, three radio stations and four news agencies. ALEA was technically private, but its directors were ministers or party officials and its aim, as Aloé later conceded, was to 'form opinion'. Yet in 1950 Perón could still tell a group of visiting journalists that there was no censorship and be technically correct; there were no censors sitting in newspaper offices, as there had been before his election. But Perón's understanding of the functions of journalism was not that of the visiting journalists. 'Our press is purified,' he told them. 'It has been subjected to an extraordinary process of perfection. There is no more adversary journalism, only pure journalism.'[6]

Yet Perón's repressive acts were performed simultaneously with the enactment of numerous and significant social reforms, some of which had the effect of making Argentine institutions more democratic. His substantial majority in Congress and in the Senate meant that he could pass whatever legislation he liked. After ratifying everything the previous government had accomplished by decree, Perón's Congress, at his behest, pushed through an ambitious programme of social legislation. In 1947 Congress, again with Perón's blessing, gave Argentine women the vote.

Fifteen separate private bills for women's suffrage had been introduced between 1911 and 1946 and each of them had died through hostility or negligence. But by the time Perón came to power it was widely agreed that women should be given the vote. Six bills were introduced in the first weeks of Congress. One of them would certainly have been passed without undue fuss.

Evita has been widely credited for having brought the vote to Argentine women, and it is this that is the basis of the claim that she was 'an early feminist'. In fact her actions were limited at the very most to supporting the bill of one of her supporters, Eduardo

Colom, a bill which was in any case later dropped.[7] Yet she had made a number of speeches in favour of the vote and *Democracia,* her newspaper, ran a series of articles urging male Peronists to abandon their prejudices against women.

There was a celebration to mark the passing of the bill, number 13010, and it took place in front of the Casa Rosada, rather than Congress, where the project had originated. In front of the government palace were banners, and a truck carried an allegorical tableau depicting a female Liberty next to a voting-box. Perón signed the law, making it public; and then he handed it to Evita, making it hers, along with this substantial new constituency of women voters.

As pressure was put on the media through which criticism of the government could be voiced, the frustration of the parliamentary opposition increased. There were all sorts of sanctions that could be applied to them. A motion of censure could be brought by the government and, if the opposition speaker did not retract his words, he could be deprived of his immunity and expelled from Congress. This is what happened in August 1948 to Ernesto Sammartino, leader of the Radical bloc in the Chamber of Deputies, after he had criticized a series of articles Perón had written for the US press. But Sammartino had his hour in the debate on his expulsion. 'We have not come here to bow reverently before the whip or to dance jigs to please a Madame Pompadour . . . this Chamber should never again listen to the voice of command of old colonels dressed in long shirts, or to orders in perfumed invitations from the boudoir of any ruler.'[8] Sammartino was expelled after this speech and his forty-two Radical followers walked out of Congress in protest after him. But they returned next month; Congress was there and it was all that remained.

There had previously been discussion of changing the Constitution, enacted in 1853, on the grounds that it was no longer adequate for a country with modern needs. Specifically, though this was never stated, it was felt that Article 77, which prohibited the President from ruling more than one six-year term at a time, should now be changed. While the Radicals were conveniently absent from Parliament the first step in the creation of a new Constitution was taken, so that by the time they returned, both houses had supplied the two-thirds vote necessary for the summoning of a constitutional convention. Perón proclaimed his disinterestedness with regard to Article 77, but since Evita was campaigning in favour of its repeal this deceived no one. In the debates of the convention its removal was justified by the argument that at present Article 77 was an impediment to popular sovereignty, for the people could not elect whomsoever they wished.

Perón's acceptance of the new Constitution, on 16 March 1949, seemed to remove the last hindrance to the almost indefinite extension of his authority. He had cowed, if not quite dominated, every Argentine institution opposed to him, and it seemed inconceivable that in the next few years he would not push further in the direction of the authoritarianism he had adopted.

His attitude towards his old friend Domingo Mercante was indicative of what Perón proposed. In recognition of his loyalty in 1945, Mercante had been given the important post of Governor of Buenos Aires. He was considered most likely to succeed Perón. He had put forward the project of constitutional reform because he was loyal to Perón and because he hoped to be made Vice-President in the elections. But during the proceedings word was passed around that he had fallen from favour. Evita began to omit Mercante from her speeches. He was expelled from the party in 1953 for unspecified 'acts of disloyalty'. The fall of Mercante marked the end of this first, relatively open phase of Peronism. It was in the second and more closed phase that Evita became really powerful.

On 20 July 1949, 6,000 members of the Peronist party met in the Luna Park stadium. After a speech of Perón's the women delegates left the men and went to the Cervantes Theatre, where they listened to a long speech by Evita in which she outlined the prospective aims of a Peronist Women's Party, which she proposed to create and over which she would preside. She spoke rousingly of the injustices of working women, but the main point of her speech was the prescription of complete and unconditional loyalty to Perón. 'Our movement is inspired theoretically and doctrinally by Perón's words . . . . To be a Peronist is, for a woman, to be loyal and to have blind confidence in Perón.'[9] Thus, in the shadow of Perón, but, as she also made clear, entirely separate from its male equivalent, Evita's political party emerged. She dominated it, and with it she produced an entire generation of loyal Peronist women. It was her first specifically political post and it constituted a recognition of her power in Argentina. Unlike the male Peronist party, Evita's organization was an astounding success. By 1952, it had 500,000 members and 3,600 headquarters.

In the next elections it was able to increase Perón's majority by giving him over sixty-three per cent of the new woman's vote. It performed prodigies of organization. But it remained subordinate to Perón's wishes and its organization was stiflingly hierarchical.

Some of the women who worked for the party Evita had met years before and used for social works; others she remembered from various occasions and now summoned. The Steward of the Residence, Atilio Renzi, had told her a long time ago of the brother and sister who ran his neighbourhood bakery and who would defend Perón and Evita in long and impassioned debates with their customers, and Evita now asked Renzi to fetch the sister. A tango singer called Juana Larrauri had supported Perón in 1945, composing a song in his honour, and had later approached Evita, unable to find work. Evita had not liked her, but she found 'Juanita' a job at Radio Belgrano, and now ordered her to come forth. The women came in groups either to Evita's office or to the Residence where they waited patiently for Evita to see them. She told them she needed 'good Peronists', 'fanatics', devoted to the party and prepared to place it above all things, including their careers or families. 'When a woman goes into politics, the man eats cold *puchero* (stew),' she told one prospective recruit.[10] Wherever they lived, and in whatever circumstances, they must be prepared to travel ceaselessly around the country setting up houses from which the work of registration and indoctrination could be organized. Only those in a position to 'give their lives' would be recruited, and those who passed this test often took this prescription of fanaticism quite literally. One woman fell to her knees before Evita and said, 'It isn't servility and it isn't just adulation, but I have never touched a saint of flesh and blood. Let me kneel before you and kiss you.'[11] It soon became apparent that there was no room in the party for anyone who was not a staunch loyalist, and many of the more intelligent people around Evita, when they realized this to be the case, left. Those who stayed, but questioned her authority in any way, were often expelled.

No tradition of women's work existed; the organizers had to deal not only with the great antipathy to Peronism that remained among many classes in many parts of the country, but also with a traditional opposition to them as women. Evita was an admirable organizer herself, ceaselessly hectoring or encouraging 'her women', calling them persistently in the middle of the night to ask about their difficulties, or bringing them back to Buenos Aires for consultations. 'She was behind us the whole time, pushing us on,' said Delia Degliuomini de Parodi, one of the first census-takers, who lived apart from her husband and mother for the first time in her life when she left Buenos Aires to organize the province of San Luis. 'When I arrived there, there were only fifty cells. When I left a year later there were two hundred and fifty and I weighed twenty-five pounds less and had a shadow on my lung.'[12]

Evita had never been specially interested in the question of women's suffrage, and she similarly displayed little concern with more theoretical questions of women's rights. She devoted very few of her speeches to questions that exclusively concerned women and where she did address herself to some of the implications of feminism, it was merely to dismiss feminists contemptuously as women who did not know how to be women. Her ideas about feminism were Perón's and Perón's ideas about feminism were much what one might expect.

Yet Evita's effect on the condition of women in Argentine and on their political life was decisive; what she accomplished here was as important as anything else she did. A mass of women who cared little about women's rights and were indifferent to the concerns of middle-class feminists had entered politics because of Evita. They were the first Argentine women to be active in politics, they gave Perón a large majority in 1951 and they remained loyal to him and what they saw as the principles of Peronism long after their inspiration and figurehead had died.

These were years in which Evita was incessantly in the public eye. No occasion – the opening of a swimming pool, a factory, a trade union building, a presentation of a medal, a lunch with a visiting foreigner – was too trivial for her presence. If a company launched a new product, it would require her sponsorship and thus the government's approval. If a sportsman, a football player or motor-racing driver left the country or returned, then he too was required to be photographed with Evita.

The rituals of Argentine politics prior to Perón and Evita had mostly consisted of formal meetings, such as long political banquets at which magniloquent speeches were made. In the 'New Argentina' babies were kissed, ribbons snipped and medals presented, but these occasions were different in aim and in intensity to their equivalents in other countries. It was said that the 'New Argentina' was all propaganda and, while this is not strictly true, its end could sometimes seem not so much the construction of public works as the generation of emotion. Each *acto* – for so the daily encounters of Perón, Evita and the people were called – no matter how trivially it began, soon developed into an intense public reaffirmation of love. 'In Argentina today,' an American reporter noted not entirely frivolously, 'it's love, love, love. Love makes the Peróns go round. Their whole act is based on it. They are constantly, madly, passionately, nationally in love. They conduct their affair with the people quite openly. They are the perfect lovers – generous, kind, and forever thoughtful in matters both great and small.'[13]

Crowds, for Perón and Evita, reflected the origins of their movement on 17 October 1945 and a notion of popular legitimacy that existed outside the old tradition of legal rule. To be before a crowd (and the crowds were vast, loving and ebullient) was to sense in the most immediate way the source of their power. In his study of crowd psychology, Elias Canetti has spoken of the phenomenon of discharge in crowds. This occurs when people of various origins are thrown together. 'In that density, where there is scarcely any space between, and body presses against body, each man is as near the other as he is to himself; and an immense feeling of relief ensues. It is for the sake of this blessed moment . . . that people become a crowd.'[14] The great crowds of Peronism were, as Canetti indicates, under an illusion, since this was not actually the case, but it was a very powerful illusion. No matter how organized the crowds became, they could relive the first 'sacred moment' of Peronism and its sequel, the creation of Perón and Evita. For Perón and Evita did not just act on their behalf, they became them.

The two *jornadas* ('great days') in the Peronist calendar were 1 May and 17 October; and on each day more than a million people would be packed into the Plaza de Mayo. On 1 May there was a beauty contest to determine the 'Queen of Labour', an outdoor concert by the Colon orchestra, and in 1949 a specially composed ballet with an allegorical motif. But it was 17 October that was the centrepiece of Peronist ritual. The city filled with buses and trucks, and the *descamisados*, bearing huge banners, re-enacted the taking of the bourgeois city on a scale surpassing that of the original. What occurred each 17 October was much too disorganized to be compared to a fascist rally, but it was accomplished in part to threaten the regime's enemies, and the 'love' proclaimed each 17 October before the great crowd could in fact be justified by the hostility which was offered to those outside it.

An entire liturgy had developed making it possible to re-enact the encounter of leader and people. In the early years, Perón spoke to the people alone, but by 1948, Evita had acquired her own place in the ceremony. There had been a march called 'The Peronist Boys', now, different lyrics were set to the same tune:

Las muchachas peronistas
Con Evita triunfaremos
Y con ella brindaremos
Nuestra vida por Perón.
Viva Perón! Viva Perón!
Por Perón y por Evita
La vida queremos dar
Por Evita capitana
Y por Perón General.

We Peronist Women
We'll triumph with Evita
And with her we'll dedicate
Our lives to Perón.
Viva Perón! Viva Perón!
For Perón and for Evita
We want to give our lives
For Evita our captain
And Perón our general.

By now the history of 17 October had been written to provide a part in the 'revolution' for Evita; as protagonist, loyalist, and spiritual support. She had many 'titles' – 'The Lady of Hope', 'The Mother of the Innocents', 'The Workers' Plenipotentiary', 'The Standard-bearer of the *descamisados*' – but the one she used most often on this occasion was the simplest; 'The Bridge of Love'. Where Perón's lengthy and raucously delivered speeches might deal with any matter of policy or contain an explication of his ideology or his theories of leadership, Evita dealt essentially with herself, with Perón and with the *descamisados*. She would speak on Perón's behalf to the crowd or on the crowd's behalf to Perón and then for herself, the person who brought the leader and his people together.

Evita had earlier been an indifferent public speaker, shrill and monotonous, but by 1948 she had acquired a masterly ability to convey emotion publicly. Even those opposed to her who affected to find the content of her speeches boring came away with a strong sense of the intense, reciprocal emotion that passed through any meeting she addressed. Usually, she began 'My dear *descamisados*'. She spoke of the benighted days of the Oligarchy, of a past in which the only important event to have occurred was the Revolution of 17 October, and of a present defined by ominous threats and betrayals on the part of 'selfish, traitorous' enemies. Only with the coming of Perón had Argentines received 'social justice', and now it would be maintained 'inexorably' or 'at all costs'. Evita spoke fluently, dramatically and passionately; often she would abandon her text and improvise in her own words and she stabbed at the air as if to touch the audience. At the midst of each speech, she spoke of her own heart. Perón had worked for the people because he loved them and they had shown their own gratitude by freeing him from prison. Then she, out of her own gratitude, had given herself first to Perón and then to them.

Evita dealt, not in political terminology but in that of the emotions. Her language came from her own feelings and the conventions of the soap operas, and they made the notions of love and loyalty to Perón vivid and urgent. These were important in Peronism because for many people they were the content of Peronism. But they also played a large part in the progressive elevation of Perón to divine status. Evita's cult of Perón probably first occurred in her speeches to shore up her own political identity and to reflect her own real admiration for Perón, but by 1949, the cult was institutionalized and Evita was its priestess. More than any alleged defect of character this hero-worship, arising out of great love, corrupted Perón and debased his movement. The press was gagged and Congress was cowed; it became an offence to speak slightingly of Perón. When Evita spoke of him so adoringly, who around him could contradict, or halt for a moment the grotesquely excessive expressions of admiration that surrounded every public mention of his name?

'Sometimes,' said Evita, 'I think that Perón ceased to be an ordinary man and became an ideal incarnate';[15] or, on another occasion, and more excessively, 'Perón is everything. He is the soul, the nerve, the hope and the reality of the Argentine people. We know that there is only one man here in our movement with his own source of light and that is Perón. We all feed from his light.'[16] In this context of revealed truth, there could be no grounds for opposition to Perón whatsoever, on any count, and no alternative to the 'fanaticism' and 'sectarianism' that Evita now laid down as the criteria for political conduct. These terms had come from the florid vocabulary of radio melodramas, but within the political context of great power, and great volatile crowds, and spoken by the wife of the President, they acquired a rather different meaning:

> The opposition says that it is fanaticism, that I am a fanatic for Perón and for the people, that I am dangerous because I am too sectarian and too fanatic on Perón's behalf; but I answer them with Perón: fanaticism is the wisdom of the spirit. What matter if one is a fanatic, if one is that in the company of martyrs and heroes . . . In any case life has its real value not when it is lived in a spirit of egoism, just for oneself, but

when one surrenders oneself, completely and fanatically, to an ideal that has more value than life itself. I say yes, I am fanatically for Perón and the *descamisados* of the nation.[17]

Many people, confronted with such statements, have preferred to assume that they were spoken with intent to deceive, or that they were figures of speech, or even the ramblings of someone who had little education and was incapable of distinguishing between the encoded excesses of radio melodrama and other forms of expression. But Evita understood and meant everything she said in these public confessions of love. That is what she felt for Perón and why she acted on his behalf.

8

The Gift of Giving

The Eva Perón Foundation was not a charity, nor was it a genuine device for taking from the rich and giving to the poor. Nor, though this has been suggested, was it a covert method of depositing money in Swiss bank accounts. It was frequently used as a blueprint for the 'New Argentina' and it came to be part of the Peronist state, but it was not created for these purposes. The most convenient way to think of it is in terms of Evita's personality and her career. It began as the simplest response to the poverty she encountered each day in her office. As it grew its purposes changed until it came to constitute an entire welfare organization, albeit one of a very special kind. But it began with people's needs and the appalling backwardness of social services – or charity, as it was still called – in Argentina.

In 1946, the exercise of charity in Buenos Aires was mostly in the hands of eighty-seven ageing society ladies who collectively represented the *Sociedad de Beneficencia*. The Sociedad still occupied the colonial convent in Calle Reconquista, which had been deeded to it in 1823. At the time its functions had been to 'manage and inspect schools for girls, homes for orphans, hospitals for women and all establishments for the welfare of that sex'.[1] There had been a period when the free time and largesse of the ladies was adequate to the organization's functions, and in those days the Sociedad was undoubtedly efficient if not specially enlightened, caring for orphans and the impoverished sick. But these days were long past.

With the growth of the country, the Sociedad had also grown, and it now operated a sanatorium, several hospitals and a great many homes for the elderly. The ladies still thought of it as belonging to them, and still met each month under the tutelage of an elderly male accountant to dispose of the accumulated funds of the Sociedad. But these funds were no longer provided by them or by their husbands' business connections; they came from the State, either indirectly, through a levy imposed by means of the national lottery, or directly through cash grants from the National Budget. And the organization's employees were becoming restive. In 1939, a speaker in Congress estimated that nurses of the Sociedad worked twelve or fourteen hours a day, received one day off every two weeks and were paid a salary that was half the minimum wage.

It was not only in matters of pay that the Sociedad was old-fashioned. Children at its orphanages wore blue smocks and had their heads shaved. Young women earned part of their keep by sewing clothes for the Oligarchy. Each Christmas these children had their heads shaved and were sent through the streets in dark clothes to solicit funds on the Sociedad's behalf, pathetic figures to tug at the public conscience. Once a year, for one of the city's more important social functions, the orphans were scrubbed, dressed up, and taken to the Colon Opera House, where as the newspaper *La Nación* put it, with no apparent irony, they received 'the encouragement of and the help of small contributions, as they had shown they knew how to fight with heroism and submit with resignation and faith to the rigours of destiny'.[2] The small children were seated in rows like singers in a chorale, facing their social betters and benefactors. At a dais on the stage sat these ladies of good family, the Papal Nuncio, the Cardinal, many Cabinet Ministers and officials, and the wife of the President. A table on the dais was stacked with scrolls, prizes for virtue, for morality, for industry, for humility and for self-denial, and as the afternoon wore on, the table was slowly emptied of paper, as the unfortunate recipients filed past to shake hands with the ladies, the First Lady and the Cardinal, to the accompaniment of periodic but subdued applause from the well-dressed audience.

In 1945 Perón attended one of these ceremonies, but Evita was not with him. At that time they were still not married, and this was certainly one of those occasions to which it was impossible to bring one's mistress. It is unlikely that he derived pleasure from the occasion, and it is certain that it would have greatly distressed Evita had she been able to see it. There had been many criticisms of the Sociedad in Congress, and in one of the earliest sessions of the new House in 1946, a resolution was introduced to the effect that the organization had been designed to promote 'noble and philanthropic activity', but that it had deteriorated into a social club and had no further place within the New Argentina, either as symbol or as functioning institution, the only important question about it being how it could best be dismantled.[3]

It has often been said that the ladies, confronted with the prospect of Evita's appointment as Honorary President, were so appalled by the bad example she might set the orphans that they sent word to her that she was too young and therefore unsuitable.[4] Evita was hurt and angry and replied, 'If they do not accept me, they can have my mother,' a suggestion she knew would not meet with their approval. When this indeed proved to be the case, Eva was able to use the pretext of the ladies' wilfulness to shut down the Sociedad. In fact there is some indication that there was a meeting between her and the ladies, but if there was, it occurred under rather different circumstances, after 'intervention' had been suggested, and at a time when it was already clear that little could be done to save the Sociedad. The ladies probably invited her as a last recourse, after all other strategies had failed. It is said that the meeting was amicable until the ladies asked Evita to be Honorary President, suggesting she help with such fund-raising drives as canasta or bridge parties. It was then that she told the ladies that the policy of the government was one of replacing charity with social justice. Now, she said, was 'the time for social justice'. The Sociedad was taken over by the State because it was thought to be anachronistic, and it was only two years later that Evita began to think of her own social works.

Evita's earliest distributions of clothes and food took place under the auspices of something the Peronist press referred to as 'The Crusade of Social Aid'. This was never much more than a slogan. At Christmas time, 1946, Evita had handed food to old people and to strikers at a shoe factory, and the next year she and Perón received poor people in the gardens of the Residence and nationally distributed hundreds of thousands of packages of cider and panettoni. The Steward of the Residence, Atilio Renzi, had been Perón's chauffeur, and Evita began to use him to help her distribute food and clothes; she would drive with him to the poor sectors of the city and personally hand over the packages. It was only after she had begun to give things that she realized the importance of this: 'There were letters and then more letters and men and women, children and old people would come to the Residence and knock at the door.' They also came to see her at the Ministry. When the persistent presence of these people was better known and articles had been published to the effect that Evita wished to help them, contributions began to be sent to her. Delegations of workers visiting her would bring donations, usually of what they produced or manufactured: furniture, sugar, shoes, tinned food or pasta, and these would be entered in a ledger by the reliable Renzi and stored at the Residence in an abandoned garage which they called 'las Delicias'. When Perón had gone to bed Evita would go down to 'las Delicias' with Renzi, with the Presidential cook Bartolo, and with the two footmen, Sanchez and

Fernandez, and they would sort the merchandise, pack it up and label it for shipment. 'Sugar was our greatest difficulty,' Renzi said, 'for in her enthusiasm, the señora dropped more on the floor than she was able to pour into the packets.'⁵

Evita had visited a number of welfare institutions in Europe, but they had mainly been religious organizations (she had not gone to Britain, where State institutions were at that time most advanced), run by the wealthy classes. These, as she later said, had only taught her what to avoid, since they had been created 'according to the criteria of the rich . . . and when the rich think about the poor they have poor ideas.'⁶ But it is hard to imagine which existing institutions could have provided Evita with any guidelines. By May 1948, according to *Democracia,* she was receiving 12,000 letters each day requesting help; she had the funds to assist some of these petitioners, because the Minister of Finance had now augmented the donations in kind by creating a special fund for her out of the accumulated surpluses of several ministries, but she had no means of distributing goods other than Renzi and his pick-up truck. On 8 July 1948 the María Eva Duarte de Perón Foundation was created and given legal rights by the signature of Perón and the Minister of Justice. It had a nominal sum of working capital in the form of a cheque for 10,000 pesos made out by Evita to her own Foundation. Two years later, when the 'Foundation for Social Assistance' was fully operative, its name was changed, because Evita herself had changed her name, to the 'Eva Perón Foundation' and so it was thereafter called, even after her death.

According to its statutes of incorporation⁷ the Foundation had the following objectives:

(a) to provide with monetary assistance, or in kind, furnish with working tools, give scholarships to any person who lacks resources and requests them, and who, in the founder's judgment, deserves them;

(b) to build houses for indigent families;

(c) to create and/or build educational establishments, hospitals, homes and/or any other establishments that may best serve the goals of the Foundation;

(d) to construct welfare establishments of any kind which can then be given with or without charge to local, provincial or national authorities;

(e) to contribute or collaborate by any possible means to the creation of works tending to satisfy the basic needs for a better life of the less privileged classes.

As for how the Foundation should be organized, the statutes were worded simply and unequivocally: it should be and should remain 'in the sole hands of its founder . . . who will exercise this responsibility for life and possess the widest powers afforded by the State and the Constitution.'

By the time these magniloquent statutes were made public, the Foundation was equivalent in size and importance to a substantial government department. It was capable of projecting and executing its own works, of imposing its priorities on the government, and of interrupting the course of other State projects if there was a shortage of labour and materials. No figures exist to give an idea of its operations while Evita was alive, but its assets in cash and goods were probably over three billion pesos, over $200 million at the exchange rate at that time.[8] It employed 14,000 workers on a permanent basis, including 6,000 construction workers and twenty-six priests, and it purchased annually for distribution 400,000 pairs of shoes, 500,000 sewing machines and 200,000 cooking pots. These were stored in enormous warehouses in Buenos Aires, and as late as 1973, significant quantities of undistributed material, sealed and forgotten, were still being discovered. The Foundation had given scholarships, and had built homes, hospitals and other welfare establishments, and some of these accomplishments had, in their own way, satisfied the 'basic needs for a better life' referred to in its statutes. And it was indeed in Evita's sole hands, for everything that it accomplished had been planned, supervised and carried through by her.

The creation of the Foundation coincided with the fat years of Peronism. Argentina was rich indeed, its products fetched high prices on the international markets, and Perón's economic policies added a hectic consumer boom of the type with which Western economies have since become familiar. Money was printed and wages rose; industrialists, workers, and members of the professional classes alike enjoyed a sudden and substantial increase in their standard of living. There was inflation, but as yet wages were increasing even faster. A wealthy and large-hearted country was therefore in the mood to give to the Foundation. In addition, Evita's distinctive status made it unwise to refuse her requests for gifts. If one was a representative of a trade union, one might hope for a larger than usual increase in return; if one was the manager of a factory, one might hope for a smaller one. Even if there were not always such direct benefits involved, the hazards of not giving were plain enough.

There are a few cases of firms which suffered financial losses because they refused to contribute to the Foundation. Arnaldo Massone, the owner of a pharmaceutical laboratory, had been President of the Argentine Chamber of Commerce, an organization opposed to Perón in the elections. In 1950, it is alleged, Massone received a 'request' for vaccine from the Foundation, and when he refused to comply the Ministry of Health first cut off his electricity supply and then inspected his plant. 'Obviously the refrigerated rooms were going to contain decaying produce,' his son later explained.[9] Massone escaped by launch to Uruguay, and his factory remained shut for three years. Another case concerns Mu-Mu, one of the largest sweet manufacturers in Argentina. According to one of the three Grossman brothers who owned and managed the firm at that time, the Foundation had ordered a large quantity of sweets, but had confusingly done so through another ministry. When Mu-Mu then submitted its bill, the factory was immediately visited by health inspectors and closed on the grounds that rats' hairs had been found floating in the caramel vats. According to Samuel Grossman, Mu-Mu was allowed to open again only 'three years, five months and twenty-four days later . . . thanks to a "spontaneous donation" of two per cent of sales, paid to the Foundation every three months.' It is possible that there were many more cases of extortion, and that these were the only ones where the matter actually came to a head. It is said that the Foundation's practice usually was to order its food, clothing, or building materials and not pay for them, leaving businessmen with the recourse of giving by default or running the risks of asking for their money. On the other hand, those who did not bill the Foundation sometimes received calls asking them to submit their expenses; it was all quite unpredictable.

A commission sitting for three years after 1955 offered to hear complaints against the Foundation. In all that time only one plaintiff came forward, a furniture manufacturer, and the case was not decided in his favour. But this alone may not mean so very much, for the practice of 'giving' was perhaps so widespread that it had come to be viewed as an alternative form of taxation, and since the stigma of corruption can be equally attached to those who extort and those who submit, it is very possible that those who did give against their will chose later to forget they had done so.

Evita, as might be expected, viewed the Foundation not as a business but as a vocation. On one occasion an American correspondent asked her if she ever kept accounts. She said that figures belonged to the cold world of capitalism and had no place in her work. 'She knew nothing about accounts or financial procedures,' one of those who worked with her has explained.[10] 'All that did not interest her, because in the twenty-hour day she worked she had no time for numbers.' It is probably the case that

Evita could not read accounts, or did not wish to, but it is not the case that they were not kept. The Minister of Finance, Ramón Cereijo, received and countersigned each of thousands of cheques that came to the Foundation, as he was required to by law. Nor is it true that the Foundation had no procedures. Although it began with individual donations, sent through the post, within a year it had evolved into something far more sophisticated.

After 1948, when Peronists were in control of the CGT, it became possible for Evita to acquire a substantial part of the funds she needed for the Foundation through the unions. She was now in a position to do things on their behalf. José Espejo, President of the CGT from 1948, insisted that Evita 'always pressured the employers to give the workers more',[11] and though this was not always the case, it became normal procedure for a union about to strike to make a series of gestures calculated to acquire her support.

A demonstration was the first step. An American journalist described the events preceding the trucking union's announcement of a pay claim. The demonstration began, he noted, with 'a long parade of trucks that had halted, snarling traffic. The drivers were just sitting in their cabs, grinning and blowing their horns. On the sides of each truck were crude posters bearing a picture of red hearts, inscriptions reading, "Eva we love you," "Eva and Juan we love you," "Eva and Juan a blessed couple", "You will go to heaven Eva and Juan".' Next, the union would come to Evita bearing a cheque or a consignment of goods. These were listed each day in column after column of *Democracia*, Evita's newspaper: 431 pairs of shoes from the shoe-workers; 219,999.60 pesos from the Social Security clerks; 22,899.20 pesos from the meat workers; 337,500 pesos from the soda-bottling workers. These contributions were paid out of union dues or collected at factories by union officials who would ask for 'something for the *señora*'. Evita would give the union something in return for its contribution (in May 1948 she gave one union the money to buy a piece of land for their new headquarters, and to a delegation of fishermen who had formed a union, she gave enough petrol to last through the fishing season), but even if there was no gift in return, these donations, which formed the bulk of the Foundation's assets, seem to have been made freely and without complaint. Evita built union headquarters, she gave the CGT a new building, and she created and ran hotels where union members and their families could have subsidized holidays. She was on the right side, she supported the unions, so it was natural to support her. She had the prerogatives of someone inside the government but she spoke as if she were outside it, a lobbyist; and she was thus of immense importance to the unions.

After the Foundation had been operating for a year, these spurts of generosity were replaced in part by more formal arrangements. A union signing a comprehensive wage contract to begin on the first of the month would allow the first two weeks of pay rise until the fifteenth of the month to be retained by the employers and 'donated' by them to Evita. In 1950, the Foundation added to its revenues by having the CGT (the organization representing individual unions) volunteer three man-days of salary for every worker which it represented, and although several unions protested and the levy was then reduced to two man-days, the organization was able to raise 394 million pesos ($4 million) for Evita.

The only document to list the Foundation's sources of income was drawn up after Evita's death, and deals with the year 1953 alone.[12] Although it is not impressive from an actuarial point of view, it is an extraordinary indication of the organization's vast economic reach. After the 'Donations in cash' (this by far the largest figure, over $30 million and one-third of the total), come 'Labour contracts' ($6 million), another considerable sum, and after that, 'Lotteries,' 'Casinos,' 'Cinematographic tax' and 'Racing taxes' (a portion of each lottery ticket, movie ticket, admission price to a horse race and each peso lost at a casino that went after 1950 to the Foundation), which sums, taken together, represent another third. Congress was also periodically generous, sometimes when it was voting funds for welfare projects, sometimes out of the simple goodness of its own heart. On one occasion Perón felt obliged to veto the large appropriation on the grounds that it was improper for the Peronist majority 'to wish to be on goods terms with the Señora to the detriment of the national interest,' but in spite of this, many millions of pesos were donated by Congress through various devices. For instance, the State had been engaged for some years in recovering death duties from the Bembergs, one of the richest Argentine families. The head of the family had died in Switzerland in the 1930s and the family had claimed that this rendered them immune to taxation. The 'Bemberg Affair' aroused much public concern. When the Supreme Court finally decided in favour of the State, and the Bembergs were required to pay a substantial sum, 97 million pesos, a great portion of it was voted to the Foundation by Congress as an immediate and effectual way of redistributing wealth. Sometimes it must have seemed as if there was no part of the country's economic activity of which something would not, sooner or later, find its way into Evita's hands.

People who wanted things from Evita came to see her; the procedure was almost as simple as that. In the beginning, they had come without warning and simply waited for her, but slowly, under the pressures imposed by thousands of supplicants, a crude system of sorting came into operation. People who wanted things were encouraged by means of radio, newspapers or through the local bureaucracy, first to write to her, saying what they needed. They would receive an invitation card from her giving the time and the place of the meeting. In principle, Evita's afternoons were set aside for 'direct help,' the name she gave to her ritual of seeing people who requested her assistance, but in practice these afternoons began earlier and ended later, until the rest of the day's business – the visits of dignitaries, union officials, foreigners – became part of this central and engulfing feature of her day. John Dos Passos, who visited Argentina in 1949, described one such afternoon:[13]

In a small office with red-damasked walls were rows of benches packed with ragged-looking women and children facing her desk. Babies squawked. Everybody talked at once. The Señora's desk was set up under floodlights beside a big, bronze oversize bust of some hero of Argentine independence. The corridor outside was full of people waiting to get a glimpse of the Señora. When she finally arrived the floodlights were turned on and there was a great crush of cameramen in the narrow room. Distinguished visitors were posed in an admiring group behind the Señora's handsome blonde head as she leaned over her desk to listen to the troubles of the poor women with their tear-grimed children.

'She's too thin,' one of the women was muttering aloud. 'That woman's working herself to death.'

At the end of each hard-luck story the Señora reached with jewelled fingers under the blotter on the desk and took out two fifty-peso notes. Then she made out with a rapid scratch on a pink slip an order for a doctor or a doll for the baby girl . . .

When a delegation of businessmen appeared with a check in five figures for the Señora's foundation, all other business was suspended while the cameramen posed the group. The check had to appear in the photograph. The Señora's white hand was held out to receive it. The leader of the delegation was presenting it with a deferential bow . . .

The floodlights, the cameras, the expectant poor, and the powerful awaiting their audience: all these elements of the tableau were constant and they revolved around Evita's technique, as a

New York Times correspondent said, 'of a chess master playing twenty-five games at high speed'. Even the delays and the sense of confusion, admittedly imposed by Evita's schedule, could also seem calculated, a means of reducing rich and poor, powerful and impotent alike to the status of supplicant, within Evita's hands.

There were groups of workers; union leaders; peasant women with their children, [wrote the Spanish Ambassador to Buenos Aires at the time[14]], foreign journalists; a gaucho family with their ponchos, the man with his long and silky huge black whiskers; there were refugees from behind the Iron Curtain; people who had come from post-war Europe; intellectuals and university professors from the Baltic States; priests and monks; fat, clamorous and sweaty middle-aged women; young clerks and football players; actors and people from the circus . . . [And] in the midst of this apparent chaos, this noisy and confused *kermesse* Evita listened to whatever was asked of her; from a simple demand for increased wages, to an entire industry-wide settlement and along the way a request for a place for a family to live, furniture, for a job in a school, food, permission to make a film, financial assistance of all kinds, complaints against the abuse of power, interviews, homages, meetings, inaugurations, women's political gatherings, the handing-over of gifts or donations. Evita was inexhaustible. She kept the momentum of this show running for hours, often well after nightfall.

The antechamber where the poor waited was heavy with the smells of poverty. The poor who came there had not been selected for the spectacular nature of their ailments or financial problems, they were simply part of the great number of Argentines who lived in tenements, shanty towns or remote villages, in the slums outside the city or in the provinces beyond the slums. Evita was conscious of the violence done to Argentine sensibilities by the presence of the poor in this government building, with its velvet drapes and wood panelling, and that is partly why they were encouraged to come here and to see her, instead of being dealt with by social workers. But she did not use them as stage props or allegorical figures in a didactic play. On the contrary, it is said by those who worked with her that she, who could be arrogant and rude with those who threatened her as rivals or intellectual superiors, was with these petitioners unfailingly gentle and courteous, attending to them not as a bureaucrat, but as an individual who had chosen such work because she enjoyed it. Her jewellery made her seem glamorous and almost ethereal, but when she spoke, smiled, asked questions or made jokes, she appeared to them not as the wife of the President, but as the Evita who declared herself, a 'woman of the people,' unlike them in circumstances and power but ineffably still of them and with them.

Her voice rises as she rebuts a complaint about a benefit concert [a correspondent of the *New York Times* reported[15]]. She calls peremptorily for the head of the General Labour Confederation. She sends a publicist away glowing with the idea that he'd make a fine counsellor of the embassy in Washington. And she pats the Governor of Buenos Aires and guides him back to an impatient circle by the window, where small talk is running thin.

She parries a question about her personal reaction to her work. 'All these people, you see?' she says. 'I am nothing – my work is everything.' She is off on another swing. When she returns there is a little more fencing and she extends a soft, warm hand, smiling superbly; 'Time is my greatest enemy,' she says.

Meanwhile the other room overflows with children. They squirm and giggle, scramble on the floor and wail. At about 6.15, a premature murmur goes around, *'Ya viene!'* (Here she comes!) Presently, the Señora steps in briskly. She sits beneath a huge oil painting of 'Amalia', a melancholy lady in a black mantilla . . . Other pictures in the red-damasked room are of the Peróns or Christ. Four secretaries surround the table. The synchronization is like that of an operating room. One shoves a pencil into her hand, another readies a pad of clothing tickets, a third holds up a phone . . .

The first supplicant is a shapeless woman with a toil-worn face. The First Lady turns her brown eyes to her; clusters of black crystals tinkle at the brim of her open-crown straw hat.

'I live in one room,' the woman says. 'I want a house to live in.'

'How many children do you have?'

'Eight.'

The *presidenta* murmurs to one of her secretaries. 'We can provide a wooden house,' she begins. The woman asks questions. Evita is dictating. 'Clothing for nine . . . a large bed, complete . . .' She turns for a brief aside to a visiting ambassador. Then she takes the slip from the secretary's pad and signs E.P. The woman shuffles out, with the slip.

The ritual of the visit was wholly unnecessary from a practical point of view, since whatever the supplicants required could more easily have been delivered to them by an organization of social workers; that is what in fact happened once they had seen Evita. But it involved human contact that is rare in bureaucracies. These people believed that the President's wife cared about them, even loved them. In most cases, the very strictest criteria of need were summarily waived. Evita made a point of giving those who approached her more than they asked because she liked giving things and because they were likely to ask for less than they needed, so great were their needs and so little experience had they of receiving anything.

It must have been in '51 [a worker said to the Argentine writer Rodolfo Walsh[16]] when his mother received a letter from the Foundation; she went with him and they waited until she received him; the mother asked her for a sewing machine and also for some metal sheets to finish building the room in her house and then, with a great effort, she asked her for the dentures – if it was not too much. She looked at her with that humbleness that comes to the poor when they think they are asking too much and Evita told her, 'But no, no one asks for that; on the contrary we need people to ask for that so that the doctors can do their research,' and she made it into a joke, as if thanking her for asking for the dentures for her and the old man. Two or three days later the truck came with the metal sheets, the beds, the mattress, a bag of sugar, the cups, the plates, the clothes, the cheese and the dentures.

The fifty-peso notes which Evita handed to those who saw her have been depicted as the purest form of wastage, a foolish hail of devalued pesos spattered over all comers, and while there is some truth in this, they were on occasions also a useful gift since often the supplicants needed money to get home. Sometimes the crisp pile beneath her blotter would be exhausted, and then she would turn to the ambassadors, ministers and civil servants around her and say, 'Señores, the people need your money. There's a tray. Please put some of what you have in your wallets. The government is giving you lots of money and you can afford to put some of it there.'[17] When this habit of hers became widely known, those who came to see her would make a point of emptying their wallets beforehand.

In many ways the Foundation completely changed Evita. Her work acquired the importance and the sanctity of a 'mission' and this new Evita was as different from the star who had toured Europe as that star had been from the young radio actress from Junín. She now dressed not in frills but in black suits, all similarly cut like a uniform. Rather than piling her hair high, she wore it swept back, and the effect, though never unbecoming or undistinguished, was one of austerity and efficiency, and made her look far older than she was. She still wore her hats, but there were fewer of these, and less jewellery, only the odd spray of ruby orchids or a sapphire and diamond Peronist emblem. This was as much of a costume as the earlier dress, but it was now the costume of seriousness and dedication. A Peronist propaganda photograph widely reproduced and undoubtedly faked, depicts her smiling as usual and waving her hand from the back of her limousine, while a clock in the background stands at four am. But this was indeed the way her 'days' frequently ended; and often she made her limousine available to those who came to see her and had to wait until it had returned.

The more of this 'direct aid' she performed, the more she began, in her speeches and in conversations, to adopt a raucously outraged attitude towards the existence of poverty. She spoke of her rage against poverty as a wound affecting her, and her language was violent. 'Sometimes I have wished my insults were slaps or lashes,' she said in her memoirs; 'I've wanted to hit people in the face and make them see, if only for a day, what I see each day I help people.' Both the ferocity and the lack of regard for herself which she showed in the last years of her life came from her days and nights with the poor. She became passionate, a real fanatic, an obsessive.

Those who worked with her were expected to behave as she did, to be continually available and to be beyond suspicion of corruption. Evita might treat the poor as equals, using such terms of endearment as *abuelito* ('Grandpa'), but she required a deference, even a reverence, from those around her, which sometimes had its comic side. Arturo Jauretche found amid 'the cries of babies, the bureaucrats watching those who were waiting and the aureole of sanctity that emanated from Evita' an aging neighbourhood tough who had once worked for the Radicals and was now carrying a large pile of rubber teats. When Jauretche smiled, 'he replied with his seasoned, bar-room voice; "so what am I supposed to do, doctor, if this woman is a saint?" '[18] But there were many who would treat the question of Evita's sanctity not with irony or as a half-truth, but as a possibility to be seriously considered. For Father Hernán Benítez, who frequently attended these sessions, it was not the transfer of objects, whether blankets, sewing machines, cooking pots or slips of denominated paper, that constituted the real importance of Evita's work, but the gestures that went with these gifts. 'I saw her kiss the leprous,' he said, 'I saw her kiss those who were suffering from tuberculosis or cancer. I saw her distribute love, a love that rescues charity, removing that burden of injury to the poor which the exercise of charity implies. I saw her embrace people who were in rags and cover herself with lice.'[19] Father Benítez was unable to consider Evita to be potentially a saint since she had never renounced the riches or honours of the world, but he did feel she had attained a state of quasi-sanctity because she had been 'faithful to her people. Faithful because she loved the poor and condemned the rich. Not because they were rich (for she was too), but because they had remained enemies of the poor (which she was not).'

In 1950, José María Castiñeira de Dios, a young Catholic poet, had watched Evita at her work:

> There were human beings in that room with dirty clothes and they smelt very bad. Evita would place her fingers into their suppurating wounds for she was able to see the pain of all these people and feel it herself. She could touch the most terrible things with a Christian attitude that amazed me, kissing and letting herself be kissed. There was a girl whose lip was half eaten away with syphilis and when I saw that Evita was about to kiss her and tried to stop her, she said to me, 'Do you know what it will mean when I kiss her?'[20]

People around Evita were usually upset by such gestures, but she hated to be interrupted. When her maid was worried after she had kissed a man suffering from syphilis and tried to dab her face with alcohol, Evita took the bottle from her and smashed it against the wall. Perón and Evita were once walking off the gangplank of a yacht when a man came up to Perón and kissed him and Perón told him not to be a pig ('the cry,' he says, 'came from my heart because being kissed by a man, I don't know . . . it disgusts me'[21]). But Evita went to him, apologized on Perón's behalf and kissed the man to make him feel better. 'She even allowed herself to be kissed by lepers,' Perón observed, seemingly bemused.

Evita's 'distribution of love' were considered vulgar by many people opposed to her, and so they were by some standards. No one had suggested that she do such things; she simply felt she had to do it. Many people were much moved by them. The poet Castiñeira de Dios immediately felt that his life lacked 'that element of sacrifice' and that he was unworthy in Evita's presence, noting:

> When I watched her for a few days, she said, 'How are you, *Oligarcha*, are you beginning to understand how people suffer?' . . . It was hard for me not to love her when I had seen her at work, as though she thought I was not worthy of everything that went on in that room. Even when I had been there three months I felt I couldn't wash the feet of those people . . . I had had a sort of literary perception of the people and the poor and she had given me a Christian one, thus allowing me to become a Christian in the profoundest sense . . .

Argentina, though secular in many respects, was essentially a Catholic country, and when Evita touched the leprous or the syphilitic she ceased to be the President's wife and acquired some of the characteristics of saints as depicted in Catholicism. Whether she actually saw herself this way or not, it was effective, a transformation of an essentially secular role by the surrounding religious emotion. This beautiful woman loved the poor and gave up her life to them. She would see them, she would kiss them, and all the cameras and lights did not alter the simplicity of this religious tableau. Questions of why she did this, to whom the goods really belonged, and in whose name they were really being distributed were waived in the intensity of this ritual, performed five days a week for some years. Many of those who experienced these days were not as restrained as Benítez or Castiñeira de Dios; they were sure that Evita was a saint.

In 1948 Evita created the Children's Football Championship. This started as a response to soccer hooliganism, but it became, through her guidance, first a 'pretext for social work'[22] and then, in the way that things did with the Foundation, something rather more ambitious. Each village in every province of the country was asked to form a team, choose a name and choose its colours. The Foundation supplied each team with all the boots, shirts, shorts and socks it needed. The shirts were made up in the team colours and each was embroidered with a shield bearing Evita's profile and name. When the qualifying matches began, the Foundation sent its health trucks to examine the children enrolled, give them X-rays, and collect information about their homes and school performance. If the children had been mistreated or the family was suffering from money problems, the social workers could either take the child for a time to one of the Foundation's homes or else give the family a fully furnished new home, and pay several months of its rent in advance. The championship games were held in Buenos Aires, at the great grounds of Boca Juniors or Racing, and were publicized as if they were professional contests. Supporters came by bus from the interior with their own banners and chants. In the first year there were 8,000 prizes (motorcycles, bicycles, scholarships to technical school or university), the winning team receiving in addition the means in cash or building materials for creating its own clubhouse on land which the Foundation would then purchase on its behalf. In addition to the national anthem, a march was played with the chorus, 'To Evita we owe our club, and for that we are grateful to her,' and Evita went down into the stadium and kicked off for the finals.

The quality of public medical care in Argentina was limited by shortages of personnel and decaying hospitals built in the French style, with vast halls lined with beds in which nursing was perfunctory and patients could easily be forgotten. Nurses were really orderlies or servants, ignorant of medical procedures. The old nursing schools (some of which had been part of the Sociedad) were now part of the State system, but at Evita's request they were merged to form a new four-year school, named after her. Interns from all over the country attended this school free of charge; everything was paid for by the Foundation. But Evita, according to the head of the institution, Teresa Adelina Fiora, was not simply interested in improving the standard of nursing. She wanted the graduates to be 'her soldiers', forming an élite capable of fulfilling the increasingly diverse requirements of the Foundation. Discipline was militaristic; the girls were forbidden to wear jewellery, and they graduated, according to Teresa Adelina Fiora, with 'a mystical sense of their importance and their fellowship through Evita'.[23] Evita believed they could take the place of doctors, drive jeeps and work alone in the interior. In military parades, dressed in sky-blue uniforms embroidered with her profile and initials, they marched behind the soldiers.

In Argentina, as elsewhere, there had been a great difference between the quality of medical care in private hospitals and that in public hospitals; one standard for those who were able to pay and another, greatly inferior, for those who could not. Evita decided to improve vastly the standards of free care and make her hospitals competitive with the best international standards of medical care. She built twelve hospitals, the two main ones, named after Perón and herself, in Buenos Aires. It is probable that for the money that was spent she could have produced more institutions more cheaply, but she chose instead to make a showcase of public care, as a propaganda statement, and also prescriptively: in the sense that the poor should have the same as rich people. The hospitals had marble foyers and staircases, large windows, rooms where patients could watch movies, wards which contained only three beds. The surgical equipment, imported from the United States, was the best available at the time, and the staff was highly paid, so that the best doctors in the country worked there. The 'Policlínico Presidente Perón' serviced the poor neighbourhood in which it was located, but it also became a medical centre and teaching hospital training Evita's nurses and caring for people from remote parts of the country who would be flown in on aircraft provided by the Foundation. All medical supplies were provided free of charge by the Foundation, including drugs for out-patients. In 1951, the 'Presidente Perón' was able to equip a hospital train and send it throughout the country to provide free X-rays, free inoculations and free drugs. In the early 1950s, the Foundation sent the hospital's staff to give medical care after earthquakes in Peru, Colombia, Ecuador, and as far away as Turkey.

Under the auspices of the Foundation, Evita built 1,000 schools in the poorest areas of the country and handed these over to the State to operate. She had created the Peronist Decalogue of Old People's Rights in August 1948, she had sponsored universal pension schemes before the State assumed this responsibility, and now the Foundation built and operated four nursing homes, one of them with its own workshop and stable, more a village than a home. In five months and twenty days of 1949, working in twenty-four-hour shifts, the Foundation turned a four-block site of Belgrano, a northern suburb of Buenos Aires, into the 'Amanda Allen Children's City,' named after a nineteenth-century Argentine pioneer of health care. It was indeed a city, with streets built to scale, a church, a functioning petrol station, a bank that issued scrip, pharmacies, supermarkets and a town hall that displayed a number of portraits of Perón and Evita in addition to the paraphernalia of government. A slogan of the 'New Argentina' was that children were 'the only privileged ones', and while the regime never imposed this vision on the entire country, it did become a reality with the Children's City. To the dormitories capable of holding four hundred and fifty children came children from the poorest, most problem-stricken families with whom the Foundation workers came into contact. There they were clothed, taught to look after themselves and educated. By the time they left the home they were supposed to be capable of attending public schools without falling behind. The children's toys and clothes were ordered from the best shops in Buenos Aires; there were even dance and music teachers on the staff. Often Evita would arrive without warning in the middle of the night and walk through the dormitories to see if everything was as it was supposed to be.

In addition to the Children's City, the Foundation subsidized a city for university students nearby, with a complete replica of the Casa Rosada, including, of course, the photographs of Perón and Evita and the propagandist statements about the 'New Argentina'. In Buenos Aires there were three transit homes where single women with children might find temporary refuge, while the Foundation looked on their behalf for permanent housing and work, and, in Avenida Mayo, a huge building was made into a home for girls who had come to the city looking for work. The latter contained two restaurants, and shops where the girls could buy things at subsidized prices. 'The salon,' an English visitor noted, 'might well have been a reception room in the Casa Rosada. It was lit by eight or nine chandeliers of crystal pear-drops; thrown across the grand piano in Edwardian style was a most exquisitely embroidered mantilla, a museum piece, given to

Evita in Spain; the Louis XV chairs were covered with the palest silk brocade on which there was not the slightest mark; on the mantelpiece and on tables stood Dresden figurines and in the corner huge Sèvres urns. At each end of the salon were oil paintings, large as the wall would allow, one of Eva and one of Perón.'[24]

Evita's social works have been persistently criticized for being wasteful, ill-conceived and unrelated to people's needs. The conservative military government that succeeded Perón concluded that the institutions of the Foundation were 'disproportionate to the aims, culture and customs of those who were going to use them' and, though in a quite unspecified way, 'liable to encourage customs bringing about moral and family deviations.'[25] However, although the Foundation adopted 'luxury' as a matter of policy, it did function better than many more rational and more frugal institutions. For the first time, there was no inequality in Argentine health care.

Allegations of waste are difficult to substantiate if a high proportion of whatever the money is spent on is actually delivered. Evita's hospitals were expensive, but they worked and they lasted; so would most of her other works had they been permitted to. Many of the objectives of the Foundation (obsessive tidiness in the homes and hospitals, an addiction to decoration) reflected her great concern with appearances, but many of the things that she made available – pots and pans, beds, houses, sewing machines, footballs – had meaning and usefulness because Evita was aware exactly what difference it made to the life of a poor family to have these things. The work of the Foundation was deeply practical and personal, far more so than it might have been had it been bureaucratically exercised.

As propaganda, of course, the Foundation was extraordinarily successful. Nobody who came into contact with any of Evita's works was allowed to forget how grateful they should be for what they received. Perón's sayings were on each wall of each hospital or home and Evita's initials were painted on every iron bedstead, embroidered on each tablecloth or football shirt and stamped on each vial of vaccine used by the Foundation. The Foundation had begun as a response to poverty, but it was now a blueprint of Evita's version of the 'New Argentina,' a benign but authoritarian system in which the entire Argentine people were the children and Perón and Evita the smiling parents.

Even in 1950, when an inflation rate of fifty per cent and a loss of confidence in the peso made a number of national economies necessary, the Foundation continued to increase in size and capabilities. It was one of the government's cheapest projects, since so much of its money came from the unions, and one of the least subject to inflation since its gifts – hospitals, holidays, houses, pots and pans – were real; and it remained as effective propaganda since the arbitrary, spectacular nature of its gifts made it seem larger than it was, a lottery distribution where the Peronist Revolution now lacked the means to do much else. In 1950, the Foundation began to operate food and liquor stores in Buenos Aires, in which, the *New York Times* correspondent noted 'scarce articles can magically be found and prices are delightfully low'. And that year too, it entered into an arrangement with the largest of the country's funeral homes to provide bargain burials for those whom it had assisted.

It was in 1950 also that the first families occupied the six hundred new houses of the Foundation's *'barrio* Presidente Perón' in Saavedra, out on the green edge of the plain to the west of Buenos Aires, beyond the formal limits of the federal capital. Some of them were given apartments in small, low houses, others were given one- or two-family houses. In accordance with the Peronist interest in sports, the town had been built in the shape of a half-moon around a large sports stadium, its streets laid out into the plain like the spokes of a wheel. Rents were fixed at 5.50 or 3.50 pesos a week (about 45 cents), far below the level of any other available comparable housing. The *barrio*, with its chalets, white plaster and orange roofs was superior to any public development in Argentina and as well-designed as any public housing in Europe or in the United States. It had a store, to whose doors Foundation vans each day brought cheap food and liquor, a church from whose pulpit Evita's confessor, the fervent Peronist Hernán Benítez, would each week preach sermons, and, of course, it had its own party headquarters, the house which Evita had given to Renzi's baker, María Rosa Calviño de Gomez, one of Evita's senators. This was a social centre as well as a party headquarters, though there were periodical 'indoctrination classes' given by visiting speakers. Women could take classes in reading, writing, sewing, stenography or first aid. They could leave their children with María Rosa, who had her own children, or could bring her requests for help in resolving problems; if María Rosa approved of them, these requests would be forwarded to the Foundation and then one day the Foundation vans would drive to Saavedra fulfilling everyone's wishes. Evita often came to her *barrio*, and when she did, people came out to see her. Once a woman fell to her knees before Evita and sobbing, asked for a house. Evita 'said nothing, neither yes nor no,' but she called María Rosa that day and asked her who the woman was and whether she needed a house. When María Rosa replied that the woman was a 'good *Peronista*' and lived in a slum, Evita gave her a house. It was thus sometimes by first wishing and then pleading, that one entered the 'New Argentina'. Between the wish and its fulfilment lay all the resources of the Woman's Party and the Foundation and always controlling them, there was Evita.

9
The Bridge of Love

1950, which was the fourth yèar of Perón's government, began badly for Evita. During a ceremony in the suburb of Avellaneda, at which she was to snip a ribbon commemorating the opening of a new branch of the pro-Peronist taxi-driver's union, she fainted and had to be rushed to the hospital. For the next four days, the press, usually over-attentive to the least of Evita's doings, contained no mention whatsoever of her name, and then, on 13 January, after the announcement that her appendix had been removed the day before, the country gave thanks for the avoided danger – while ministers, ambassadors and churchmen, including the Papal Nuncio, came to her bedside, and in churches throughout Argentina masses were said for her recovery. Evita spent her convalescence watching movies in the Residence, among them her own La Prodiga, for which she retained great affection; and then, two weeks later after two days of half-work, she resumed all her activities, with the Foundation, the unions, and the Women's Party.

One of the doctors who had examined Evita prior to her operation was Oscar Ivanissevich, who was at that time also Minister of Education, and he would later suggest that he had conducted a number of tests on her while she was in hospital, which revealed her to be suffering from cancer of the uterus. Evita had agreed to the tests, but when Ivanissevich suggested a hysterectomy, she would not listen to him and became furious. She was convinced that he was not giving her disinterested medical advice, but that like many other people, he had different concerns than those he professed. 'You won't touch me because there is nothing wrong with me,' she told the doctor, who represented himself as startled by this outburst. 'All of them want me out of politics, but they won't succeed.'[1]

The question of when Evita first experienced the symptoms of her illness is far from resolved, nor is it likely that it will ever be. Ivanissevich resigned his post shortly after Evita's first illness, but it has been suggested that it was not his frankness with her, but his dealings on the black market which led to his leaving the government. Perón, the one person to whom Ivanissevich might naturally have told the truth, persistently and wrongly referred to his wife's illness as anaemia and dated its onset over a year and a half after this first diagnosis. By that time, it was apparent to everybody that Evita was ill. Perón's repeated suggestions that her illness and death were inevitable, arising from a desire to be destroyed by overwork, came oddly from someone whose first wife had died of the same illness. It is as if, hazily and sentimentally, he was engaged in some form of special pleading.

It is highly unlikely, even if he did indeed diagnose the illness, that Ivanissevich actually told Evita that she had cancer. He probably said that she was ill and that she should rest, and she probably did ignore his advice, out of fear or because she did not believe him. In the months immediately following this operation she worked harder than she had done before, and though this does not prove – as has been said – that she was consciously engaged in a race against time, knowing that she would die, it does show that she had ceased to care about herself. Even when she was exhausted and obviously ill, she continued to work. Of all the many distortions surrounding her life the least outrageous and the closest to the truth is the suggestion that she elected to die for Perón and Peronism.

In these years, the height of Evita's power, her public existence began early each morning in the private suite on the second floor of the presidential residence. 'She sat in the entrance hall,' recalled the photographer Gisèle Freund,[2] 'from which she could look straight down into the large drawing room. She was being combed out by her hairdresser and having her nails done by a manicurist, while her private secretary set up her schedule for the day and took notes. Just a few steps away several men carrying heavy leather briefcases waited patiently.... It was eight in the morning but the drawing room downstairs was already beginning to fill up.'

At Evita's *levée* there would be present her secretary, Emma Nicolini, the young daughter of Evita's friend Oscar, who had decided, against her father's wishes, to 'work with Evita' in politics, and who called her *madre*; Atilio Renzi, the Residence Steward who helped her with the Foundation; and such Ministers as Armando Méndez San Martín or Nicolini himself, of whose loyalty Evita was quite convinced; or such union officials as José Espejo, whose devotion was similarly beyond question. Elena Mercante, the wife of Perón's old friend, was no longer there. Isabel Ernst, Evita's previous secretary, had decided to leave in 1948 and was not encouraged to stay. Liliane Guardo had also disappeared: her husband had been expelled from Perón's circle of advisers. Shortly after returning from Europe to the Residence, Liliane came to give Evita back some money and as usual went upstairs to see her, but she was stopped by the guard, who took the money on Evita's behalf. Liliane never saw Evita again.

Off this main drawing-room was a suite of small rooms where Evita kept her clothes and jewels, which she was happy to show to photographers or journalists like Gisèle Freund.

'Here I keep only my dressing gowns. They all come from Paris,' she noted. A maid helped her take some of them out. Dozens of dresses filed past my eyes and my camera. Then came the fur coats. In another room, nothing but hats; I counted more than a hundred of them. Evita posed willingly and tried on a hat. Then there was the room reserved for shoes.

Evita's jewels were now stored in another adjacent room. Perón remarked of this notorious collection: 'One can be poor in spirit without actually being poor. Had Evita been a hypocrite, of whom there are many, or a miser, she would have made herself look like a tramp, hiding the things she liked. If people were giving her these things, what was to stop her wearing them?'[3] Evita could tell Gisèle Freund 'with emotion' that all these jewels were gifts, and so they were in a way, but they were rarely given out of simple affection. In 1976, the Dutch Parliament, while investigating the implications of the Lockheed scandals in Holland, made reference to the substantial 'commissions' paid by a Dutch railway supplier in order to do business in Argentina, among them the provision of a specially-equipped railway carriage for Perón, and jewellery to the value of $12,000 for Evita.[4]

Perhaps because there was no one left around her capable of criticizing anything she did, Evita did not realize that her passionate interest in clothes, hair and jewellery might not appear entirely harmless. With Fleur Cowles, an American journalist accompanying her publisher husband on a week's visit to Buenos Aires, she 'displayed a willingness (later eagerness) to talk "girl talk" about clothes, jewellery, coiffure' to the extent of spreading sheets of photographs of herself on the Residence carpets in the presence of Perón, and asking her guest which of her hairstyles she preferred.[5] Fleur Cowles somewhat disingenuously told Evita that her latest hairstyle was best, and then went home to New York to write a book about Evita and Perón. Evita, she concluded,

was not a woman's woman with a warm remembrance of moments spent like any woman with her friends . . . not a man's woman either, even if she may once have been, but a woman politico . . . a woman too fabled, too capable, too sexless, too driven, too overbearing, too slick, too sly, too diamond-decked, too revengeful, too ambitious – and far, far too under-rated far, far too long by our world.[6]

Certainly, Evita could on occasion be vain or overbearing, as many critics pointed out, but these critics missed, perhaps because they chose to, the utter lack of self-regard she also displayed. Her clothes and her jewels were by this stage symbols that she used consciously. Each Evita – the 'President's wife' of Colon galas, the 'saint' of the distributions to the poor, the *compañera* of union gatherings – was subordinate in the strictest sense to what was expected of her politically. Even the remoteness and coldness of which people complained arose out of this sense of political vocation. As for the ruthlessness with which Evita has so often been credited, it was certainly there, but it was primarily directed towards herself.

'In every real sense,' Perón wrote of the years 1950 and 1951, 'I had lost my wife. We saw each other only occasionally and then only very briefly, as if we lived in different cities. Eva would work all night for many nights and come back at dawn. I used to leave the Residence at six in the morning to go to the Casa Rosada and I met her at the front door, exhausted but satisfied with her work. One day I said to her: "Eva, get some rest, remember you are my wife." She looked at me seriously and said, "Doing this makes me feel that I am your wife."[7] Perón insisted, at Evita's doctor's behest, on her spending long weekends at the *quinta* at San Vicente where, as she had done in the first days of her marriage, she cooked a little, rode with Perón and wore his lieutenant's tunic, but she was always reluctant to go there and would be on the telephone much of the time. When Perón had the wires cut, she had them reconnected and placed the phone under a cushion so that he would not hear it ring. In Buenos Aires, she foiled by small deceits Perón's attempts to make her eat regularly: if she came in late, she would have the servants serve the full number of courses but remove them again at once, uneaten, and when Perón arrived she would be eating dessert as though she had just finished all the rest. Sometimes, when she worked all night, she took those who had been with her back to the Residence. 'We would take a taxi home with Evita,' the union official Angel Peralta said, 'and we would get there at dawn, sometimes when Perón was having breakfast and then, lest the General find us, we would all hide behind a curtain and wait until he had gone to the Casa Rosada.

Then we had breakfast and went to our homes. Eva Perón slept for about two hours and her workday began again.' On one of these occasions a guest of Evita's slipped on the stairs and Perón woke up, came in while they were having breakfast, and said sadly to Evita, 'Just look at the time, Evita, just look at the time.'

By this time neither her husband nor her family had much control over what Evita did. Doña Juana occupied her old apartment in Calle Posadas but, having discovered she liked gambling, spent more and more time at the great casino of Mar del Plata. Evita made a civil servant available to carry her chips and, when her pile was exhausted, to fetch her more. The business of giving people things filled Evita's life. Whenever she met people whom she had known when she was an actress, her response was always the same: to give them presents. Thus it was with the designer Paco Jamandreu, whom she had long since left for Dior and Rochas and whom she found attempting to start his car in the street at 4 am. She found it natural to give him what he called 'a superb convertible Packard...in one of the five shades in which it had recently become available in the country.'[8]

The progressive idealization of Evita came from her beauty and her power but also from this habit of giving. The only people with whom she felt totally at ease were those who accepted what she was doing unconditionally, as did the members of the large, dark-suited retinue which went everywhere with her. For Guillermo de Prisco, a union official and staunch 'Evitista', her most remarkable characteristic was this 'capacity to give before anything was asked of her'. 'Evita,' he said, 'was incredibly beautiful but no one could ever treat her as if she was a woman. It was as if she was a different being, untouchable, not cold in the least, but without any sexual presence whatsoever.' He had never, he said, met anyone else who resembled her.[9]

There was a canteen in the Foundation's hostel for working girls where Evita often ate with de Prisco and the rest of her followers and it was here, in the last months of 1950, that the 'Peña Eva Perón' began to meet. The poets had watched Evita at work, had eaten dinner with her and now they gathered their chairs in a circle to listen to each other's work. All their poems were about Evita, devotion, beauty and sanctity. *Alabanza* (Glory) describes the Catholic poet José Castiñeira de Dios's response to Evita's work:

Eva y María estan juntas en la mujer que mi voz canta
Que más que nombres son un nombre, como dos ojos es igual a una mirada,
Y más que manos, es la mano de quién la tiende en las desgracias,
Y más que ojos, son los ojos de quién da fe con su mirada

Para que el hombre solitario alce su rostro hasta sus plantas
Y vea en la luna y las estrellas, sobre la tierra de la patria.
A Eva y María. María Eva. María Eva, transfigurada en la Esperanza.

Eva and Maria are joined in the woman my voice celebrates
For more than names they are one name, as two eyes make up a gaze,
And more than hands, the hand proffered in time of troubles,
And more than eyes, the eyes of her who gives faith with her
    look
So that the lonely man may raise his face towards her feet
And see in the moon and the stars, above the earth of our fatherland,
Eva and Maria, Maria Eva, Maria Eva transfigured into Hope.

Shortly before her trip to Europe in 1947, Evita had been introduced to Manuel Penella da Silva, a Spanish journalist who had emigrated to Argentina from Switzerland. Penella da Silva had attempted to interest Evita in an autobiography to be ghosted by himself. She agreed, da Silva was paid a fee of 50,000 pesos and at some point in 1950 work began on this project. Evita burst into tears when she was shown the first pages of the manuscript, 'as if it was a novel. "It was just like that," she kept saying.'[10] However, there were a number of difficulties in the production of these memoirs. Evita was uncertain about how she wished to be depicted. At first, according to da Silva, she 'wished to appear perfect, idealized, a bourgeois myth'; she then changed her mind and instead of projecting this saintly view of herself, put into her sessions with the journalist all her rage and sense of inadequacy. She told Penella da Silva that she loved Perón, but she herself was nothing, a *grasa*, a common person. Penella da Silva had always been interested in the feminist aspects, such as they were, of Evita's work and it seems that he incorporated this interpretation of her importance in the first draft of his manuscript.

Father Benítez, to whom it was first shown, merely remarked that it 'contained a lot of Spanish [as opposed to Argentine] expressions,'[11] but Perón, to whom the manuscript was finally passed at the end of 1950, was displeased with it. It was then given for reworking to Raúl Mende, who had written a number of speeches for Perón and who was considered reliable. It was Mende, according to Penella da Silva, who substantially rewrote the book, excising the chapter concerning 'feminism' and replacing it with one composed of selections from Perón's speeches, approvingly presented by Evita. The final draft had little in common with the original, which had been crushed to pieces, 'so that the book now had nothing to do with her'.

Yet Evita accepted *La Razón de mi Vida* (the English title was

My Mission in Life, though it should perhaps have been 'The Purpose of My Life'). It was cast in the form of a long conversation, by turns intimate and rhetorical, and it repeated all the themes of Evita's speeches, often in the very same language and with the original defective syntax. It contained almost nothing about her life before Perón; a distorted account of 17 October, and lies about her work (the assertion, for instance, that she 'did not interfere in government affairs'). The book supported the myth of Perón, the generous, good, hard-working, self-sacrificing, fatherly male, and through that myth it contributed to the myth of Evita, incarnation of every feminine virtue, all love, humility, and even more self-sacrifice. The reason Evita had no children, according to her autobiography, was because her real children were those she protected – the poor and the old and the helpless of Argentina – together with whom she joined in adoration of Perón, their father. Thus, pure, virginal, without sexual desire, she had become the ideal mother.

Evita's ceremonial prominence in Perón's regime was second only to that of Perón himself. She took precedence over the Vice-President on all occasions except military ones, where the rigid spirit of protocol would not allow it, and when it came to the naming of gasworks, ocean liners, bridges, constellations and bus terminals, her name was used more often than Perón's. No precedent existed for the power she exercised, and because it was unofficial, surrounded by the government in a haze of half-truths or lies, its precise extent was always a matter for speculation. The assertion that Evita ruled the country became so common in Buenos Aires that at the beginning of 1951 an Argentine resident returning to the country could ascribe to her 'the cloudy proportions of a myth', suggest that she was 'virtually omnipotent', and observe that the rest of the country daydreamed wistfully at each sign that her power might be on the wane.

Great though this power certainly was, it was not quite so great as it appeared to be. It was not limited by any institution (there was no longer any institution in Argentina capable of criticizing Evita or of holding her accountable), but its ultimate source, Perón, did have some control over what it had bestowed. Despite all the freedom he allowed his wife, Perón never ignored the implications of what she was doing, and if her activities appeared to jeopardize his interests he would at times prove that he could control them. And the unions, loyal though they were to their 'standard-bearer', could not disregard their rank and file. The link between the unions and Peronism was forged of promises delivered, and had been enormously strengthened by Evita's activities in the Ministry and in the Foundation; but if promises were not delivered and Argentina ceased to be a true 'workers' state', the relationship would become strained. As high inflation, trade deficits and the general disintegration of Perón's economic plans diminished his ability to make good his promises, so did this become more evident. By the beginning of 1951 the unions would still vote for him and join enthusiastically in the rituals of Peronism, but there were circumstances in which they were unable to waive their proper functions because their members would not let them.

The Unión Ferroviaria was the largest, the oldest and the best-organized union in the country, representing the railway workers, the first skilled workers in Argentina. Although it was dominated by Socialists, it had supported Perón since 1944. Its workers had suffered from inflation and now found themselves with a lower standard of living than they had enjoyed in 1946. There were demands for a substantial pay rise, but Perón's nominees refused to press these claims, because they had been told not to. In January 1951, the union members formed a clandestine committee to organize a nation-wide strike, thus closing the country's entire railway network.[12] The strike jeopardized the country's balance of payments by closing the ports and it was encouraged by the opposition, particularly the Socialists, and watched closely by the Army, some of whom by now hoped to see the first cracks in the Peronist edifice. The role of mediation fell to Evita, who first attempted to influence the strikers through their official leadership. She went in person to the Buenos Aires terminals and told the pickets they were 'playing into the opposition's hands'; she even rode down the tracks from station to station on a handcranked cart. At some stations she was cheered, since the railway workers, despite their strike, still supported the government and liked her; at others the word *viudo* [widower] had been scratched next to the common graffiti of Perón's name. Despite her entreaties, the railway workers obdurately remained on strike. Perón had blamed the strike on a few agitators but he now took personal responsibility for its resolution, using his full legal powers of coercion. After issuing a decree permitting him to draft all strikers into the army in case of an emergency, thus removing their legal right to strike, he removed the Minister of Transport, arrested hundreds of workers and suspended 2,000 strikers from their jobs. Within a week the strike had collapsed and the railways were in operation once more.

Perón's drastic resolution of the railway strike seems to have led him to one of the oddest mistakes of his career. One of the few newspapers to have reported the strike accurately and in detail was *La Prensa*. This old and respected publication was a consistent exponent of 'liberal' oligarchic views; it had been virulently opposed to Perón since 1944. Its circulation was small, but it was internationally known, which is perhaps why Perón had allowed it to continue its reporting unmolested. During the month following the railway strike there was a strike of *La Prensa*'s pro-Peronist newsvendors' union, which caused rioting at the plant in which an employee was killed. The newspaper's supply of paper was rationed, an inquiry was instituted into its accounts and when it was established that *La Prensa* owed the government a substantial sum in back taxes, the judge in charge ordered the paper expropriated, after which it was turned over to a committee formed of the representatives of trade unions. They produced a very different-looking newspaper with predictably different editorial concerns.

In 1951, a year of presidential elections, the resolution of the railway strike and the closure of *La Prensa* became important issues for the opposition. The paper spoke on its readers' behalf for a distinctive notion of Argentine civilization. It had recorded births, marriages and deaths of well-to-do Argentines and, though its style was ineffectually pompous and its vision of Argentine politics derived from the 1890s, it had seemed an important and sacrosanct institution. Its closure made the paper into a symbol of abused press freedom. The officer corps had become reconciled to Peronism on the grounds that it was the only regime capable of restoring social order, but it now seemed as if Perón was bent on 'the subversion of social values'. Officers had been angered by the 'reform' of the Constitution. Even those who were not members of the Oligarchy were distressed by the *nouveaux riches*, the strong and favoured unions, and what they perceived as an arrogant working class ruthlessly supported by the State.

By this stage, not only the Argentine middle class but also skilled categories of workers had begun to suffer from inflation. They were not richer than they had been in 1946 and they could see that many less skilled than themselves were. Much of their resentment was directed towards Perón, but there was Evita, too. It was she who exercised power within the unions and she who now represented, in the idiom of that year, illiteracy against culture, vulgarity against measured thought.

Evita had worked for Perón's re-election since 1948, but it was by now widely recognized that she had also been furthering her own cause. The numerous 'declarations' on her behalf were spontaneous only in appearance and for form's sake, and they could not have been made without her assent. At that date, no woman had been elected to a post as important as the vice-presidency in any country. Evita certainly wanted this honour, though she would consistently deny it. Her reticence arose from the opposition any open move would be bound to incur. Under the Argentine Constitution, the Vice-President automatically succeeded the President in the event of the latter's death in office, and the prospect of any woman, let alone Evita, holding presidential office was bound to seem deeply offensive to many Argentines.

It is not clear whether the Army ever formally complained about Evita to Perón, but Perón was certainly aware of the disquiet her candidacy would cause. He never spoke of it and his attitude towards it has been the object of much speculation. If he was against it because of the Army's opposition, as has been claimed, why did he countenance the campaign posters bearing Evita's name pasted on walls all over the country? Perhaps the key to his attitude arises from the sense he must have possessed by this stage that both the support her candidacy received and the pressures against it would soon be equally irrelevant.

Evita herself may not have understood how ill she was, but her condition was now apparent to those around her. She had become thin and even paler than usual, her face was drawn, there were shadows around her eyes and her legs were permanently swollen. She hid her haemorrhages and her attacks of fever from everyone except her maids, but she now complained of intense abdominal pains. When her doctors suggested a series of tests, she left the Residence early each morning to avoid them.

Perón let things take their course. At the worst, Evita's candidacy could be halted at the last minute and some new title that would satisfy the *descamisados*, if not her, might be presented to her in its stead. And perhaps Perón, who was not above such calculations, was also aware of the impression of sacrifice a last-ditch cancellation would make, particularly in the Army. What more could he do for them, after all? But Perón was to be startled by the depth and intensity of support for Evita; he did not realize, until it was too late and his calculations were upset, that she had now become as important to his followers as he.

The meeting called by the CGT to proclaim labour's adherence to the Perón-Perón candidacy was named after the *Cabildo Abierto*, the first spontaneous political gathering of *porteños* called on 25 May 1810 to overthrow the Spanish colonial government. Unlike the first *Cabildo*, this second one, scheduled for 22 August

1951, was carefully planned. Buses and trains were chartered to bring the *descamisados* from the most remote provinces, with meals, board, and movie tickets thoughtfully provided by the government. On the great Avenida 9 de Julio, so wide that it seemed empty even in rush hour, a giant scaffold had been erected to support a long dais, two sixty-foot high portraits of Perón and Evita, and a connecting 'bridge of love' which bore the inscription *Perón-Eva Perón, la fórmula de la patria.* 'By dawn the city was dominated by an intense feeling of anticipation,' a reporter wrote in that day's evening edition of *La Razón,* 'and throughout the day it retained the appearance of a *fiesta,* its streets covered with flags and overflowing with people.' There were encampments at the base of the dais, where the first arrivals had slept in order to get the best seats, and there were banners slung between the palm trees up which many people had now climbed for a better view. By the afternoon, more than a million people occupied the great open space of the avenue, chanting and waving their banners, while an aircraft flew over the city writing PERON, EVITA and CGT in the cloudless sky. Perón mounted the dais at five pm, accompanied by the various elements of the Peronist hierarchy: ministers, deputies, party members and CGT officials, but without Evita. José Espejo, the president of the CGT, then began his speech, but since he was continually interrupted by cries of 'Evita' he stopped, no doubt as had been arranged beforehand, and declared to the cheering crowd that 'the modesty of Eva Perón, her greatest virtue' had stopped her from attending the meeting. Then he left the dais and returned almost at once, with Evita.

After this crude but theatrically effective entry, Evita made her speech, full of obscure threats to the Oligarchy and violent expressions of love. There were frequent interruptions, chants taken up by one sector of the crowd and then moving across until they were shouted as with one voice: *'Con Evita', 'Evita con Perón'.* But Evita did not refer to her own candidacy, at least not directly. 'I shall always do what the people wish,' she ended her speech, 'but I tell you, just as I said five years ago, that I would rather be Evita than the wife of the President, if this Evita could do anything for the pain of my country; and so now I say I would rather be Evita....'

Was this a refusal? It was certainly taken as such by the crowd, which persistently interrupted the next speech, Perón's own, and when it was over and Perón had declared his own acceptance, began to chant 'Evita' in a mood of growing frustration until Espejo went to the microphone and, repeating the crowd's demand, asked Evita to accept. When she said that she could not speak, he brought the microphone to her, so that her pleas could be distinctly heard by the crowd and thus, in the dusk, began an extraordinary exchange, Evita facing the great mass that cried out for her with the sadness and anger of frustrated devotion.

'My beloved *descamisados*,' she began again, her voice hoarse and broken with emotion and exhaustion,

> I ask the comrades in the CGT, the women, children and the workers gathered here, not to make me do something I have never wished to do. I ask the CGT and I ask you, by the affection which unites us, by the love that we feel for one another, that for so overwhelmingly important a decision in the life of this poor woman, you give me at least four days for consideration . . .

'No, no, now, general strike, let's go on strike!' the voices replied.

'Comrades,' Evita said, repeating the word four times before there was finally silence: 'Comrades, I am not giving up my place in the struggle, I am only giving up the honours. I am keeping my hopes, like Alexander . . .* for your glory and your love and that of General Perón.' And then, while the crowd still shouted 'Now', Evita began a rambling and confused self-justification, explaining, arguing, pleading for time as if holding off the crowd.

> Comrades, it's said throughout the world that I am a selfish and ambitious woman; you know very well that this isn't the case. But you also know that everything I did, it was never so that I could have any political position in my country. I don't want any worker of my country to lack arguments when those people full of resentment, those mediocre people who never understand me and do not believe that everything I do, I do for the lowest motives . . .

She never finished this sentence because she was again interrupted, and then she asked again for a day's grace and again they shouted 'No'.

> This has taken me by surprise [she said]. For a long time I had known that my name was being put forward and I did not discourage it; I did it for the people and Perón, for there is no man capable of coming anywhere near him and for you, so that those men with the idea of being *caudillos* would know and so that the General, with my name, could for a moment stand above party disputes, but never in my ordinary heart of an Argentine woman did I think I would be able to accept that post . . .

*Evita means Alexander the Great.

While Evita went through these unconvincing excuses, beneath the huge portrait of herself, the dais had become another chorus of arguing voices, with Perón's raised above the others. No one had expected the meeting to take this course. 'Tonight,' Evita pleaded, and when the crowd said 'No, no, NOW', she asked for two hours' grace, and when they said 'NOW' again, she passed the microphone to Espejo, who said: 'We shall wait here for her decision. We shall not move until she gives us a reply in accordance with the desires of the people.' The crowd cheered deliriously and then, as night came, newspapers were rolled into torches, as they had been in 1945, and they settled down to wait for Evita's reply. But she did not really reply, at least not in the unambiguous terms they had demanded. When she finally came forward again her words were simply: 'Comrades, as General Perón has said, I will do what the people say.' There were more cries, more complaints, but after that the meeting was closed. The next day was declared a public holiday and the crowd peacefully left the city, not at all sure, after all, whether the question of Evita's candidacy had been finally decided.

She received much homage and many decorations in the course of her political life, yet none of these tributes matched *Cabildo Abierto* in intensity. For the first time in his career, Perón found himself relegated to a secondary role, mute and astonished by the passion inspiring his wife's bond with the *descamisados*. But while that bond had given Perón power, propelling him to the Presidency, Evita's marked both the zenith and the end of her political career. She had successfully left the issue of her candidacy open. *Democracia*, which of all the press had the best reasons to know what was going on, next day reported the *Cabildo Abierto* under the banner headline, *Aceptaron!* (They have accepted), but nine days later Evita broadcast a radio message announcing her 'irrevocable, and definitive decision to renounce the honour' which had been offered to her. This decision was 'totally free' and had arisen out of the conviction first glimpsed the day of the *Cabildo Abierto*, and sustained on subsequent reflection, that she should not 'exchange one battle position for another'. She referred to 17 October as her birth in politics and concluded: 'I did not possess then, nor do I possess now the slightest ambition for myself other than this: that it should be said of me when the marvellous chapter in history that will surely be devoted to Perón is written, that there was by the side of Perón a woman who devoted her life to the task of conveying to the President the people's hopes and that the people lovingly used to call this woman "Evita". That is all I wish to be.'

For her part, Evita must have known that it was unlikely that she would be able to be a candidate, yet if that was indeed the case, why did she attend the meeting or allow this exchange at all? It is possible that by the time she knew this, it was too late to stop the course of events and that she, like Perón, was surprised by the intensity of support for her; but it is much more likely that, knowing her chances were slight, she created and sustained these demands for herself as a means, the last and only means, of bargaining for the vice-presidency with Perón. In the end it was not enough: Perón had determined she should not be a candidate, and she could not go against his decision.

22 August 1951 became known in Peronist iconography as Evita's 'day of renunciation', and her gesture, as might be expected, aroused tributes to her spirit of sacrifice, her sense of discipline, her loyalty and her humility. Three days after the broadcast, the unions declared that 17 October that year would be specially dedicated to her renunciation, and three days after that Congress held a special session in her honour. On 10 September, Perón, as Supreme Chief of the Peronist Movement and of the Order of the Peronist Medal, called a press conference to announce that he would shortly create a new honour in remembrance of Evita's gesture.

Evita did not choose to renounce her political ambitions – the decision was forced on her. But the fact that the zenith of her career and its end came so close to each other, and were marked in such a spectacular way by the *Cabildo Abierto*, ensured the survival of the myth of deliberately chosen sacrifice, of a woman electing to give up the world out of sheer goodness. This powerful image remained unaffected by the reality that even had she been encouraged by her husband to stand, she could not have done so. She fell ill immediately after the *Cabildo Abierto*, and within a month it was apparent even to her how serious her illness was.

10
Death and its Public

The evening after her speech at the *Cabildo Abierto*, Evita fainted from pain and exhaustion. In the following weeks she suffered increasingly from acute pains in her abdomen, and was unable to resume her work; some days she was unable to get out of bed at all. Perón and the doctors pleaded with her to allow a series of tests to be made, pointing out that her refusal laid her open to more pain and worse illness, and at last, in mid-September, she agreed to spend several days in bed in the Residence while these tests were carried out. On Monday, 24 September, Perón was taken aside by the doctors and told that Evita was suffering from 'cancer of the uterus, in an advanced state and with dangerous side-effects'. Father Hernán Benítez, who was present when Perón was told, said that 'this blow struck Perón as hard as anything he had ever experienced. His life would be entirely altered. He knew exactly what was in store for him the moment he was told, as his first wife, Aurelia, had suffered from the same illness and, after they had tried and failed with every type of treatment, she had died in great pain, which affected him more than her.'[1]

Because of Evita's physical weakness the doctors were reluctant to perform a hysterectomy until she had received a series of blood transfusions. However, Evita, who was never told the real nature of her illness, refused to be treated, forcing her doctors to resort to the first of a series of what Father Benítez would call 'pious lies' in order to secure the compliance of their patient. They told her that she had the alternative of being treated with drugs or of undergoing an operation, and she chose the treatment.

She was receiving a blood transfusion in the Presidential Residence on the morning of 28 September when units of the Army, the Navy and the Air Force, led by General Benjamin Menéndez (the perpetrator of a number of failed coups) attempted to overthrow Perón. This was the first military rising against the Perónist regime, and was hastily conceived and incompetent. It was soon apparent that much of the Army was still loyal to Perón, and when the CGT had first declared a twenty-four-hour general strike and then filled the space in front of the Casa Rosada with columns of *descamisados,* Perón made a violent speech from the balcony rallying his followers. A squadron of planes had been detailed to bomb Casa Rosada while Perón was speaking, but they were too late and the officer in charge decided against the 'fruitless massacre' that was inevitable with so large a crowd and flew his planes to Uruguay. As Perón said, the day turned into a *chirinada* – a disastrous mess.

Evita's absence from the balcony during Perón's speech was noted by the crowd, and they shouted for her to appear. The government information service was thus forced to release the first public acknowledgment of her illness, calling it 'an anaemia of great intensity'.

As a result of the doctor's recommendations, news of the uprising had been kept from Evita, though she must have sensed something was amiss from the disrupted routines and anxieties of those around her. When Perón returned to the Residence that evening, she insisted on recording a radio message to be transmitted nationally. From her sick-bed, she thanked the *descamisados* for having gone to the rescue of Perón at the Plaza de Mayo, and as she began to sob, promised them 'to be back in the fight soon'. She asked them to pray for her health, not on her own behalf, but on Perón's behalf and theirs, her *descamisados*. The danger to Perón, however slight it had ultimately been, made real Evita's persistent fears of plots and treacheries. The next day, after telling those around her that 'if the Army will not defend Perón, the people will have to', and without consulting or informing Perón, she summoned to her bedside three members of the CGT's executive committee; Atilio Renzi; and the still loyal Commander of the Armed Forces, José Humberto Molina. She ordered 5,000 machine pistols and 1,500 machine guns, which were to be paid for by the Foundation, stored in a government arsenal, and made immediately available to members of the CGT in the event of another insurrection of the Armed Forces. Thus the *descamisados* 'would be able to defend themselves'.[2] Prince Bernhardt of the Netherlands had recently discussed the possibility of his acting as an intermediary in supplying arms to the Argentine Armed Forces, and according to one of those present, it was through him that Evita's private arsenal was now purchased.

Another bulletin was released, this one alluding to Evita's 'great weakness . . . intensified by the emotional stress caused by the events of last night', and it was after this explicit use of her illness for political purposes that the first groups of workers and Peronist militants began the practice of holding masses for her health – though many of them would, of course, have needed no prompting. In the first two weeks of October, according to *Democracia,* ninety-two masses on her behalf were heard at the request of various organizations. At Luján, thirty miles from Buenos Aires, there was a massive, putty-coloured, imitation-Gothic basilica filled with plaques and trophies commemorating miracles performed by the Virgin of Luján. Catholic Argentines had traditionally come to Luján for comfort or favours and now they came in their thousands on Evita's behalf. People began to perform 'feats' or 'sacrifices' for her health: cripples or boys with broken legs walked to Luján from remote parts of Argentina, groups of people travelled great distances carrying the image of the Virgin, pin-headed, chrysalis-shaped, swaddled in blue and white, with the inscription underneath *'Por la salud de Evita'.* Altars were raised in the street or in individual homes, an image of Evita and one of the Virgin, flowers and candles. 'It would be difficult to find a similar phenomenon in history,' observed Father Benítez, with only a slight degree of hyperbole. 'People who had never in their lives entered churches now found themselves doing so and old people now ransacked the attics of their memories in search of the *Pater Noster,* kneeling in the dust and weeping as they prayed.'[3] Demonstrations of a more secular sort were performed by the unions, as, for instance, that of the construction industry's trucking union, which on 6 October assembled more than one thousand trucks and drove them as slowly as possible around the topiary-and-palm bordered asphalt walks of Palermo park, in a fume-shrouded 'march of silence'. At the end of this demonstration two trucks left the convoy and drove up to the nearby Presidential Residence, to leave a large bunch of flowers and a message of sympathy for Evita at the gate.

Evita was well enough to get out of bed for Perón's birthday on 8 October, but she was not able to attend the reception held to mark the publication of her autobiography, *La Razón de mi Vida,* a week later. Editorial Peuser, the publishers, had agreed to publish the book on the terms that all the profit would go to Evita (their expenses on the book would be covered by the government). 300,000 copies had been printed in three editions: de luxe, hardback and paperback. According to *Democracia,* which published several issues made up almost entirely of articles about the book and excerpts from it, 150,000 copies were sold on the first day of publication; one bookstore employee in Buenos Aires sold 1,500 copies single-handed. A month later sales were well past the half-million mark and Evita's autobiography had sold more copies in Argentina than any other book.

17 October 1951 was dedicated by the unions to the memory of

Evita's renunciation, and over a million and a half *descamisados* crowded into the Plaza de Mayo hoping to see her. She had been given a strong dose of morphine and though she was able to stand on the balcony, she looked exhausted, a wasted and tragic figure in a black suit that seemed to have been made for another person. She received two medals, one from José Espejo on behalf of the CGT for her renunciation, which 'had the greatness of the actions of saints and martyrs', and another presented by Perón, the Grand Peronist Medal, Extraordinary Grade 'awarded for the first time'. When the moment came for her to speak she stepped to the microphone but was unable to say a word. There was silence, a scuffling on the dais, and Evita was lifted away. Perón began again with a tribute to his wife, which resembled a funeral oration in both tone and content, a complete summation of Evita's career. Perón had never before spoken in public about his wife in any detail and now that he was doing so, it was as if she had already died. He spoke of her three roles: as link with the unions, creator of the Foundation, and the creator of the Women's Party.

> With her natural capability of organizing politically on a mass scale, she has given the Peronist movement a new orientation and a mystique . . . Her daily work in the Labour Ministry, in which she has lost part of her life and health, has been a holocaust on behalf of our people, enabling me to live some of each day in contact with the people . . . Above all, with her marvellous good sense, she has kept watch on my behalf with intelligence and with loyalty, the two most powerful determinants of destiny and human history.

Evita had never received such compliments from Perón. She listened to him and when he finished, got to her feet again unassisted, and while the crowd waited in silence, she fell towards him, sobbing and hugging him. The crowd, as Father Benítez said, 'witnessed this extraordinary scene in utter silence, a lump in its throat.' Her own speech, delivered in a faint and hoarse voice, began with an eerie commitment to be present each October, with Perón and the *descamisados,* 'even if I have to shed the tatters of my life to do so'. She thanked Perón for her life, and then turned to the great crowd to thank them too:

> I could never repay him, even by giving him my life, to thank him for how good he always was to me and is to me. Nothing I have, nothing I am, nothing I think is mine; it all belongs to Perón. I will not tell the usual lie. I will not say that I don't deserve this, my General, I deserve it for one reason alone, greater than all the riches of the world; I deserve it because everything I did, I did out of love for this people. I am not anything because I did something, I am not anything because I

renounced anything; I am not anything because I am somebody or have something. All that I have, I have in my heart, it hurts my soul, it hurts my flesh and it burns on my nerves, and that is my love for this people and for Perón. And I thank you, my General, for having taught me to know that love and value it. Were the people to ask me for my life, I would give it to them singing, for the happiness of one *descamisado* is worth more than my own life . . .

While the crowd stood in awed silence, Evita began to plead with them to be vigilant on Perón's behalf, as she could no longer be. 'I ask one thing, comrades. We should all now swear in public to defend Perón and fight to the death on his behalf. And our oath will be proclaimed by shouting for an entire minute so that our cries will reach the end of the earth: *"La Vida por Perón".'* The crowd of a million and a half shouted these words not for one minute, but for several. As if in a trance of devotion, Evita, strong enough finally to finish her speech, stretched her hands across the balcony to them to give them her love and then, exhausted again, fell back into Perón's arms sobbing while the crowd still cried out her name.

Evita would speak many 'last words' in the last year of her life, and though the occasions on which she did so were undoubtedly theatrical, they were movingly so. Whatever artifice there was in Perón's and Evita's prolonged romance with the *descamisados* – and it had, indeed, often seemed a huge, carefully-managed melodrama – with the onset of her illness the rhetoric of love, loyalty and sacrifice came to seem entirely appropriate. Nothing else would have been adequate to express the extraordinary emotions of pain and loss experienced by Evita, Perón and the crowds. There are writers otherwise sympathetic to her, such as V.S.Naipaul, who have perceived in this only the implication that Evita's 'private tragedy' was thus being 'turned into the passion play of the dictatorship',[4] but for Evita, as for Perón and for the crowds, this 'passion play' was real, a long and appallingly painful death in public. Her death was not only of political importance, it also became, for almost a year, the most important political event in the country, a national experience of deep and lasting impact.

Evita's health worsened after this public appearance, and it was decided that in spite of her physical weakness surgery could not be delayed. By a coincidence so conspicuous that it led many people to the conclusion that this decline in her health had been organized for political ends, the operation was scheduled for early November, shortly before the Presidential elections. Evita was well enough to choose the slate of women candidates. She made two campaign broadcasts, the first celebrating the opening of her Children's City, the second directed to Peronist women, urging them to vote, but both times she seemed tired, nostalgic and frustrated by her absence from politics and her inability to help Perón and Quijano, who, though himself dying, had been induced to stand again. The opposition, the Unión Cívica Radical, had chosen two strong candidates, Ricardo Balbín and Arturo Frondizi for President and Vice-President, respectively, and the campaign was as violent as the previous one had been, with rallies in Buenos Aires, police attacks on the opposition meetings, injuries and deaths. On 3 November, shortly after recording a speech to be broadcast six days later on the eve of the elections, whether she was alive or not, Evita was taken by ambulance to the Policlínico Presidente Perón, the hospital built by the Foundation in Avellaneda. No public announcement was made, but the news was passed by word of mouth, and the street outside the hospital filled with a crowd of twenty thousand, some of whom remained there the entire time Evita was in the hospital.

The Argentine Embassy in Washington had approached Dr George Pack, a surgeon at the Memorial Sloane-Kettering Center in New York, one month previously, and he was now summoned to Buenos Aires in the greatest secrecy. He was met at the airport by Evita's brother and an English-speaking friend, and immediately conveyed to the Presidential weekend retreat in Olivos, where he stayed during the time he remained in the country. Evita never saw Pack. She, like the rest of the country, was under the impression that the operation would be performed by Dr Ricardo Finochietto, the Argentine surgeon who was also director of the Presidente Perón hospital. Two days after performing the hysterectomy Pack left the country as quietly as he had come, satisfied that at least the spread of the cancer had been arrested and that Evita would recover from the operation itself. On 9 November, the last day of the Presidential campaign, the Argentine Electoral Council, with the support of the opposition parties, passed a resolution allowing Evita to vote from her hospital bed. On 11 November, the president of the district in which she was to vote, two electoral supervisors and two policemen entered her room bearing the ballot papers and the boxes in which she was to deposit her votes. The Peronist ballot paper, disregarding her 'renunciation' and her physical condition, displayed Perón's likeness on one side, and hers, not that of the vice-presidential candidate, on the other. The officials left the room while she voted, respecting the ballot's secrecy. One of them was the writer David Viñas who wrote later: 'I was disgusted by the atmosphere of adulation surrounding Eva Perón, but the image of the women outside, on their knees, praying on the sidewalk, touching the urn which contained Evita's vote and kissing it, moved me deeply. It was a dazzling tableau, like something out of Tolstoy.'[5]

The room at the Residence in which Evita recuperated had red velvet curtains, pink carpets, a sofa upholstered in pink and an ornate bed in the haut-bourgeois style of official Argentina. 'To think,' said Evita when she saw it, 'that I had to die to get a room like this.' There was a crucifix in black silver on one wall, and a cot standing against another for her night-nurse. The balcony overlooked the gardens, and beyond them the Avenida Libertador on which, throughout the next few months, there would always be a crowd. Even in bad weather well-wishers waited there for a sign, or praying. If she were well enough Evita would go out and greet them from the balcony.

When it was possible her sickroom assumed some of the functions of other nearby rooms from which she had exercised genuine power. She could not receive the poor, because of the danger of infection, but she did see deputations of union officials and Peronist women, and her circle of political dependents could come and spend time with her, their presence sustaining the illusion that she still controlled the Foundation and worked with the unions. Favourite guests – Nicolini, de Prisco, her brother – were allowed to sit on her bed, the others were assigned the sofa. Perón ate in Evita's room while she was still confined to her bed, but when she recovered a little, they spent the evenings watching films in the great hall of the Residence. At night, when he had gone to bed, she would summon her friends and, much as they had done in her office, they would talk about politics.

For a time, as she recovered from the operation, it seemed to Evita that she would be able to resume some of her activities. The election results had given Perón a substantially larger margin of victory than in 1945, with most of his new support coming from Evita's supporters, the women voters. On 2 December she made a broadcast expressing her hopes of 'returning to the fight', and treated the electoral victory as if she had won it, by thanking the people for having voted for Perón as she had asked them to. At Christmas, she was once again able to distribute some of the millions of the Foundation's toys and bottles from the Residence gardens. In January she spent a week on the Presidential yacht, but by February she was complaining of the same abdominal pains as before, and another biopsy revealed that the cancer was spreading. But this time little could be done to arrest its growth.

'No one ever told her what she was suffering from,' Father
Benítez said, 'but she knew that things were not going well, even
that they were going rather less well. She suffered from the same
acute pains, the same loss of appetite and she had the same terrible
nightmares and bouts of despair . . . .'[6] The summer was humid,
and Evita lay on her bed in her pyjamas, her poodle, Canela, at
her feet. Amulets, stones and printed images, which supposedly
possessed miraculous curative properties, and many flowers
arrived every day, and were passed on at her behest to local
churches, particularly to the shrine of the Virgin at Nueva
Pompeya. 'I believe in the Virgin,' Evita said to her nurse, 'but I'm
not a *chupacirios* [a licker of candles].' One of the many things
promised her on her recovery was a voyage to the Middle East, but
when the wardrobe ordered from Paris arrived and was rushed to
the Residence, it was as if it had been ordered for another woman,
so thin had Evita become. She could not wear any of it, and Irma
and Pilar, her two maids, had to model the dresses for her,
together with her jewels.[7]

Whether because of the pain or the drugs or simply because she
knew she was dying and had little time, Evita's public utterances
became more violent, with threats of destruction, and messianic
references to the afterlife. Later, these speeches would seem to be
the quintessential Evita and would be used in an entirely different
political context, and by a different generation of Peronists, to
legitimize the use of political violence. In reality they were cries of
pain and impotence. On 1 May, Evita was able to walk
unsupported on to the balcony of the Casa Rosada to greet the
descamisados. She defended Perón as the real 'leader of the
people' and attacked her enemies ferociously. 'If it is necessary,'
she said, 'we will execute justice with our own hands. I ask God
not to allow these madmen to raise their hands against Perón, for
beware of that day when I will go down with the working people, I
will go down with the women of the people, I will go down with the
descamisados . . . and I will leave nothing standing that is not *for*
Perón.' With these words she was carried from the balcony by
Perón. 'In the room, behind windows through which the sound of
crowds calling her name could just be heard,' Perón said, 'I could
hear only my own breathing, for Evita's was so slight as to be
imperceptible. In my arms, there was nothing more than a dead
woman.'[8] Again, four weeks later, Evita was able to get out of
bed, this time for a meeting of Peronist governors; again she used
these 'last words' to make violent threats in turbid language.
'Those who believe in sweetness and love,' she said, adapting the
Bible for her purposes, 'forget that Christ said, "I have come to

earth to bring fire, so that it may burn more". He gives us an example of fanaticism and for that reason we must be fanatics for Perón unto death.'

Raul Alejandro Apold, the Under-Secretary of Information, came to the Residence on 4 June, the morning of Perón's inaugural ceremony, with a propaganda work for Evita entitled *Argentina Forwards!* Perón expressed his concern to Apold, lest she insist on taking part that day in the long procession to Congress and the Casa Rosada. Apold should tell her just how cold it was. 'The *señora* was wearing a pair of blue pyjamas. She leafed through the illustrated book and when she saw a photograph of herself, she began to cry, "To think what I was and what I am now." ' Apold, to change the subject, began to talk about the cold, and Evita became very angry. 'That is an order of the General,' she said, 'but I will go all the same. The only thing that will keep me in this bed today is my own death.' An employee of the Residence put together a frame of plaster and wire and, thus supported, Evita, wearing a fur coat too large for her, was able to stand beside Perón in the back of an open car, waving and smiling vaguely at the crowd. She had needed a triple dose of pain-killer before the inaugural ceremonies began, and when she reached the Casa Rosada, she needed another double dose.

By June 1952, ten months after the beginning of her illness, Evita weighed only 80 pounds (38 kilos), and every day she was losing more weight. Atilio Renzi used to unscrew the regulating wheel of the scales to conceal this, but 'sometimes my hand would slip, I would correct too much and she would be happy as she thought she had gained some weight.'9 By now she had been moved to another room containing a hospital bed from the Foundation on which her initials were stamped in blue; her own room now contained the machinery needed for radiotherapy. This method of treatment had little effect, except that during the course of it Evita was badly burned and suffered greatly. 'Those days were an inferno for Evita,' Perón said. 'She had become skin alone, through which could be seen the whiteness of her bones. Only her eyes seemed alive and articulate. They moved from person to person and they asked questions of everyone; sometimes they were serene, sometimes they expressed feelings of utter loss.'10

Sometimes, as in the case of Perón's inauguration, events were reported without allusion to Evita's state of health, as if she were perfectly well, a state of affairs which was denied by the photographs accompanying the reporting. Where there were bulletins, they said enough to excite concern and sympathy but gave no details of the surgery which had been performed or the nature of Evita's illness. Among the anti-Peronists and representatives of the foreign press, her illness had been at first interpreted as a nervous collapse of psychosomatic origins, 'the natural reaction of a woman of her ambitious character to the supreme political defeat she had experienced'[11]; and then, when it became apparent that she had not recovered, another interpretation gained credence, barely nearer the truth. This began with the supposition that Evita was Perón's source of mass appeal, and that with her imminent death the dictator and his works would swiftly crumble away. Perón's repeated 'exhibitions' of his dying wife were seen as desperate final acts, and in this lurid context, the debate over who actually used whom was revived, its terms now inverted, with many stories of how Perón was obliged to drag his reluctant wife, screaming with pain, on to the public stage. When not depicted as reckless, Perón was usually described as cowardly in the face of his wife's sufferings. The most curious of many such stories, told and retold, and frequently proffered as historical fact, concerned his behaviour with respect to the odours that allegedly emanated from Evita's dying body. He was supposed to enter her room only very rarely and when he did, to keep a muslin mask over his face, like a keeper of bees.

A great number of odd fantasies concerning revenge, illness or death were repeated in Buenos Aires at the time of Evita's long illness, which have been attributed by the psychiatrist Marie Langer to feelings of guilt and fear harboured by many Argentines with respect to Evita. Many of Langer's patients had confessed to wishing her dead, and now she was dying they felt guilty and anxious and they suffered from hypochondria. 'Thus they expressed their fear of biblical punishment – an eye for an eye, a tooth for a tooth – brought on by their hatred.' In the *barrio norte*, the city's richest residential district, the rumour ran abroad that mothers should not take their children to doctors' offices and hospitals, because Evita needed 'young and fresh blood' every day and it was collected and taken to the Residence by Foundation vans.[12]

Among supporters of Perón the celebration of masses, the pilgrimages and processions had continued, creating a climate of feeling in which no tribute could be satisfactory and no superlative could any longer encompass Evita's virtues. *La Razón de mi Vida* had received remarkable critical notices, one reviewer in Democracia asking what voice 'had awoken similar feelings in men's hearts?' and going so far as to conclude: 'only the voice of Christ'. Portuguese, Arabic and Braille versions of the book were now announced, and Congress decreed it a compulsory textbook for all State-run or State-financed schools. One Peronist cell had even raised an altar to the book on its premises. The reluctance of New York publishing houses to handle the English translation of Evita's autobiography led, on 4 June, to a brief General Strike summoned by the CGT and a large rally at Luna Park in 'glorification' of Evita, in which, after many 'anti-imperialist' speeches and windy exaltations of her spirit, José Espejo, president of the CGT, compared what was being accomplished on her behalf with the deification of Caesar by Augustus in the first century A.D. In the 'New Argentina' of 1952, he said, 'the entire country is effecting the apotheosis of its heroine.'

As Evita's health continued to deteriorate that month, the city of Quilmes resolved to change its name to 'Eva Perón', and Congress, after a special legislative session devoted to eulogies of 'the most remarkable woman of any historical epoch', gave her the title *Jefa Espiritual de la Nación* (Spiritual Leader of the Nation). In recognition of this new title without precedent, she was awarded the 'necklace of the Order of the Liberator, San Martín', a massive piece of jewellery containing 753 precious stones and incorporating six distinct emblematic configurations: the Peronist shield, the national flag, a crown of laurels, a condor, the shields of the fourteen provinces and, of course, the national emblem itself, made of gold, platinum, diamonds and enamel.

For some years the government had contemplated the possibility of erecting a monument to the Revolution of October 1945, but nothing had been accomplished until early 1951, when Evita entrusted the task of preparing a scale model for the project to León Tomassi, an Italian sculptor. Tomassi showed his model to her shortly after her operation and the government would later suggest that she had thus responded: 'It must be the largest in the world. At its summit, there must be the figure of the *descamisado*, and inside the monument we shall build the Peronist museum. Beneath this, there will be a crypt containing the remains of the *descamisado*, in honour of those who died during the Revolution.' Evita had been impressed by the tomb of Napoleon at Les Invalides in Paris, and she told Tomassi that she had something like that in mind. October 1945 had taken place without the death of a single *descamisado*, so for the tomb Evita suggested 'one of those . . . [and there were a few] who, after crying *Viva Perón!* fell beneath the wheels of the train', in which Perón had made his campaign tour. As it was now apparent that Evita herself would shortly die, the Senate gathered on 7 July to debate the issue of whether the monument should be dedicated to her. During the session the senators listened to a recording of Perón's tribute to Evita of the previous October, and gave eighty-four speeches in her honour. These speeches were later collected in a leather-bound volume and presented to her by a delegation of faithful senators. The volume was entitled 'Eva Perón in Bronze'. Of the many inflated speeches uttered that day, the most inflated was possibly that of Senator Juana Larrauri, the tangosinger whom Evita had chosen to work for her:

> All the honours sought by mankind have shrivelled beside the marvellous greatness of Eva Perón; she was able to renounce the spirit of flattery because of her sublimity and her strength; her soul never needed flattery and flattery always had need of her in that it was ashamed of having less light than her, who was the cleanest light, the light of infinite love. [Shouts of 'Hear! Hear!'. Prolonged applause. Senators and public in the gallery rise and shout the names of General Perón and Eva Perón.] Eva Perón is the honour of honour. I cannot accept, Mr President, that she be compared with any woman, any heroine of our time, for many of these have had eminent writers to immortalize their individual histories; there is not, nor will there ever be a writer, no matter how intelligent, capable of following faithfully the history of the realities of Eva Perón. [Hear! Hear! Prolonged applause. Senators and public in the gallery rise and shout the names of Perón and Eva Perón.]

Evita can have been only intermittently lucid throughout May and June, the last two months of her life, but she began to take leave of those she had worked with and valued, summoning them to her bedside and giving them many mementoes, pieces of her own jewellery, or medals bearing her profile, which had been struck to her personal specifications. She knew that she would soon die, she knew that her veneration was assured; already she could see it everywhere around her, and it is more than likely that she derived some satisfaction from the spectacle of these elaborate farewells disguised by assurances that she would speedily recover. She would indeed frequently interrupt such assurances to indicate she was not deceived by them. To Father Benítez, for instance, in front of Atilio Renzi and an audience of union officials and ministers, she said, 'You are lying to me as if I were a coward. I know I have fallen into a pit and no one can get me out,'[14] and to Raúl Apold, head of the government propaganda bureau, she said she had dreamt of dying and 'you, Raúl, were calling up the newspapers to get them to run headlines about my death.'[15] She asked Delia Parodi, one of the new women deputies in the assembly, 'Who really loves me?' Delia, as a good Peronist, replied, 'The people', and Evita said, 'Yes, but I mean really, for myself.' She began to cry, and when Delia also cried and handed Evita her handkerchief, Evita said to her nurse, so that Delia could hear, 'Things must be really bad if Parodi is crying.'[16]

The French historian Philippe Ariès has suggested that the major change in attitudes towards death in the last hundred years has been the progressive 'expulsion of death' both as a conscious experience for the dying, their family and friends, and for society at large.[17] This attitude, most prevalent in Anglo-Saxon countries, but also extended to the industrialized Catholic West, has ended the 'era of beautiful death', death as an occasion to be consciously experienced, a means of communicating information or consolation to those living on. Except in rare and momentous cases, public death has been replaced by deaths which are private and unobtrusive, in much the same way as the anonymous motorized hearse has replaced the plumes and black velvet of its horse-drawn predecessor.

It is unlikely that Evita expressed a wish to be embalmed or chose her own resting place. Suggestions that she did so, merely reflect Perón's response to the many criticisms of what happened to her body after her death.[18] But her desire to die publicly, in the archaic sense of which Ariès has spoken, is beyond doubt. She wanted to thrust the fact of her death, with all its pathos and dramatic circumstances, into the public consciousness, and thus into a niche in history.

During her last weeks when she was conscious, she started to write another book, *My Message,* which was never published. It was most probably, like her last speeches, a dissertation on the greatness of Perón and a ferocious attack on his enemies, particularly the Army, which had now taken the Oligarchy's place in Evita's mind as the most serious threat to Perón. She also wrote her will, two versions of which have survived: the first version was made public immediately after her death; the second was handed to an Argentine journalist by Perón at the end of his own life, in 1975. Both begin with the same apocalyptic drum-roll:

> I want to live for ever with Perón and with my people. That is my absolute and unchangeable will and it is also my last wish. Wherever Perón may be and wherever my *descamisados* may be, there too, my heart will always be, to love them with all the strength left of my life, all the fanaticism burning my soul.

The will that was made public and which Evita did indeed sign, began with a series of reverential mentions of Perón and then proceeded to an orderly disposition of her possessions. All of these – jewels, clothes, royalties from books – were to be placed 'at

Perón's disposition as sole representative of the people'.

> I desire that a permanent fund be constituted with all my assets . . . [to be used] in the case of disasters affecting the poor and I want these to be seen as another proof of my love for them.
>
> I desire that in each case a subsidy equivalent to one year's salary be given to each family.
>
> My jewellery does not belong to me. Most of it was given to me by my people, but even the pieces I received from friends, from foreign governments or from Perón, must return to the people.
>
> I do not want them to fall into the hands of the Oligarchy and that is why I want them to stand . . . as a permanent source of credit which banks may then use for the benefit of the people.
>
> I also want the poor, the old, the children and the *descamisados* to continue writing to me as they did in my lifetime and [I wish] the monument that Congress wishes to erect to combine the hopes of everyone and convert them into reality through my Foundation . . .
>
> My last words shall be as my first ones; I want to live eternally with Perón and my people. God will forgive me if I prefer to remain with them because he, too, is with the poor and I have always understood that in each *descamisado* God was asking me for love which I never withheld.[19]

The other 'last wishes' are quite different and could be those of another person. They are not written in typescript, but in Evita's almost illegible hand:

> I confess that I suffered, but I suffered a lot out of the sense of impotence of a poor woman who wants to do good [and] isn't understood, and also to see the poor, the people, not making use of their victories not only because the betrayers of the people had as their interest their continued exploitation but because they [the poor] themselves slighted [these victories] I want the people to know how much I loved them and how much I loved Perón himself . . . If God doesn't help all the peoples [of this earth] millions of workers, women, children and old people will be exploited by these evil men. I never wasted time warming the seats of churches because I could understand God without any intermediaries and because when I helped a poor man, cured a sick man, gave food and homes, fought for the equality and dignity of workers, I believed myself to be closer to God, I now ask him to accomplish this miracle and bring about the hour of the people because the strength of a man like Perón, an honourable, patriotic man is slight before the evil of money . . .[20]

The Foundation, Evita continued, was to become part of the CGT, which would administer its assets on behalf of its members. Had it ever been executed, this request would significantly have fulfilled her wish to leave what she had to her *descamisados*.

Lastly, before the jewels were handed over to the poor, a good piece should be given to each of her sisters – Blanca, Elisa, Erminda – and her last wish was, 'I ask the General to give, as long as she is alive and God wills it, 3,000 pesos a month to Mama and he should never forget doña Juana, whom I am unable to forget.'

It is not hard to understand why this handwritten will was never offered for public view. It was a despairing document which would have introduced a jarring note into the official mood of mourning. It is quite possible that it was 'revised' with Evita's consent and became the other will; but it is more likely that she was by now far too ill to have much idea of what was going on around her.

On 18 July, at 3 pm Evita went into a coma, but at midnight she awoke again, saw her family and her doctors around her and said, 'What has happened to me? I have to get out of bed. If I don't I will die,'[22] and, to the great astonishment of those present, she got up out of bed and was able to walk a few steps on Perón's arm. Her family – her sisters, her brother, doña Juana and Perón – were by her bedside much of these last days. She asked often for Father Benítez and spent many hours alone with him. On 28 July, after two cancer specialists had been flown specially from Germany to Buenos Aires and after they had informed Perón that nothing could be done for Evita, Perón told Father Benítez that he must 'prepare the people' for her death. It was a cold, rainy afternoon and the Colon Opera House orchestra could not, as had been planned, play the Schubert Mass in the open air, yet thousands of *porteños* came to hear the mass sponsored by the CGT at the base of the great obelisk on the Avenida de Julio. In his sermon, Father Benítez spoke of Evita as 'our sister and our mother', and, while instructing the crowd to pray for the miracle of her life, he drew their attention again and again to the many other miracles which she had wrought: miracles of Christian heroism, miracles of Christian resignation, the miracle of 'having ascended, at the peak of her worldly glory, to sacrifice herself on behalf of the people' and of having finally, through her long and terrible agonies, 'opened the doors of the churches' to the working class, thus redeeming them from their wayward 'communist atheism and anti-Christian nihilism'. Someone had told Evita that Father Benítez was to preach that afternoon, though they had not told her what was the theme, and she had wanted to listen to the radio; but Renzi pulled the wires from the set and told her that there was no electrician in the Residence that afternoon.

On Saturday morning, 26 July 1952, a damp grey winter's day, Evita said to her maid, 'I never felt happy in this life. That is why I left home. My mother would have married me to someone ordinary and I could never have stood it, Irma; a decent woman has to get on in the world.' At 11 am she went into a coma, and at 3 pm Father Benítez gave her the last sacraments. From that hour, there were periodic radio announcements on the national network from a hook-up in the Residence, first that her state of health had declined, then, by 8 pm, that it was 'very serious'. Around Evita's bed were Perón, her mother, her sisters, her brother, Renzi and members of the Government, Nicolini, Aloé, Cámpora and Apold; and at 8.25 pm – a minute of the day which many Argentines would have occasion to remember – Evita ceased breathing. She had celebrated her thirty-first birthday only two months previously, but she was thirty-three years old.

A minute later, Raúl Apold of the Secretariat of Information broadcast to the nation, saying that *a las veinte y veinticinco*, at 8.25 pm, the Spiritual Leader of the Nation had died, and that her remains would be brought next day to the Ministry of Labour, where the public might see them. Although no instructions had been given to this effect, the entire city and the entire country instantly went into the deepest, most heartfelt state of mourning. Cinemas stopped their movies, theatres interrupted their plays, restaurants, bars and *boîtes* immediately showed customers to the door, their shutters slamming down over suddenly darkened streetfronts. Within a matter of minutes the city was silent and dark. The enormous crowd that nad made its way into Buenos Aires that night, either after the football games or for other entertainment, wandered idly around the streets, waiting for the extra editions of the evening papers, which contained for the first time information about the medical aspects of Evita's illness. A large crowd gathered outside the Residence, many of them kneeling despite the intense and increasing cold, and saying their rosaries. Among these mourners was Chuenga, seller of sweets at the River Plate soccer stadium, who had understood that there would be no games the next day and had come to the Residence to sell his sweets, dressed in black, his voice lowered.

Inside, the Residence was filled with members of the Peronist hierarchy. One of those waiting in the many rooms on the ground floor of the palace was Dr Pedro Ara, Professor of Anatomy, Cultural Attaché and by preference, though he had great disdain for that title, an embalmer. Ara had studied in Vienna, followed an academic career in Madrid, and had produced over the years many examples of what an Argentine newspaper article about his work could justly call 'the art of death'. Through his skills beloved daughters were turned into sleeping beauties; old men were preserved in dignified agony. His method of embalming depended on replacing blood with glycerine, thus retaining all the organs of the body and preserving its lifelike appearance, and his work was specially distinguished for its aesthetic qualities. He was able to apply the *art nouveau* look of mortuary sculpture to the human body, giving death the appearance of artistically rendered sleep. Ara was small, bald and discreet about his vocation and was not widely known in Argentina, but he was known in Buenos Aires society for, among other achievements, having embalmed the body of the composer Manuel de Falla. He had been summoned to the Residence to discuss the possibility of embalming Evita when she had been in her previous coma, and now, after sending Perón and the other mourners away, he and his assistant set to work, not to perform the complete task of preservation, for that would require more time and substantially greater facilities, but to render the body fit for a sustained encounter with the public. By early morning, according to Dr Ara, 'the body of Eva Perón was completely and definitively incorruptible'.[23]

Dr Ara was still in attendance when they came to dress Evita; first the dressmakers with a white shroud, then her hairdresser Julio Alcaraz, then Sarita, who had always done her nails. Shortly before her death Evita had told Sarita to remove her red Helena Rubinstein nail lacquer and replace it with transparent nail varnish. 'Her hand was so cold! I had never touched a body before and when I couldn't open the fingers, Doctor Ara placed his own fingers between the *señora's*. Thus I was able to do my job and when I had finished, as if in a dream, I took my things and left.'[24] The body was lifted into a cedar coffin, a rosary placed between the crossed hands, and covered with the Argentine flag. The upper portion of the coffin's lid was glass, leaving the face and upper body visible; before it could be locked into place, Ara sprinkled inside some detoxicant tablets 'rendering impossible the life of any microbe or insect'.

Preparations had been made for a national period of mourning on a substantial scale. The government suspended all official activities for two days, and all flags on government buildings were flown at half-mast for ten days. The CGT declared a two-day general strike in all but the most essential industries and a month's compulsory observation of mourning – black tie, white shirt, black jacket – for its members. But as the Foundation ambulance bearing Evita's body left the Residence, it was quickly apparent that these measures, of unprecedented elaboration for someone who was not a head of state, fell short of reflecting the people's grief. The crowd was dense outside the Residence and denser still around the Ministry of Labour, to which people had begun to come the moment her death was announced, and the streets were congested for ten blocks in each direction. When Evita's body was moved from the ambulance to the Ministry eight people were killed in the crush, and in the next twenty-four hours 2,100 people would be treated for injuries. Wreaths of white flowers filled the high lobby of the Ministry of Labour, overflowed into the street, and were stacked in great piles against its walls or trampled underfoot. Within a day after Evita's death it was impossible to find flowers of any kind in the flower shops of Buenos Aires.

It had rained on and off all Sunday, and those who had waited all night beneath umbrellas and newspapers were exhausted from the cold and from lack of sleep. They were regimented into lines by soldiers, and at noon the first ones were allowed into the Ministry, where they stood in line again, moving up one side of the large double staircase to the space at the top, where the coffin was displayed, and then down the other side. Around it was an Argentine flag framed in crêpe, a crucifix of ivory, silver and gold, and two candle-holders. Some of those who came just touched the coffin lightly, others bent to kiss the glass, others crossed themselves, and many broke down and cried uncontrollably, so that they had to be helped away by a nurse of the Foundation or by one of the cadets on guard. At the end of the three days which had been set aside for people to see Evita, it had become apparent that many people who wished to see her had not yet been able to do so, and the government decided to extend the ceremony indefinitely. No count was ever made of how many people came to see her in the next thirteen days, but the several lines outside the building stretched as much as thirty blocks in different directions, making it necessary to wait several hours before one could get inside.

That weekend and for some days afterwards, all restaurants, shops, theatres and cinemas, and public transportation were closed down. Giant photographs of Evita had been placed at intersections throughout the city, and at the obelisk were screens on to which a hastily-edited movie about her works was continuously projected. The city was grey with rain, the avenues were shiny and black, and the sky was dense, unbroken grey. Each night there were processions of people with lighted torches while candles burned before the giant likenesses of Evita. There were also thousands of small altars erected in the *barrios*, each with an image of her surrounded by flowers. From the open doors of churches could be heard, according to *La Nación,* 'the murmur of responses, the echoes of continual masses for Evita's soul', and from the loudspeaker by the obelisk the sound of funeral chants.[25] As the days went by, popular grief was stimulated by a number of government measures: schoolchildren were taken by bus, workers were allowed paid time off to stand in line to see Evita, and some of those who were discovered failing to make the proper use of this act of kindness, found themselves without jobs. But for the most part the sense of intense loss was personally experienced and quite genuine. It is probable that more people saw Evita after her death than had entered her office during her lifetime, and for many of them the experience was one which they would never forget – a great death in the great family to which they belonged. Even the harshest critics of Peronism, at home or abroad, would have to agree with the *Life* magazine reporter who wrote that these Argentine sorrows were not the result of coercion by Juan Perón. 'They were genuine and deep and demonstrated that Evita, who had contributed so strongly to the totalitarianism and bankruptcy of her country, had also won its love.'[26]

Evita's body had not been preserved with a view to so sustained an exhibition, and the limitations of Ara's work eventually became apparent. A mist developed inside of the glass plate, obscuring her features, and the coffin lid had to be removed several times so that the glass could be cleaned. The doctor finally bored some holes in the coffin, thus equalizing the temperature inside and clearing the mist. Ara felt that this 'placed in danger the aesthetic effects of conservation . . . [by] dehydrating the most vulnerable parts, like the fingers and the lips.'[27] Ara complained about this development to Perón, and it was Perón's concern rather than any slackening of public interest that led to the next phase of this long period of national mourning. On 9 August, the coffin was sealed, placed on a six-foot-high gun-carriage and dragged to Congress, not by horses, but by thirty-five union members, men and women selected by the CGT and dressed in white shirtsleeves and black trousers. In Congress the coffin was opened again, and that night, after Evita had been given the honours due to a head of state, the crowds were briefly allowed to file past once more. Outside there was another torch procession which ended at 8.25 pm when hundreds of thousands of torches were extinguished simultaneously. Next day, 10 August, the *descamisados,* preceded by allegorical floats from the CGT and the union of petroleum workers, pulled the gun-carriage down the Avenida de Mayo. The sky was grey again, the streetlamps had been covered with crêpe, and the enormous crowd was held back by 17,000 soldiers. Beside the catafalque walked the nurses of the Foundation, cadets, union members, more soldiers, and then Perón, Evita's family, and government officials. A military band played Chopin's funeral march, and the crowd wept in silence. The windows and the balconies were crowded with people throwing flowers. It took more than three hours for this cortège to negotiate the twenty blocks between Congress and the Casa Rosada, and then it turned right into Calle Azopardo, finally coming to a halt before the concrete-and-glass building which Evita had built as headquarters for the CGT. It was here that Dr Ara would complete his work while her last resting-place was being built.[28]

11

The Body and the Myth

The three rooms on the third floor of the building in Calle Azopardo were always heavily shuttered and the lobby beside the lift was guarded by uniformed firemen. A small office furnished with cabinets and tubular steel chairs had been installed next to the laboratory itself, with its extra-large bath, shelving, bottles, tubes and hoses and a large table. All was painted white, clean and artificially lit. The rest of the floor was still used as offices by the unions. Evita's sisters and mother came once a week to pray outside the lift, facing the closed doors, and leaving their flowers with the firemen. Sometimes when the air-conditioning had broken down, chemical odours seeped through the building and there were emergency evacuations, but for the most part the discreet activities of Dr Ara went unnoticed, so accustomed had those who worked for the Confederation of Labour become to his unobtrusive presence.

Ara worked with his assistant, Pepe, or sat in his office, read his anatomy books and made entries in his diary, going to inspect his creation when necessary – perhaps more often than was necessary. His memoirs and diaries are certainly the work of a man obsessed with the technical problems he had chosen to solve, and profoundly satisfied at having accomplished a masterwork.

Incisions had been made in the heels and below the neck, by which the body was drained. It was then placed in a bath of 150 litres of acetate and potassium nitrate, weighted with the coffin lid to keep it submerged. Then it was injected and reinjected with mixtures of formol, thymol and pure alcohol, dipped in bath after bath, month after month, reinjected each time and finally coated with a thin but hard layer of transparent plastic, so that it could be displayed and touched. The entire process took a year and when it was completed, as Ara wrote in his report to the government commission in charge of the monument, the cadaver was 'impregnated with solidifying substances' and able to sustain indefinite contact with the air; it contained all its internal organs, 'whether healthy or not', and these could be examined at any time with the appropriate technology. 'Basic measures with regard to the body,' he wrote, 'are, first to keep the temperature in the room where it is kept below 25 degrees C. Second, keep the glass case containing the body away from the rays of the sun. Third, do not under any circumstances allow the glass to be opened or the cadaver to be touched in our absence. With this in mind, I propose to keep the key to the case, if I am to observe the results of the embalming for the next few months, or permanently, as the case may be. . . .'[1]

This last offer of Ara's had been made necessary by delays in the construction of Evita's tomb. Originally, the monument was to have been surmounted by a gigantic statue of a *descamisado*, shirt unbuttoned, torso bared, a pillared pedestal supporting him leading to the crypt and museum of Peronism, his hollow interior space containing the lifts and stairways to the observation post inside the head. But then the committee had suggested that since the monument was to be dedicated to Evita, the statue should be of her, not of the *descamisado*. The sculptor, Leon Tomassi, had been opposed to this plan on the grounds that her 'graceful form' would translate badly into the colossal dimensions required by the scale of the monument. The committee first accepted this argument and then considered the alternative of leaving the *descamisado* on top of the monument, but commissioning Dr Ara to embalm four more mummies as statuary – a *descamisado* and a member of each of the Armed Forces – to carry Evita's preserved body inside the crypt. This idea was abandoned when Ara told the committee he could not possibly handle so much work with the resources at his disposal. A year after Evita's death the committee was being criticized for having accomplished nothing, and could only announce in its defence the prospective size of the monument, the number of lifts it would contain, and the number of cubic metres of reinforced concrete which would one day be shaped to Evita's memory. Meanwhile her body had to remain with the unions and in Ara's hands.

A funerary chapel of sorts, with shrouded lights and a crucifix, was set up in the ante-room of Ara's suite, and it was to this way-station that Evita's family and a select few of her associates came to see the body and pray. Perón had been given personal access to the suite by means of a private lift from the basement, but he did not use it. He went to see the body only three times. The first time he was apprehensive about what he might find; but when he saw her, he was impressed and moved:

> I was under the impression that she was asleep [he wrote]. I could not take my eyes away from her breast because I hoped at any moment to see her arise and the miracle of life repeat itself. Eva was wearing a

long, white tunic covering her feet. On the tunic at shoulder level, there was the Peronist emblem of gold and precious stones that she had worn in life. Her hands were visible through the cuffs of wide sleeves and they were knit together, holding a crucifix. Her face was as if of wax, clear and transparent, her eyes closed as if she was dreaming. Her hair had been beautifully dressed and she shone with a special radiance.

He wished to touch Evita's face, but he was 'afraid that the heat would reduce her to dust as occurs when air disturbs old graves.' Dr Ara said in a low voice, 'Don't be afraid. She's as whole, *intacta*, as when she was alive.'[2]

Only a month after Evita's death, the newspaper vendors' union put forward her name for canonization, and although this gesture was an isolated one and was never taken seriously by the Vatican, the idea of Evita's holiness remained with many people and was reinforced by the publication of devotional literature subsidized by the government; by the renaming of cities, schools and subway stations; and by the stamping of medallions, the casting of busts and the issuing of ceremonial stamps. The time of the evening news broadcast was changed from 8.30 pm to 8.25 pm, the time when Evita had 'passed into immortality,' and each month there were torch-lit processions on the 22nd of the month, the day of her death. On the first anniversary of her death, *La Prensa* printed a story about one of its readers seeing Evita's face in the face of the moon, and after this there were many more such sightings reported in the newspapers. For the most part, official publications stopped short of claiming sainthood for her, but their restraint was not always convincing. From 1953 Argentine schoolchildren learned to read in primary school from a book which, among many other such lessons, contained this prayer:

> Our little Mother, thou who art in heaven,
> good fairy laughing amongst the angels . . .
> Evita, I promise to be as good as you wish me to be,
> respecting God, loving my country;
> taking care of General Perón; studying
> and being towards everyone the child
> you dreamed I would be; healthy, happy,
> well-educated and pure in heart.[3]

In the illustrations of this primer, as in most images of Evita published by the government, there is only the slightest suggestion of radiance, a haziness at the periphery of the image; but in the calendar for 1953 of the Buenos Aires newspaper vendors, as in other unofficial images, she was depicted in the traditional blue robes of the Virgin, her hands crossed, her sad head to one side and surrounded by a halo.

In the first months after Evita's death, Perón had stood in on her behalf, personally distributing the goods of the Foundation and attending meetings in his new capacity as President of the Peronist Women's Party, but when it became clear that he lacked the time and the patience for these tasks, he was obliged to delegate them to other people, who performed them with conspicuously less success than had Evita.

There was less money for the Foundation, so it could accomplish less: losing Evita it had lost its heart and its impetus. Perón devoted the 17 October following her death to a reading of her will and a broadcast of one of the great speeches she had made the previous year, but there were limits to the political effectiveness of memories. Without Evita, the rhetorical sweep of Peronism, and with it the vivid emotional relationship linking Perón, Evita and the *descamisados,* were greatly diminished.

Perón had mourned Evita conspicuously and seriously, and while it would be an exaggeration to suggest that he was definitively altered by this loss, he could seem on occasions sadly, even grotesquely diminished by it. Without her the process of his isolation was complete, for he had long expelled people of intelligence from his presence. Having once been an excellent fencer and equestrian, he now took to driving cars and motor scooters. There was an occasion when he rode through the streets of Buenos Aires at the head of a large procession of scooters dressed in a windcheater and baseball cap. Although never quite obese, he began to look puffy and soft, losing his physical grace and dignity. He had given the grounds of his Presidential weekend house in Olivos to the Union of Secondary Students, who used it as a playground, and it was said by his enemies that he spent his lunch hours playing there with teenage girls, stuffing his pockets with pesos for them to pull out.

Only three years were to separate Evita's death and the day in September 1955 when Perón would pack a few belongings into a suitcase, board a Paraguayan gunboat and go into exile. His rapid decline was not caused by his wife's death – or not to the degree which has sometimes been assumed. It resulted from much more complex causes which had been in operation while she was still alive.

The serious condition of the economy, exacerbated by two bad harvests, was the main cause. The terms of trade, so favourable in 1946, had now turned against Argentina. The effects of inflation, which had at first touched only the middle classes, were now being felt by the working class, which made its resentment clear through more frequent strikes. And against this background of scarcity and hardship, corruption, which had alwas been present, began to seem more glaring. This had a particularly damaging effect when Evita's brother, Juan Duarte, committed suicide in 1953. There had been public complaint about the shortage of beef, and its high price, and Perón had ordered an investigation. Juan Duarte, who was widely suspected of dealing in beef on the black market, first went to Switzerland, then returned and killed himself only a few hours after Perón had made a violent speech against 'pimps and thieves'. It was rumoured that Duarte had been sent to Switzerland by Perón to collect funds deposited on Eva's behalf, and that he had returned empty-handed because his sister had lost the key or the combination. Perón's attempt to counter this sort of rumour by explaining that Duarte had become a depressive 'as a result of the syphilis he had picked up in a night-club' was hardly more convincing or more savoury. It began to look as though Perón himself was at least partly responsible for the strong odour of corruption given off by those around him; and – even worse – that he might possibly have had Duarte murdered to prevent the emergence of worse scandals.

To economic collapse and corruption were added the methods of Perón's security forces. They had successfully muzzled his enemies, and this had left them with an appetite for more. In the late 1940s Argentina had not been a police state, although the opposition often asserted that it was. By now their forebodings had been fulfilled. Perón no longer felt it necessary to bring charges – even implausible ones – against those he imprisoned, and the *picana,* an electric cattle-prod traditionally used by the police on suspected felons, was now used on union members and academics who were believed to be dissident. Torture had been used in Argentina before Perón, and would be used even more after him. His contribution during the last years of his government was to make it a part of police procedure.

In 1955 Perón embarked on his fatal confrontation with the Catholic Church. It had always supported him, and it was the one institution which had so far escaped Peronization. Now he moved against it. Religious holidays were curtailed, religious instruction in schools was made voluntary, and divorce and prostitution were legalized. Nothing else since 1945 had so united the opposition against Perón. There was a vast demonstration before the cathedral in Buenos Aires, followed by a counter-demonstration of *descamisados* during which the cathedral was stoned and several churches were burned. Perón held two prelates responsible and they were hustled out of the country, martyrs of anti-Peronism. As a result Perón was excommunicated by the Vatican, the first head of state to receive this treatment since 1890.

The battle with the Church led to many defections in the armed forces, and it was from the Navy that the first attacks came. On 16 June 1955 a squadron of naval aircraft taking part in a military display flew over the city and instead of dipping their wings in homage, dropped full loads of bombs which missed the Casa Rosada, their target, and killed several hundred bystanders. A naval unit attacked the palace, but Perón was no longer there. In the fighting around the Casa Rosada a great number of CGT members who had rallied to Perón, were killed.

This attempt against him was followed by a period in which Perón tried for reconciliation with his enemies, for a while permitting the genuine functioning of political parties. The opposition responded by increasing its attacks on the government. The truce was ended on 31 August when Perón made a bloodthirsty speech in Evita's style. In the week beginning 16 September, units of the Navy again rose against him – and were supported, once it was apparent that the revolt was coherent and serious, by many Army units based in Córdoba. Perón could probably have crushed the uprising with the forces still loyal to him, but he chose not to. He was to explain later that he had not wished to plunge his country into civil war, having himself seen the aftermath of civil war in Spain. It is possible that he briefly considered arming the CGT, as Evita had done in 1951, but it was by now apparent that the unions were no longer disposed to 'give their lives' for Perón. The end had come.

On 21 September 1955, the day after Perón left the country, the great square was filled with people, much as it had been so many times during his ascendancy. There were banners, chants, processions. But this crowd representing the 'Liberating Revolution,' as it would be called, was very different from the *descamisados*. It was better-dressed, less rowdy.

Dr Ara had been alerted by a friend the day the bombs came down, and he spent the day at home with his family. But Evita's body was not damaged by the bombs, since the CGT had been spared. Ara attempted to see Perón on one of the days of the uprising, and when he was not successful went instead to the Commission for the Monument, which was still in existence, though the monument itself was no more than a huge hole in a public park. Here he was more successful, giving his assurance that he would continue to attend the body come what might and receiving, only two days before the disintegration of the Peronist machine, the last payment of the $100,000 due to him for his work.[4]

Ara's main preoccupation during these days was with the proper clothing of the body, which for some reason was still dressed only in a sleeveless shift, its bare feet revealed to the world. A dressmaker friend, following Ara's specification, made up a long linen gown modelled on the sculptured robes of medieval statuary, and thus attired, the body was photographed and X-rayed from all angles. Ara prudently sent copies of this documentation to a number of friends outside the country. He was pleased that the Revolution took place without any damage to his charge or disruption of his routine, but surprised that in the days following the Revolution nobody came to the CGT or approached him about the body.

The new President, General Eduardo Lonardi, adopted a cautious attitude towards the remnants of Perón's system, but he had to give way after only five weeks in office to his Vice-President, General Pedro Eugenio Aramburu, who represented those determined on a swift and total purge. A commission under the chairmanship of another violent anti-Peronist, Vice-President Admiral Isaac Rojas, was set up to investigate methods by which the country could be renovated, and one of its first actions was to jail most of the prominent followers of Perón still in the country. The CGT called a general strike in protest, whereupon the government intervened, placing the whole CGT, including its headquarters, under the control of an Army officer.

As a result, first a trickle, then a stream of military men made their way to the 'liberated' third floor of the CGT, and Dr Ara's function extended to take in the role of tour guide. It appears that in spite of his explanations, many officers refused to believe what they saw.

'I heard that only the head was saved. . . .' 'It is said that when it was on display it became black and had to be burnt and replaced by a statue. . . .' 'No one believes that what you have in your possession is the real thing. . . .'

According to one of these visitors, Captain Francisco Manrique: 'It was the size of a twelve-year-old girl. Its skin was wax-like and artificial, its mouth had been rouged, and when you tapped it, it rang hollow, like a store-window mannequin. The embalmer, Ara, hovered over it as if it was something he loved.'[5]

The attitude of the new government towards the body of Evita would be incomprehensible outside the specific context of frustration, fury and hatred that possessed these men of 1955. A few of the victors, those who had taken part in the 1951 coup, had spent four years in camps in Patagonia. Their hatred of Perón was understandable, and it was they who set the tone for their colleagues. These revolutionary officers wished to believe that Peronism had been an aberration, a huckster's trick perpetrated on a gullible people by unscrupulous persons, and although a rational consideration of what had occurred would not have supported this view, this was no time for rationality. As a final means of 'destroying the myth', a phrase they often used in conversations with Dr Ara, they would have liked to demonstrate publicly that Evita's body was a fake; and they clung to this illusion despite the large amount of documentary evidence produced by Ara. Such evidence, they felt, could be forged. It required a second X-ray session and another series of medical examinations, including the excision of a finger from the body, to convince them that the body was authentic, whereupon it became a deeply disturbing problem for them, much harder to solve than reason would suggest.

'We were not really interested in the cadaver because we had more important things to think about,' said Admiral Isaac Rojas. 'We had no idea how to proceed, but we were resolved on two guiding principles: first, that not the slightest profanation should occur and second, that the body should immediately be taken outside politics.'[6] 'Taken outside politics' were the key words, since what they feared was the body as a symbol, as a powerful relic of Perón's regime. In the following months they would make it an offence punishable by prison to possess photographs of Perón or Evita or use the expression 'Peronism' or 'Peronist'; they would disband the Peronist Party, make it illegal for those who had belonged to it to hold elective office or public employment, and make it an offence to display the Party's emblem, 'because it reminds us of an epoch of pain and ridicule for the population of this country'. The last thing they wanted was a tomb round which a cult would almost certainly develop; a tomb which would attract defilement by those hostile to Evita's memory and pilgrimages by those who loved her.

The new Junta met on three separate occasions to discuss what should be done.[7] After the first meeting Dr Ara was asked if there were any circumstances in which the body might decompose – if, for example, the breakdown of the air-conditioning equipment would produce this effect. When he answered that it would not, and let it be known that he was reluctant to assist the officers on this question, enquiries were made on an informal basis as to whether there were any circumstances in which the Catholic Church might countenance cremation. But the Church returned the answer that no exception could be made, and although there were those within the Junta who thought this ruling should be disregarded, the opinion of President Aramburu, a devout Catholic, prevailed, and the possibility of destroying the body was explored no further.

On the President's instructions, the Junta passed a secret decree allocating to the government a numbered but not named plot in the Chacarita, the largest cemetery in Buenos Aires, and it was decided that Evita's body should be secretly buried there for the time being. The President stipulated that flowers must be placed on the grave and masses must be said regularly once a month.

The job was given to Carlos Eugenio Moori Koenig, the plump and erudite head of military intelligence. On 24 November 1955, he summoned Dr Ara and twenty officers dressed in civilian clothes to come at midnight to the third floor of the CGT building. The elaborate coffin in which the body had first been displayed to the public had been recovered from the funeral home in which it had been stored and was brought up to the third floor by office cleaners. When they came into the ante-chamber with the velvet curtains and the image of the Virgin, Moori Koenig told them they should stay to watch the event – they were workers who had loved Evita, fit witnesses to his good faith – and they, with the military men, formed a large circle. The flags were removed, the body was uncovered. 'Her form was stylized, seeming longer than it actually was because of the linen folds, as if of alabaster, that entirely covered it; her hands, the fingers crossed as if knitted together by the beads and string of the papal rosary, were reminiscent of those prostrate stone images on old European tombs,' Ara recorded.[8] Two of the cleaners, 'pale and sweating with emotion and terror', carried the body from its platform to the coffin, put the ribbons from the surrounding wreaths inside the coffin and fitted the lid. Dr Ara, meticulous as usual, had established beforehand what the procedure would be and knew that the lid was now supposed to be welded down. Was this about to happen, he asked; but Moori Koenig told him that either through oversight or for some other reason, the welders had not turned up. At that point the ceremony ended abruptly. The welders did not come the next day, nor the day after. Indeed, they never came; and Dr Ara found himself barred from the building, his calls to Moori Koenig unanswered. Some days later, he received a telephone call in the middle of the night and a voice said: 'Professor, they have taken her away.'

The events that followed this midnight ceremony were recalled by Moori Koenig, but not until he was a sick man and therefore a not entirely reliable witness. It seems that the body, still in its unsealed coffin, was first placed in a military truck, which was parked for the night in the courtyard of the 1st Regiment of Marines. Next morning a bunch of flowers and a candle were found beside the truck. The coffin was transferred to an unmarked civilian vehicle and moved to another location in the centre of the city. When the flowers and the candle appeared there, too, and at several other locations, Koenig finally decided not to bury the coffin at all, and not to tell anyone about his decision. The body was placed in a long wooden box that had recently contained radio transmitting equipment used in the revolt against Perón (it was labelled 'the Voice of Córdoba') and was stored in the attic above Moori Koenig's office, on the fourth floor of the building where the headquarters of the Argentine military intelligence was located. It was still there a year later when Moori Koenig showed it to a friend, who told Captain Francisco Manrique, now an aide of the President, what he had seen. Moori Koenig was judged to be suffering from a nervous breakdown and was relieved of his job. Once again the 'problem of the cadaver' claimed the government's attention.

Those mysterious flowers and candles to which Moori Koenig bore witness led the Junta to the conclusion that it would not be safe to keep the body in Argentina. The President was still anxious to observe all the proprieties, so the Church was consulted. At some point early in 1957, Father Rotger, an Argentine priest, appeared at the Casa Rosada with a bearded Italian colleague, and it was once again arranged that the body should be interred in the utmost secrecy. This time only four or five people apart from the President were to know about it, and no one in the government, not even the President, would know exactly where the body lay. There would thus be no possibility of the body's being 'brought into politics' by anyone. The government undertook to cast further mystery on the ultimate destination of the body by filling a number of coffins with ballast and sending them off to Argentine embassies in Germany, Italy and Belgium; anyone excessively curious about the body would assume that one of these coffins contained it, though none in fact did.

The bearded Italian priest then took formal possession of the real coffin, and six weeks later came back to the Casa Rosada with an envelope, which by prior arrangement contained details relating to the body's actual whereabouts. President Aramburu gave it to his lawyer with instructions that it was to be kept unopened until four weeks after his own death, when it must be delivered to whomever was then President of Argentina. That person might then open it or not, as he thought fit. To those enquiring about the coffin's whereabouts – doña Juana for instance – Aramburu could now say in good faith that he personally knew nothing, but that the body was certainly in 'Christian hands' and that at some later date, when passions were cooled, it would be returned for family burial.

In the first days of the Revolution, the neo-classical statues on top of the Foundation's headquarters had been toppled and smashed, and its principal warehouse vandalized. In Foundation homes and resorts Evita's name was cut out of linen sheets, which were then patched, and in hospitals it was scraped off the beds. It is said, and it may be true, that the government would not use the Foundation's polio vaccine because her initials were stamped on the vials. A National Investigating Committee, chaired by an admiral, had held hearings on the Foundation, summoning many witnesses, and although it had failed to uncover any malpractices, the government passed a decree on 4 July 1956, transferring all the Foundation's assets to the National Treasury. It was asserted in justification that the Foundation had been used 'for political corruption and acts of favouritism that by themselves constitute the denial of any healthy concept of social justice and are typical of totalitarian regimes'.

Equally rough treatment was given to Evita's jewels, which had been exhibited, itemized and labelled with their probable cost in an exhibition at the Presidential Palace entitled 'The Fabulous Treasures of the Peronist Dictatorship', and were then offered for sale in November 1956, at the premises of the Argentine Automobile Club, the proceeds to pass through a Commission of National Recuperation into the public treasury. 'The sale will no doubt have international repercussions,' the Commission said. 'In the last few years it can only have been exceeded in importance by the auction of King Farouk's possessions.' The items to be auctioned, which included some cases of Perón's wine, had been valued at 100 million pesos ($7 million), but as early as the first night, when only four of Evita's pieces met their reserve prices, it was apparent that the government had been over-generous in its estimates. Her jewels were bought in bulk by jewellers, and finally found their way into the 'hands of the Oligarchy' only after they had been dismantled and reconstituted.

The Argentine press, inhibited or muzzled throughout the years of Perón had celebrated its freedom with many revelations of 'the secret life of the former dictator', mostly gossip which had animated foreign commentaries on the Peróns. This material later found its way into a series of books purporting to tell the truth about Perón and Evita. What these writings did was to take the lies of the first 'official' myth and invert each component, substituting for a totally unreal set of virtues an equally unreal set of vices: bad for good, black for white. Evita's transformation was accomplished even more thoroughly and viciously that that of Perón. He himself had already started on the work of destroying his original image, but she had died young and beautiful, before failing, her legend intact, and it was because she was recognized to be still potent, still dangerous, that this 'desanctification' was taken so seriously.

Sometimes the attacks on Evita would have an almost religious character and would depict her as a sort of fiend, evil beyond rational explanation; but more usually their frame of reference was secular and drawn from the conventions of yellow journalism, pulp fiction or bad movies. She was dubbed 'the Woman with the Whip' (she had in fact been called by a Radical politician 'a woman who would stand by and see someone to whom she had made love, whipped to death'[9]) – and became an utterly flat character of monomaniacal intensity. According to all of these mid-1950s accounts, Evita had been taught to hate the world by her poverty and to hate men by her illegitimacy. Everything she had achieved – her movie career, her entry into politics, the Foundation – was the result of a single-minded quest for revenge on the world, while she revenged herself on men by seducing them in order to humiliate them. Perón she had tolerated because he was soft enough to pander to her drive for power, but she had not loved him because she could not have done so; she was strong, he was weak; 'he is the woman and she is the man' – and with such an inversion there could have been no real love, only its surrogates: 'the excessive love of luxury' (here the jewels were cited), the love of flattery (here Evita's 'failure' as an actress was related to the huge dramatic spectacle which she had in revenge devised and imposed on the country). To the writer Ezequiel Martínez Estrada, she was 'a sublimation of vileness, abjectness, degradation.... Her resentment towards the human race, a quality one might expect in a third-rate actress, was only satisfied when she displayed herself to the Oligarchy. . . . Before that her public had been the lower classes and *descamisados*.'[10]

Even one of the least unsympathetic of these writers, Luis Franco, who could concede Evita's real connection with the 'less privileged classes', described her as 'a sort of Lady Bountiful before whom ministers, generals, doctors, financiers, bishops, intellectuals, even her husband made obeisance like castrated dogs. . . .'[11] But Franco was charitable by the standards of most of these polemicists, who either denied Evita any real achievements, or explained them by recourse to another theory, first expressed by the socialist writer, Américo Ghioldi, that 'A robot might have accomplished these things.'[12] A creature of malign power, or a robot with no existency apart from 'a headquarters, a certain amount of hired brain-power, a team of administrators, journalists, photographers, hairdressers and fashion designers' supplied by the government': there were occasions when these two contradictory images were presented within the same piece.

Jorge Luis Borges has written in one of his short pieces that in July 1952 an Indian 'with the inexpressive face of a mask or a dullard' arrived in a small town of the Chaco, a province of northern Argentina:

With the help of some local women he set up a board on the two wooden boxes and on top a cardboard box with a blonde doll in it. In addition they lit four candles in tall candlesticks and put flowers around. People were not long in coming. Hopeless old women, gaping children, peasants whose cork helmets were respectfully removed, filed past the box and repeated, 'Deepest sympathy, General.' He [the Indian], very sorrowful, received them at the head of the box, his hands crossed over his stomach in the attitude of a pregnant woman. He held out his right hand to shake the hands they extended to him and replied with dignity and resignation: 'It was fate. Everything humanly possible was done.' A tin money-box received the two-peso fee and many came more than once.

What kind of man, I ask myself, conceived and executed that funeral farce? A fanatic, a pitiful wretch, a victim of hallucinations, or an impostor and a cynic? Did he believe he was Perón as he played his suffering role as the macabre widower? The story is incredible, but it happened and perhaps not once, but many times, with different actors, in different locales. It contains the perfect cipher of an unreal epoch; it is like the reflection of a dream or that drama within-the-drama we see in *Hamlet*. The mourner was not Perón and the blonde doll was not the woman Eva Duarte, but neither was Perón Perón, nor was Eva Eva. They were, rather, unknown individuals – or anonymous ones whose secret names and faces we do not know – who acted out, for the credulous love of the lower middle classes, a crass mythology.[13]

Borges's mother had been briefly imprisoned after an anti-Peronist demonstration in Calle Florida, and Borges, who worked as a librarian, was 'promoted' out of the library to the inspectorship of poultry and rabbits in the public markets. Like many members of his class, Borges hated Perón, whom he usually called 'the fugitive' or 'the dictator'. In 1979, asked by Paul Theroux about Evita, he would still say she was a whore. 'We had a sense that the whole thing should have been forgotten,' he said in 1972.[14] But it was not forgotten so easily, no matter how much Perón and Evita were ridiculed or how seriously the government took its process of de-Peronization, and indeed, after only a few years of government-imposed oblivion, the 'crass mythology' returned to enjoy a surprising revival.

These attempts to purge Argentina of Peronism gave rise to what Peronists have called 'the Resistance': a period of violent strikes and acts of sabotage. In June 1956, civilian and military Peronists struck throughout the country at radio stations and police headquarters. The government responded with the most severe repressive measures. A thousand Peronists were arrested, and twenty-seven of the coup's civilian and military leaders, including General Juan José Valle, were condemned to death after the most cursory 'administrative' examinations and executed by firing squad in the National Penitentiary. It now became an indication of loyalty for Peronists to risk imprisonment by displaying photographs of Perón and Evita in their homes. Each assault by the police or the Army, each destruction of a bust in a local union, or burning of photographs, was added to the many grievances that could be held against the *gorillas,* as the Peronists dubbed the militant anti-Peronists. Since Evita had no tomb, Perón's family mausoleum was chosen as her memorial, and each birthday, each anniversary of her death, each weekend even, there were wreaths and flowers piled around it. Sometimes these demonstrations were permitted, but at other times there were police at the cemetery, and the men and women carrying flowers were dispersed with tear gas and truncheons.

'There is an altar to Evita in every Peronist home, and no saint of the Catholic Church has received so much devotion in Argentina,' Perón observed from his exile's viewpoint. A real and persistent 'cult' of Evita did indeed begin with the Resistance. Analogies have often been made between this and the sort of reverence paid to – for example – Ceferino Namuncura, the son of an Indian chief revered in Chompay in the province of Rio Negro. Such 'popular canonizations' are not uncommon in Argentina. But an anthropological study of Evita's 'cult' suggests that these analogies are false: that they are attempts to make 'a myth of a myth' which reflect what people wished to believe – or feared might happen – rather than the truth.[15]

It is, after all, quite a common custom, and a largely secular one, to keep photographs of a dead relative in the house. Prayers may be said for or to the dead person as a way of remembering, but no worship or attribution of sanctity is involved. And this appears to have been what happened with regard to Evita. All people did was remember her. Most of what they remembered about her was that she had been good, and had helped them, and if they called her a saint it was in a familiar and colloquial way; not usually – although there were exceptions – because they believed she had performed miracles or given other evidence of supernatural holiness. Argentines have always been faithful to their dead heroes. For many years they honoured the tango singer Carlos Gardel, who died in a plane crash, by placing flowers on his tomb and using his films and records to celebrate the month of his death. It is only in this imprecise sense that reference can be made to a 'cult' of Evita.

During the 1960s the government relaxed its strictness towards the press, whereupon Evita joined Gardel as a subject for annual pictorial commemoration. There would be the brief life (bowdlerized and sketchy), the spectacular death (photographs of the open coffin were often used), and finally the great mystery, 'the scandal of the cadaver's pilgrimage'. It was here, in the writings of relatively sophisticated journalists who often had polemical motives, that the language of political indignation met and joined with the hyperbole of popular religion.

Journalists were forced to theorize about the body's fate, since no government since that of President Aramburu had chosen to disturb his effective disposal of the matter. It was said that this most emotive of Peronist relics had been cremated (despite government denials), buried in the Perón or Duarte crypts (despite denials from Perón and doña Juana), or secretly lodged in a remote cemetery of the interior, of which there were, of course, a great many. Or perhaps it had been kept on Martín García, the island fortress to which Perón had been taken in 1945? Journalists scoured the windswept site, challenging the naval authorities to explain the existence of a tomb inscribed with the legend 'unknown drowned man', or why someone had seen a container the size and shape of a coffin thrown from the stern of a naval launch. After it had been suggested that the body had been dropped out of an aircraft into the Rio de la Plata, demands for a dredging of a large section of the river were made.

For some time the only person willing to give an account of his role in the operation was Moori Koenig. Numerous attempts had been made on his life, and he was fearful of other attacks. It was he who continued to elaborate on the circumstances of the body's disappearance, suggesting that mysterious disasters struck all those concerned with it. A captain who had (for undisclosed reasons) been keeping the body in his apartment had fired at what he supposed to be a body-robber and killed his pregnant wife. Sometimes Moori Koenig would tease journalists with the suggestion that he had buried Evita upright, 'like a gaucho'. The writer Rodolfo Walsh made a short story out of the Colonel's ramblings and the confused self-criticisms of a left-wing journalist visiting him. Was the journalist really interested in the body or was he doing this for money? Did Evita's body matter as history or was its fate a mere footnote to larger things? 'She means nothing to me,' Walsh's journalist rants, 'but I will get behind the mystery of her death. . . . If I find her I'll have a sense of anger, fear and frustrated love, a sense of vengeance accomplished and I will not feel alone.' The journalist does not find the body, however. 'That woman,' the colonel tells him in a moment of sobriety as he leaves, 'that woman is mine.'[16]

It was not long before the 'Liberating Revolution' which drove Perón out gave his adherents reason to call themselves Peronists once more. What followed Perón made the failures of his last few years seem unimportant. The years of his government became a golden age in the eyes of Peronists, and having survived the Resistance, they remained a cohesive voting force at the disposal of their exiled leader. At his orders, they would spoil their votes or vote for candidates he named. They spoiled their votes in the 1958 elections, voted in 1962 and spoiled them again in 1964. The indestructibility of the Peronist vote presented the armed forces with a problem to which the only solution was not congenial. The military since 1955 had committed itself formally to the re-establishment of democracy: free elections, a functioning assembly, civilian governments. But they did not believe the followers of Perón to be democrats, because Peronism was synonymous with totalitarianism. So the Army found itself backing up governments elected without Peronist support and thus maintaining the country in a condition far short of democracy. Attempts by civilian governments instituted by the Army to reinstate Peronism were carefully watched and ultimately forestalled, if necessary by coup d'état, with the result that the armed forces, ostensibly with precautionary motives, ended by becoming a permanent feature in Argentine political life.

During these years Argentines spoke of the decadence of their country. In fact there was growth in spite of all that worked against it, and for each year of crisis there was one of prosperity, so that the greatest Argentine myth, that of limitless prosperity, was never entirely destroyed. But Argentines had always taken it for granted they would be prosperous and they wanted something more than wealth. At the very least they wanted coherent political institutions and if they were more demanding, they wanted the idea of a national future which Perón had, however briefly, realized in his first Presidency.

Because of the 'problem of Peronism' such civilian governments as the military permitted were obliged to tread carefully. They were never more than caretakers awaiting changed circumstances. But how could circumstances change? If a President was bold, as Dr Arturo Frondizi was in 1962, he was removed; if he was not bold, like Frondizi's successor, Dr Arturo Illia, in 1964, he was also removed. The military, too, wanted a national future, but nipped it in the bud by their prohibitions. By the mid-sixties, the military had become so disillusioned with the civilian governments of their own making that a serious attempt was made to circumvent party government in favour of a military technocracy which would modernize the country first and hand it back to the politicians only after that task had been accomplished.

This time the coup was prepared with the aid of public opinion soundings, and a large segment of the Argentine establishment – businessmen, commentators – declared themselves *golpistas*. It was bloodless and efficient and by-and-large welcome, except by that great proportion of the electorate that cared only about Perón's return. For a while it was successful and then it became like other military governments. The problem was less corruption (though there was some of that) than the impossibility of running this vigorous and complex country by mere decree. Disenfranchised, the Argentines were afflicted with a genuine sense of lacking something, no matter how loudly the military leaders spoke of national purpose. And because they were not listened to, the leaders began to shout even louder.

In this *callejón* – this dead-end – Peronism was rediscovered by the intellectuals of Argentina. What had been abhorred in the mid-1950s began in the 1960s to look like the only way out. It was here in the Argentine past, rather than in the derivative technocracy of the military, that the answer lay. Perón had twice been elected with overwhelming popular support; soldier though he was, his regime seemed closer to democracy than that of his successors; and great though his errors had been, they had the virtue of ambition. Beside the old Peronist myth of the golden age there arose a new one of a socialist, libertarian Peronism. Its central figure, in Franco's Madrid, did nothing to discourage it. At one time it seemed possible that he might move to Castro's Cuba.

Evita was an important figure in this 'second Peronism', an Evita who now took on an almost revolutionary aura. Emphasis was put on her last, violent speeches, and there were those who concluded that these speeches made her, rather than Perón, 'the true heart of Peronism'. There was much discussion of how she would have developed – in 1967 the essayist David Viñas found himself in the position of asserting that Evita, had she lived, might well have left Perón rather than endorse his reactionary policies.[17] Another essayist, Juan José Sebreli, set out to attack 'fixed and immovable myths' and finally resolved the contradictions in Evita by resorting to the language of existentialism. She was 'a solitary individualist in search of collectivity', which she found in her feminist work, her 'direct action' for the poor and her people's militia. Thus there emerged an Evita 'symbolically expressing the desire for justice and equality.'[18]

The phase of political life that had begun in 1955 with the fall of Perón, ended in 1969 with the *cordobazo*. This was an explosion of popular rage in Córdoba, the second city of Argentina, capital of the interior and an industrial centre. For a few days there were street battles between soldiers and a combination of students, unionized workers and even the city's middle class. The *cordobazo* upset the ailing military government and led to a switch of personnel, but it also led to the feeling in the Army that the experiment in long-term military rule had been a failure and that the country should once again be handed back to civilians. And it gave those most frustrated by the political impasse a sense of where the breakthrough might be made. After the success of the *cordobazo*, a great number of what the Peronists were to call 'special formations' came into existence. These were guerilla groups such as the Montoneros, the FAL and the FAP.

The ideological origins of these groups varied enormously, some of their members from the Left, some coming from the Catholic

Right, but they were all for the moment allied with the Peronists because they regarded Peronism as a 'Movement of National Liberation', and most of them were prepared to have recourse to political violence, which they regarded as legitimate in what they saw as circumstances of extreme repression. Banks and supermarkets were robbed, hostages taken. At one point there were over 40,000 guerillas in Argentina, children of the middle and upper-middle class, armed and well-organized, an army against the Army.

Some of the guerillas regarded Evita much as they did Peronism, as an existing element which had to be used in the absence of anything else. For others there were aspects of the Evita myth that became prescriptive. An 'Evita commando' was formed, though it never accomplished much. Another guerilla group robbed supermarkets and distributed what they had stolen in the *villas miserías,* along the lines of what they presumed to have been the Foundation's policies. Many of the guerillas believed that Evita was what they and the people had in common, and they saw at this stage no serious contradiction between the people's 'saint' and their own revolutionary icon. They were most interested in the romantic extremism of Evita's last year, her rhetoric of sacrifice and blood. The guerillas had ideas of wrongs to be righted, of the sacredness of revenge, and they romanticized their Revolution. Evita had done the same, of course, but her Revolution was not the same as theirs.

On 29 May 1970, two men in military uniform came to the front door of General Pedro Aramburu's apartment. The former President was in retirement, but he retained an interest in politics. It was said at this stage, that he, like much of the country, had 'second thoughts' about Peronism and that he was contemplating the formation of a new political grouping in which the Peronists would be included. The two men said they admired him and since the General no longer had his own security guard, offered to stand in as unofficial guards when they were off-duty. Once inside the apartment, however, they forced Aramburu to walk with them to a waiting car. After driving to a suburb of Buenos Aires, they tied up the General, placed him in the back of a van with blacked-out windows and drove eight hours out of the city by devious routes to a remote ranch. A first communiqué of the group, which called itself the Montoneros after the gaucho fighters of the nineteenth-century wars, announced that Aramburu had been kidnapped and would be tried 'by revolutionary tribunal'.[19]

Interrogation began the next day. The General was willing to answer questions about the killing of Juan José Valle and twenty-seven Peronists in 1956, for which he admitted some responsibility and which, according to the guerillas, he justified by recourse to the argument that 'such things were necessary in revolutions'. But when the guerillas asked Aramburu about Evita's body, he 'became paralysed', nodded at the tape recorder, and when the machine was switched off, told his interrogators that, 'for reasons of honour', he could say nothing. 'We insisted on knowing what happened to the body,' the guerillas' account of their 'investigation' continues. 'He said he couldn't remember. He tried to bargain with us, he undertook to recover the cadaver when the time was right, on his word of honour. We still insisted. He said "I'll have to think," and we said, "Good; you think." ' Next day Aramburu told the guerillas that the body was buried in Rome (which was false), that it was buried under a false name (which was true), and that it had been kept under the Vatican's auspices (which was at best half-true). It is possible, as has been said by Aramburu's colleagues, that the General in reality told the Montoneros nothing and that this 'confession' is a concoction, yet Aramburu, because of his elaborate precautions, knew little more than the guerillas claim he told them. This was really the only story he could have told to save himself, for the story of the envelope to be opened after his death would have sounded too improbable for them to believe.

The guerillas debated Aramburu's case, and the next day they told the General he had been sentenced to death. Aramburu said 'they were all Argentines' and they must think before spilling blood, but he saw that they meant what they said. He asked for a priest, asked to shave and when he was told he could have neither, walked to the cellar and told the guerillas to 'get on with it'. He was shot by the guerilla leader and next day a second communiqué was sent to the newspapers to the effect that Aramburu's body would not be returned to his family until 'the day the remains of our dear comrade Evita are returned to the people'.

Most Argentines were appalled by the kidnapping of a former President in broad daylight from one of the best suburbs of Buenos Aires. The Montoneros had only just been formed, and their operations to date had included nothing remotely so spectacular. There had been strong feelings about the unknown fate of Evita's body, but the inclusion of this demand in the communiqué cast doubt on the seriousness of the document.[20] Admiral Rojas, by now also in retirement, was one of those who did not believe Aramburu had been killed, and though the guerillas had never made this a condition of the former President's release, he decided to offer Evita's body as ransom for Aramburu. But neither he nor his colleagues knew about the letter left by Aramburu with his lawyer. Only after the police discovered the body of Aramburu was the letter delivered by the lawyer to General Alejandro Augustín Lanusse, the President. Then 'Operation Cadaver', planned in 1956, was at last able to come to its close.

The President – who had spent the years 1951–55 in a Patagonian gaol at Perón's behest – had determined to end the 'state of abnormality' begun in 1955 by withdrawing the Army from political life and allowing Peronists to stand for election. He saw 'the question of the cadaver' as one of the many issues hindering the implementation of this policy.[21] Having opened the envelope and learnt the name of a priest and of a cemetery in Milan – the only information it contained – he sent Colonel Héctor Cabanillas of Army Intelligence to Italy, accompanied by Father Rotger, the Argentine priest who had first made contact with the Italian government on the government's behalf.[22]

The two men found that both the priest named in the document and the priest who had originally written down the name had died. They therefore searched the cemetery's records for women's bodies that had arrived for burial in 1956. Of these, the most likely one was registered as the body of Maria Maggi de Magistris, a middle-aged widow who had apparently been born in Italy and had emigrated to Argentina where she had died. Her body had been returned to Italy for burial five years after the registration of her death.

Encouraged by the Argentine government, Colonel Cabanillas grew a moustache and obtained a set of false papers enabling him to pass as Carlos Maggi, brother of the deceased widow. In Milan he secured a permit to exhume his sister's body and to transport it to Spain; the job to be done by a Milanese funeral home specializing in 'long-distance funerary transportation'.

On Wednesday, 2 September 1971, a grave digger, an official from the Sanitation Department of the city of Milan, Father Rotger, the man who was supposed to be Maria Maggi's brother, and another young man gathered around the marble slab of plot 86, garden 41. The lamp had never been lit, the vase containing plastic flowers was cracked and dusty – evidently the nuns who had been instructed to tend the grave had been lax in their duties. The coffin was removed from the earth, and its zinc inner container removed from the crumbling wood and placed in a fresh coffin. That afternoon, after the forms had been signed, a hearse left the cemetery bearing the brother and the coffin, driving first through the Italian–French border and then through the French–Spanish border, where, according to the hearse's driver, 'a number of men who knew the man with the moustache' greeted him and escorted the hearse on the road to Madrid, driving before and behind it. Thirty kilometres from Madrid, the convoy turned off the road into the driveway of a large house where the Italian driver of the hearse was told to unload the coffin and place it in a plain van. When he protested he was told his job was done.

Dr Ara, now retired and living in Madrid, received a summons on the morning of Saturday, 4 September to go to Perón's Quinta 17 de Octubre, in the suburb of Puerto de Hierro. Perón, still well-preserved, his new wife Isabel who worked as his secretary, and his 'confidant' José Lopez Rega, shook hands with him and escorted him to a glass-enclosed patio behind the house at the far end of which was a half-opened coffin. This was certainly not the ornate coffin he had last seen, but it contained 'what it was supposed to', even the sweet smell Perón had noticed when the coffin was first closed so many years ago. According to Ara, 'The hair was dirty and wet, but still smooth. The stainless steel hairpins were rusty and broke in our hands. The General's wife began to undo the plaits of hair and remove from them the accumulated rust and earth.'[23] After further, full inspection, Ara was pleased to find only minor damage. The nose was flattened, the forehead scarred and there was a deep line across the throat, but this was 'merely a crack in the plastic coating which had occurred when the head was pushed against the coffin lid'. Otherwise the cadaver was exactly as he had last seen it the night of 24 November 1954, almost seventeen years previously.

After 1971, when Peronism was once again officially sanctioned, the cult of Evita came above ground. There were records of her speeches, comic-strip versions of her life and, of course, photographs and posters. 'Her pictures are everywhere,' V. S. Naipaul wrote of Buenos Aires in 1972, 'touched up, seldom sharp and often they seem like religious pictures made for the very poor: a young woman of great beauty, with blond hair, a very white skin and the very red lips of the 1940s.'[24] (One poster, which was used in an election campaign of 1973 had the caption, 'Once there was a girl who was all love.') The different components of the Peronist coalition preserved their separate visions of Evita even in their iconographic treatment of her. For the new Peronist movement she was the *señora,* a regal figure with a jewelled orchid in her buttonhole; for the CGT, she was a raucous *compañera,* and for the guerillas, who did not bother with posters, she was usually a large ¡*Evita Viva!* scribbled on a wall. This was what the crowds

chanted at rallies, or else, *'Se siente, se siente, Evita esta presenta'*
(We can feel it, Evita is here); or even, if they were young and
thought of themselves as sympathizers of the guerillas, *'Si Evita
viviera, seria Montonera'* (If Evita were alive she would be a
Montonera).

Between 1970 and 1972, while President Lanusse attempted to
find a formula whereby the military could safely and decorously
retire to barracks and hand over the country to civilian politicians,
there was a steady increase in terrorist operations, Trotskyist and
Peronist. The government responded to the robbing of banks, the
killing of policemen and soldiers and the kidnapping of foreign
executives, with its own, preventive terror. Suspects were tortured
or 'disappeared', guerillas held in gaol were massacred by their
captors in retaliation for the murder of soldiers. It was apparent
that the use of state force alone could not resolve anything, for all
the State could do was hold itself together; and it was in this sad
and frightening situation that Argentina turned again to Perón. He
had contacts with some of these guerillas and he had never
disavowed them; if the armed forces could not win their war
against them, perhaps he, as he had promised, would succeed in
building a new coalition of all Argentines. The alternative to
Perón seemed to be chaos. In the elections of 1972, Héctor
Cámpora, standing on Perón's behalf at the head of the Justicialist
Front of Liberation, received the votes of forty-nine per cent of
the electorate, including a far higher proportion of the country's
middle classes than had ever voted for Perón. Four months later,
the armed forces capitulated, even restoring Perón's rank, of
which they had deprived him in 1956, and allowing Cámpora to
resign from his post so that the country could 'restore to Perón the
mandate of which he was so unjustly deprived'.

Plans were made for the reopening of the Foundation, tributes
were read in Congress, and Evita's old office in the Department of
Labour was refurbished. For the process of restoration to be
complete all that remained to be accomplished was the return of
her body. But when Perón came back to Argentina in November
1973, accompanied by his third wife and his dogs, he did not bring
Evita's body with him; nor, although he attended such events as
the Mass held in 1973 on the anniversary of her death, did he show
any signs of fulfilling his promise to do so. It was Isabel Perón who
showed most concern for Evita's memory, declaring in interviews
that she hoped to 'follow in Evita's footsteps' and sometimes
leading the chants for Evita by standing at a window holding up a
photograph of her predecessor. Isabel lacked many of Evita's
qualities, but at this time of great nostalgia people were eager to

overlook deficiencies. At the Party convention of 1973, held in the theatre where Evita had announced the foundation of the Women's Party, she was given what had been denied to Evita. She, a frightened, nervous woman of forty-two who could manage no more than a few consecutive sentences in public, was to run for the Vice-Presidency on a Perón-Perón ticket. Perón was elected with the largest majority he ever received. When he died in office on 1 July 1974, Isabel succeeded him and there began, as the Army had feared in 1951, a period of great sadness, disarray and terror.

It was the Montoneros who finally reclaimed Evita's body for Argentina. They did it by re-kidnapping Aramburu, taking his cadaver from his family's vault. On 17 November 1974 a chartered aircraft brought Evita from Madrid to Buenos Aires. There were men in civilian clothes armed with submachine guns at the airport, and few people in the streets.

The government of Isabel Perón began work on a pantheon which was to be a hundred and ten feet high and would contain the bodies of eminent Argentines. Here Evita's open coffin and Perón's closed one (he had left instructions that he was not to be embalmed) would rest. This 'Altar of the Fatherland' was to stand opposite the site of the house where Perón and Evita used to live, which had been destroyed after 1955, and would carry the inscription: 'Linked in glory, we watch over the destiny of our Fatherland. Let no man use our memories to divide Argentina.' There were, however, delays, during which the bodies of Evita and Perón were kept in the Presidential Palace and shown to the faithful; and once again a grandiose memorial had been taken little further than the planning stage before the government which commissioned it was overthrown by a military coup. The new President, General Jorge Rafael Videla, was unwilling to occupy his Palace while Perón and Evita remained there, so on 22 October 1976, her body was at last handed over to her family.

The Recoleta Cemetery, near Palermo Park, is where illustrious Argentines are buried. It was conceived to stand on the edge of the city which now surrounds it, and it houses its dead in what is almost a miniature city. There are banks, pyramids, war memorials, Doric temples, bourgeois villas, statues and innumerable plaques with elaborate inscriptions. Soldiers, tobacco tycoons, aviators, great landowners, poets are all commemorated. In contrast to the modern city surrounding it, this cemetery makes a strong statement of social hierarchy. As in other Catholic countries, the living often visit the dead, but here it seems like a social call or an inspection of property, locks and paintwork.

A small tomb to the west of the main avenue bears a florid inscription paying homage to Major Alfredo J. L. Arrieta, a senator from the municipality of Junín, who died in 1951. A second plaque commemorates Juan Duarte, also from the municipality of Junín. Nothing indicates the presence of Evita's mother, who died in 1971, and nothing but scrawled and half-erased messages and a long, also half-erased, list of names, indicates that Evita, too, lies here.

It is an outwardly unimpressive tomb, but it is more than it appears to be. There is a trapdoor in its marble floor leading to a compartment which houses two coffins; and under that compartment there is another, to which a second trapdoor gives access. Evita's coffin is in this lower compartment. The installation was paid for by the government, and Evita's sister was given the only key to it. It is said to be proof against even the most ingenious grave-robbers and capable of withstanding any bomb attack, even a nuclear one. It reflects a fear: a fear that the body will disappear from the tomb and that the woman, or rather the myth of the woman, will reappear.

Epilogue

'I will come again, and I will be millions,' Evita had said in one of her apocalyptic last speeches just before her death; but even she could not have foreseen her sudden transformation, from Latin American politician and religiose national cult figure to late twentieth-century popular culture folk heroine. In June 1978, the 'rock opera' *Evita,* with lyrics by Tim Rice and music by Andrew Lloyd Webber, opened in London, to rapturous reviews. Directed by Hal Prince, a Broadway choreographer, staged with aggression and brio on a series of giant sets, it ran for more than seven years, making around $1 billion throughout the world. In London there were six Evitas, on Broadway two. In Australia, Tokyo, Paris, Istanbul, Lisbon, Tel Aviv, Budapest, Warsaw, Johannesburg, Evitas trod the boards – and throughout Latin America, too, from Puerto Rico to Chile. Only in Buenos Aires was there no production; but fashionable Argentines were ready to fly up to Rio for the show.

Although it was based for the most part on the earliest and seamiest versions of Evita's life, something happened to the tale in its retelling, and the Evita who emerged each evening, dressed first as a teenager, then a hooker and finally, in tulle and silver foil, as First Lady, was far from being unsympathetic. Success against odds was, after all, the great showbiz cliché, endlessly reworked on Broadway, from Busby Berkeley onwards; and it was as an actress (a successful one, as the existence of the musical itself made clear), not as a politician, that audiences applauded the new Evita. As for her alleged corruption, people were entitled to expect such behaviour in the glitzy never-never-land Carmen Miranda 1940s evoked by the sets; and in case they missed this not very subliminal message, the figure of Che Guevara, turned into a capitalist selling duff insecticide, was present on the stage almost throughout to give the required gloss. The choruses of generals and oligarchs were played for laughs; by their side the gravel-voiced Perón, a puppet master or undertaker (the production never seemed quite sure) did provide some element of saving gravitas. If not exactly moved to tears, audiences were at least touched by Evita's solitary death, and her curtain-closing apotheosis at the hands of a chorus of embalmers.

Evita was the first important British production to break into Broadway, imposing as it did so a new international style for the musical. It showed that the ailing musclebound tradition of Rodgers and Hammerstein, given snappy lyrics and music cunningly adapting a variety of sources, nineteenth-century symphonic schmaltz as well as contemporary 'glamour rock', could appeal to international audiences. But it was also important for the underlying not-so-subtle message which it carried – one of cynicism, above all. Throughout the world, political seriousness was out of vogue by the 1970s; and everywhere the old values of the political class had begun their long slide to insignificance. The new 'infamy chic' of *Evita* – it is a commonplace now in the 1990s – consisted in implying that because everything in public life was unauthentic one might as well settle for the genuinely factitious or even overtly criminal. The ethos of show business thus came to supplant the old rituals of politics, putting an end to their power, as it had indeed absorbed and reshaped such anachronistic institutions as royalty. If it was the done thing to perform obeisance at the shrine of fame, Evita, a politician who was supposed by her enemies to have turned national life into show business, was the perfect minor deity.

Conspicuous power drives could now be accommodated with the spirit of feminism, and actresses older than Evita had been when she died began to develop an interest in her. In 1982 Faye Dunaway starred in an NBC movie for television based in part on this book, though the producers came to rely on many of the by now hoary manifestations of the 'black myth' – the prostitution, as graphically described as possible given the lack of detail, the submarines ferrying Nazi gold to the Peróns, etc. Faye Dunaway looked rather old for a Junín teenager, but she came into her own in a scene where she showed the contents of her wardrobe, including her shoes, to a visiting American photographer. Banned in the Philippines, the film was shown in five Manila movie houses after the overthrow of Imelda Marcos – audiences applauded the shoe scene, crying 'Encore . . .'

By the early 1980s there were already plans for a film version of the musical. Andrew Lloyd Webber and Tim Rice teamed up with the showbiz entrepreneur Robert Stigwood, who was to produce the film. EMI acquired an interest in the property, and approaches were made to Robert De Niro and Meryl Streep. But after EMI ran into money troubles, the rights were sold to Paramount. Stigwood next hired the flamboyant Ken Russell, who tested Elaine Paige, who had starred in the stage version, and Liza Minnelli. But despite Stigwood's urgings Russell refused to use Paige ('she wasn't enough of a whore') and he withdrew from the project shortly before filming was supposed to start in Spain. After that the project occupied a place in showbiz limbo, kept alive by feverish press speculation. A succession of directors were associated with *Evita*, some more serious than others: Franco Zeffirelli, Herbert Ross, Richard Attenborough, Alan Pakula, Hector Babenco and Francis Ford Coppola. Zeffirelli supposedly wanted Diane Keaton to play Evita.

In 1987 the film rights were sold again, this time to Jerry Weintraub, who had managed Bob Dylan and John Denver. He approached Oliver Stone, the maker of *Salvador* and *Platoon*, who was a fan of the musical and who had become Hollywood's leading chronicler of contemporary history. Stone saw *Evita* in true D. W. Griffith style as an epic on a grand scale requiring the resources of an entire Latin American army; and he now wrote a fresh script somewhat saltier than the by now tame-seeming musical. Stone briefly met and dismissed Madonna; he wanted Meryl Streep to play Evita. But with filming imminent once again, a series of disasters hit the project, culminating in Meryl Streep's abrupt withdrawal (she was apparently annoyed with Stone), though she did change her mind ten days later. But by that time Oliver Stone had lost interest in the idea of *Evita*; instead he decided to make *The Doors*, based on the life of another rock celebrity, Jim Morrison.

The film rights now passed to the Disney Corporation, and after another false start, in which Madonna was hurriedly paired with Glenn Gordon Carron, director of the television series *Moonlighting*, Oliver Stone once again became interested in *Evita*. By now Carlos Menem, the son of Syrian immigrants, who had briefly been imprisoned as the Peronist Governor of La Rioja during the late 1970s, had been elected President of Argentina, and he expressed interest in some sort of collaboration. Stone flew down to Buenos Aires, where he lunched with the dandyish, side-burned and Italian-suited Menem, and the two men, both of them notorious womanisers, did hit it off. But Menem was either misinformed about the relationship of the movie to the Rice–Lloyd Webber musical, or he had misjudged his followers' mood, because he was taken aback by the outcry which followed his acceptance of Stone's offer.

One of the many versions of Stone's scripts had done the rounds, and it proclaimed on page nine that Evita lost her virginity aged 17. On page 18, Evita had found her vocation: 'Int. photographic studio.

A flash bulb goes off. Evita posing for a cheesecake shot, sucking on an orange . . .' Although it was already apparent to Argentines that Menem's Peronism represented a clean break with tradition, and that he wished to dismantle the old Peronist system of social protection in favour of neo-liberal policies involving the denationalisation of many industries, such disrespect for the greatest Peronist icon proved too much. 'It would be like letting Oliver Stone use the White House to say that Kennedy was a homosexual,' said Patricia Bullrich, a Peronist Congresswoman, of Stone's wish to restage Evita's story in the Casa Rosada. Menem thereupon suggested that it might be possible for Stone to film in Buenos Aires without using any public buildings, but this, too, failed to mollify his supporters. 'Any artist has the right to create his own work,' said the Interior Minister Carlos Ruckauf huffily. 'But when it deals with the most important woman in the history of the country – as no doubt Evita is – we want the right to debate with Stone.' After a week of impassioned protests, Menem finally cancelled his agreement with Stone. 'The opera is total infamy,' he announced in the old-style accents of Peronism. 'If historical truth is not respected, the movie has no chance of being filmed.'

Oliver Stone now wished to film in Spain, and he had settled on Michelle Pfeiffer as his star. He described Evita as 'a Cinderella-like creature on her short path through life from extreme poverty to power and glory'. But he withdrew once again in June 1994, citing the excessive cost of $60 million. Once again, the indefatigable Robert Stigwood did the rounds, and this time he came up with Alan Parker, who had directed *Fame* and *The Commitments*, and whom he had previously approached for *Evita* in 1978. Parker was enthusiastic, and he now approached Madonna, who still wanted to play Evita. He cast Antonio Banderas as Che, and Jonathan Pryce as Perón. By December 1995, *Evita* was at last officially declared to be in production.

It would have seemed impossible even five years previously for an Argentine government to contemplate taking part in the making of Evita, and Menem's initial eagerness was a sign of how, at last, the climate surrounding the violent past of Peronism had begun to change. Some of the archives from the early period were now open, and it was ultimately possible to acknowledge Evita for what she had been – a significant figure in Argentine politics, despite her brief career – rather than indulging in romantic political daydreams about what she might or might not have done if she had lived longer or differently. In 1995 the Argentine journalist and academic Tomás Eloy Martínez published Santa Evita, the first full account in

Argentina of the bizarre progress of Evita's embalmed corpse. Told in the style of a novel, the book recounted in detail the efforts of Dr Pedro Ara and Moori Koenig, while telling the story of Evita's life through a series of cinematic flashbacks. Among the newish or rehashed revelations, supplied by former members of the Argentine intelligence services, it appeared, astonishingly, that Perón had had made several replicas of Ara's work (there were supposed to be three, or even five, depending on who you were talking to; and they were manufactured by an Italian sculptor) so that the 'real Evita' could be identified only by a star-shaped mark behind the ear. These fake Evitas were reputedly shipped out to Europe, at the same time as the real, star-marked corpse. One of them was buried at Moori Koenig's ancestral home in Germany, to be washed away by the Danube, while another was briefly exhibited in a sex emporium in Hamburg, and then – the story is no more improbable than many others involving Evita which have turned out to be correct – somehow mislaid.

It was primarily as a relic or an obsession that Martínez now judged the importance of Evita, and he pointed out that the Argentine habit of acquiring or fighting over pieces of national heroes was as old as the country itself. The story of Evita's body reflected a bitter struggle for power – with the ultimate possession of the national consciousness as its symbolic outcome. Calculation of political advantage, highly cynical in its expression, was the dominant motivation; only thus could the savagery and obsessional behaviour of the participants be explained. Perón wished to re-acquire his wife's body for political reasons, as part of his efforts to rehabilitate himself; but once he had done so – after briefly exhibiting it on his dining room table, apparently for the benefit of the curious among his visitors – Dr Ara's creation was no longer of any importance to him. Indeed Perón returned to Argentina without Evita; only after his own death was she brought home by Isabel at a time when her own regime required shoring up.

Santa Evita was a best-seller and it was extremely successful among younger Argentines who had grown up without experiencing the cult of Evita, except in second-hand, attenuated form; and visitors to Evita's armoured tomb in the Recoleta cemetery could be seen clutching well-thumbed copies of it. 'She is the summary of our national preoccupation with death,' Martínez said. 'Nobody can see the body now. It is locked away in its vault and only Evita's sisters have the keys, but its symbolic power is undiminished. It is more than a relic; it is the expression of a deeply necrophiliac strain in our culture. In Argentina, we are never more alive than when we are contemplating death.'

As the Hollywood myth machine busied itself with Evita, Victor Bo, an Argentine producer, announced the imminent production in Buenos Aires of a rival narrative entitled *Evita: The True Story*, starring Andrea del Boca, an Argentine soap star. 'Evita was a pioneering feminist, not the prostitute others would have you believe,' Bo said confidently. 'We shall be able to tell the story of the true Evita.'

'Evita Vive!' the guerillas had once hopefully written on the walls of Buenos Aires or chanted, evoking the presence of her ghost. Many people had striven in vain over the years to find ways of definitively identifying the true Evita, but none, alas, could ever be as simple or as meaninglessly incontrovertible as the tell-tale star-shaped mark behind the right ear. Still, the evidence did show that Evita was alive – she had fulfilled the promise made to her *descamisados*, and she had come again. Within the limits prescribed by the late twentieth century, she had become immortal, as she had wanted.

NOTES

CHAPTER ONE

1. Ezequiel Martínez Estrada, *Radiografía de la Pampa,* Buenos Aires 1953, p.116.
2. Ysabel F. Rennie, *The Argentine Republic,* New York 1945, p.75.
3. Interviews quoted in *Así,* Buenos Aires, June 1973. Also interviews with Pascual Lettieri and Daniel Dilagosta, quoted in Otelo Borroni and Roberto Vacca, *La Vida de Eva Perón,* Buenos Aires 1970, pp.21-22.
4. Martínez Estrada, op. cit., p.34.
5. Interview with Eduardo Brossi, quoted in Borroni and Vacca, op. cit., p.23. It has been asserted repeatedly, even by such eminent Argentines as Jorge Luis Borges, that Eva's mother was a prostitute. Those who actually knew her in Los Toldos and Junín insist that she was not, that she wanted to be respectable and that such stories arose only when Eva became famous. But because of doña Juana's ménage with Duarte the family did have 'a bad reputation', .and it was gossiped about.
6. Erminda Duarte, *Mi Hermana Evita,* Buenos Aires 1972, p.19. This sentimental ghost-written account of the Duarte childhood was published to preserve Evita's myth and to rescue her mother from her many detractors. It describes the family as it wished to be seen. Sometimes it takes the malicious gossip, bowdlerizes it and repeats it.
7. Eva Perón, *La Razón de mi Vida,* 1973. There are many editions of this autobiography, first published in 1951. Page references throughout refer to the 1973 edition. An English translation is available, but we have made our own.
8. Erminda Duarte, op. cit., p.26; 'what hurt us most', ibid., pp.30-31.
9. *El Exmo. Sr. Gobernador y sus Ministros entre su pueblo,* pamphlet (n.d.).
10. Authors' interview with Clara Cabrera de Lequizamón.
11. María Flores, *The Woman with the Whip,* New York 1952, p.20. María Flores is a pseudonym of Mary Main, an Anglo-Argentine historical novelist who revisited Buenos Aires in 1950, when Evita's power was at its height. All her information was taken from the opposition and her book is consequently a compendium of the most virulent anti-Peronist gossip. It was translated into Spanish and published in Buenos Aires in 1955. Because it was the first hostile book about Eva to be published in Argentina it was often subsequently used by her detractors. It is the basis of the Evita in the musical *Evita.*
12. Authors' interview with Palmira Repetti.
13. Authors' interview with Sra de Alberto Haylle.
14. Manuel Puig, *Boquitas Pintadas,* Buenos Aires 1969. Puig's novel is a wonderful evocation of the popular culture and love-life of a small *pampa* town in the 1930s. The quotation is from the English translation by Suzanne Jill Levine, *Heartbreak Tango,* New York 1975, p.63.

15. Erminda Duarte, op. cit., p.43.
16. As, for instance, Main, op. cit., p.21. Sometimes the tango singer is differently named. It has been said that this story originated with the hairdresser of Junín, who began telling it in Buenos Aires when Eva was powerful, and was then encouraged by the police to return to Junín. However, many of those who knew Eva when she first came to Buenos Aires say that she was assisted by Magaldi. Authors' interview, Pierina Dealessi.
17. Erminda Duarte, op. cit., p.75.

CHAPTER TWO

1. For a deft, entertaining portrait of this 'golden age' of Buenos Aires, including its architectural interest and the social history of immigration, see Francis Korn, *Buenos Aires, Los Huéspedes del 20,* Buenos Aires 1974, ch. 1-2.
2. For a comprehensive exploration of *porteño* attitudes, see Ezequiel Martínez Estrada, *La Cabeza de Goliat,* Buenos Aires 1968.
3. Waldo Frank, *América Hispana,* New York 1931, p.111.
4. Georges Clemenceau, *Notes de voyage dans l'Amerique du Sud,* Paris 1911, p.28. The remark of Anatole France is quoted in Korn, op. cit., p.65.
5. Rennie, op. cit., p.224.
6. María Rosa Oliver, *Mundo mi casa,* Buenos Aires 1970, p.193.
7. Jules Huret, *En Argentine,* Paris 1913, p.2.
8. Quoted in Alain Rouquié, *Pouvoir Militaire et Société Politique en République Argentine,* Paris 1978, p.29.
9. Rennie, op. cit., p.224.
10. *Buenos Aires,* quoted in Dario Canton, *¿Gardel, a quién le cantas?,* Buenos Aires 1972, p.74.
11. Martínez Estrada, *La Cabeza de Goliat,* p.131.
12. Frank, op. cit., p.115.
13. Enrique Santos Discépolo, *Cambalache,* 1934. Most tangos are about betrayal or loss of women. Discépolo was one of a few composers to introduce social themes into tangos in the 1930s.
14. Raúl Scalabrini Ortiz, *El hombre que está solo y espera,* Buenos Aires 1974, p.65.
15. *Crítica,* 27 March 1937.
16. Edmundo Guibourg, *Crítica,* 15 July 1938.
17. Authors' interview with Fanny Cunéo.
18. Authors' interview, name withheld.
19. Authors' interview, name withheld.
20. Authors' interview, name withheld.
21. Tongues are still vigorously clucked over Eva's alleged ruthlessness and contempt for acting skills. Thus Tim Rice, librettist of the musical *Evita:* 'She dedicated herself to perfect the art of manipulating people (*sic*) in order to become a star, rather than dedicating herself to become a good actress,' *Sunday Times Magazine,* 11 June 1978. Eva's stage experience offered her few opportunities to demonstrate acting excellence. Perhaps she would have got better parts if she had been

more ruthless. Most of those who knew her say she was gentle and kind to those around her.

22. Interview with Carmelo Santiago, quoted in Borroni and Vacca, op. cit., p.49.
23. *Antena*, 20 June 1939.
24. Authors' interview with René Cossa.
25. Interview with Pablo Raccioppi, quoted in Borroni and Vacca, op. cit., pp.90-3.

Chapter Three

1. Alain Rouquíe, *Pouvoir militaire et société politique en république Argentine*, Paris 1978, p.275.
2. ibid., p.326; Ray Josephs, *Argentine Diary*, New York 1944, p.33.
3. Josephs, op. cit., pp.41-2.
4. *Antena*, 17 June 1943.
5. Robert A. Potash, *The Army and Politics in Argentina*, Stanford 1969, pp.220-4.
6. Juan Domingo Perón, *Del Poder al exilio*, Buenos Aires (n.d.), p.51. In some accounts it is suggested that Perón was not Eva's first colonel. Ray Josephs, for instance, says in a March 1945 article in *Cosmopolitan* that he met her at an audition with a US film producer before the 1943 coup; and that when she was turned down she threatened the producer with retaliation by 'her colonel'. Mary Main implies that Eva used to entertain considerable numbers of officers in her apartment before she met Perón. Such stories are not plausible; if Eva had indeed been *la fille du régiment*, this would have been rather better known. For once she and Perón are somewhere near the truth.
7. *Yo, Juan Domingo Perón*, Barcelona 1976, pp.51-4.
8. There are a number of photos of 'Piraña' (as it is said she was called) taken with Perón. The story of Eva and the truck comes from a close friend of Perón's; authors' interview, name withheld.
9. *Radiolandia*, 5 February 1945.
10. *Redacción*, Buenos Aires, April 1978, p.3. For Perón's childhood, *Yo, Juan Domingo Perón*, pp.2-23, and Enrique Pavón Pereyra, *Perón*, Buenos Aires 1952, pp.17-41. There are many discrepancies between Perón's authorized biography, written while he was in power, and the transcriptions of the interviews he gave to three journalists while he was in his Spanish exile. Perón is concerned to place himself in the best possible light and on some occasions what seemed good in the early 1950s has not stood the test of time and is thus rejected. But sometimes Perón's disregard for recorded truth seems attributable only to reckless complacency, so unconcerned is he about being found lying.
11. Potash, op. cit., p.77.
12. The story of Perón's lost and never recovered crown prince is from his friend Jorge Antonio, quoted in *Redacción*, p.13. The editors observe that if Perón gave his official biographer an accurate chronology of his stay in Spain 'the colonel must have seduced and impregnated [the

lady] in . . . a short time [and] the act of love must have been consummated in the facilities of Barcelona station.'

13. The importance of this organization has been greatly exaggerated. For an accurate account of its activities see Rouquié, op. cit., p.315.

14. Perón, op. cit., p.37.

15. *El Mercurio,* quoted in *La Prensa,* 12 November 1943.

16. Perón, op. cit., p.40, and Rouquié, op. cit., p.350.

17. ibid., p.54. Not only does Perón play down his romance with Eva in favour of a platonic friendship in which both parties were solely concerned with political ideals, he is also ungallant about his mistress. Eva, he says, 'did not bother with appearances [in 1945] and did not want to pass for an elegant woman.'

18. Paco Jamandreu, *La cabeza contra el suelo,* Buenos Aires 1975, pp.69-70.

19. *Radiolandia,* 7 April 1945.

20. Libertad Lamarque left Argentina for Mexico in 1946, where she continued to be very successful. It has always been assumed that she left because she was blacklisted by Eva. Since the Mexican movie industry was in better shape by 1946 than the Argentine one, there may have been other reasons, too. Libertad Lamarque's films were always shown in Argentina, and she came back frequently to see her family. The most she will now say about Eva is; 'If [she] had known what that woman would become [she] would have been more careful.' Authors' interview.

21. Scripts of *Towards a Better Future.*

22. Interview with Arturo Jauretche, quoted in Borroni and Vacca, op. cit., p.85.

23. Perón, op. cit., p.54.

24. Eva Perón, op. cit., p.22.

25. Interview with Arturo Jauretche.

26. Stories about Perón's impotence are common. Perón the great *caudillo* is perceived as Perón the great *macho;* such deflations are anti-Peronist jokes, for it is thought there would be irony in his impotence. There is no reason to suppose such stories true.

27. *Radiolandia*, 7 April 1945.

28. Authors' interview with Mario Soffici, director of *The Circus Cavalcade* and *The Prodigal.*

29. Authors' interview with Hernán Benítez.

30. Waldo Frank, *South American Journey,* New York 1943, pp.105-6.

CHAPTER FOUR

1. A graphic and detailed account of the events of this year is *El 45* by Felix Luna, Buenos Aires 1972.

2. *The Times,* 4 December 1945. Throughout 1945, *The Times'* reporting was excellent. Its correspondent was one of the very few observers to see through the rhetoric of that year to the specifically Argentine issues at stake.

3. Silvano Santander, no publisher, Montevideo 1953. For further

elaborations of this, including the celebrated but wholly spurious Bormann connexion, see *Aftermath*, Ladislas Farago, New York 1973.

4. Luna, op. cit., p.77 *et seq*. Also Spruille Braden, *Diplomats and Demagogues*, New York 1971.

5. *La Prensa*, 19 September 1945.

6. Quoted in *Primera Plana*, 28 September 1965.

7. Authors' interview, General Gerardo Demetro.

8. Quoted in *Primera Plana*, 19 October 1965.

9. Quoted in Luna, op. cit., p.215.

10. *El Pueblo*, 1 October 1945.

11. Authors' interview with Roberto Petinato, who was with Perón and Evita that night.

12. Luna, op. cit., pp.245-6.

13. This is the case with virtually all of the books about Eva listed in the bibliography, and with most studies of Peronism, an exception being Luna's work, the first to cast doubt on this official version. In otherwise sober accounts there is persistent talk of 'attacks of hysteria' and 'demoniac energy'. There is in fact no record of Eva's activity in contemporary sources and we have found no serious witnesses to corroborate this version. Momentous actions begin to be credited to Eva only when she is more important. In 1947, for instance, the Peronist newspaper *Democracia* merely speaks of Eva's 'loyalty' in 1945; by 1952, however, when the time has come for her obituary, it is asserted that she 'assured the continuity of the Revolution'. Anti-Peronist accounts of Eva's life faithfully mirror this official rewriting of history, though Eva's actions are, of course, rather differently interpreted.

14. *La Vanguardia*, 28 September 1945.

15. Eva Perón, op. cit., pp.37–9.

16. Borroni and Vacca, op. cit., p.107.

17. Authors' interview, Dr Miguel Mazza.

18. Letter of Perón quoted in Luna, op. cit., p.337.

19. Perón, op. cit., p.64.

20. According to Luna (op. cit., p.341), this episode was related by Eva to the historian Vicente Sierra in 1948. Father Hernán Benítez says that he, too, heard it around this time (Open Letter to Sr. Cipriano Reyes, in authors' possession). Perón was present when Eva told the story and he began to laugh at her. There are some union leaders (i.e. Mariano Tedesco, quoted in Borroni and Vacca, op. cit., p.112) who have said that Eva met with a number of militant groups during these days and even visited factories. But she knew no union leaders and would have been powerless to influence them. Even if she did perform some of these actions attributed to her, it is hard to see how they could seriously have influenced events.

21. Cipriano Reyes, quoted in Luna, op. cit., p.275.

22. *El Pueblo*, 25 October 1945.

23. Leopoldo Marechal, quoted in Luna op. cit., p.275.

24. Sir David Kelly, *The Ruling Few*, London 1953.

25. Perón, op. cit., p.65.

26. Luna, op. cit., p.292.

CHAPTER FIVE
1. Benigno Acossano, *Eva Perón, su verdadera vida*, Buenos Aires 1955, pp.40–1; also Borroni and Vacca, op. cit., pp.116–7.
2. Interview with Daniel Dilagosto, Borroni and Vacca, op. cit. p.20.
3. Dario Rodríguez del Pino, clerk at the Los Toldos Registry in a letter published in *Primera Plana*, 20 July 1965.
4. Details of the series of forgeries were first made public as a result of the investigative labours of a judicial committee set up after Perón's fall: *Documentacíon, autores y complices de las irregularides cometidas durante la segunda tiranía* (5 vols.), Buenos Aires 1958, vol. 1, p.520 et seq.
5. Authors' interview, Mario Soffici.
6. *Presencia de Eva Perón* (no author), Buenos Aires 1954, p.9.
7. Authors' interview, name withheld.
8. Cipriano Reyes, *Primera Plana*, 17 May 1966.
9. *Democracia*, 14 December 1945.
10. Authors' interview, Ricardo Guardo.
11. Interview, Hernán Salowicz, Borroni and Vacca, op. cit., p.141.
12. Interview with José Presta, quoted ibid.
13. Authors' interview, Liliane Lagomarsino de Guardo.
14. Paco Jamandreu, op. cit., p.72.
15. Authors' interview, Valentin Thiebaut.
16. *Newsweek*, 19 August 1946.
17. Perón, *Del Poder al exilio*, p.52.
18. US Ambassador George Messersmith to Spruille Braden (top secret), 2 August 1946, 835.00/8.29.
19. Messersmith to Braden (secret) 14 August 1946, 835.00/8–1446.
20. Philip Hamburger, *New Yorker*, 26 June 1948.
21. Spruille Braden, op. cit., p.323. Braden suggests that this joke was told him at a reception by General Farrell, Perón's predecessor as President. Braden never actually met Eva, although Perón once invited him to lunch at the studio where she was filming. Braden says in his memoirs; 'I never had another opportunity to meet Evita. She may have been a mediocre success in the two professions she tried before she met Perón; but her involvement in his career gave full scope to her real and formidable talents as a demagogue' (p.331).

CHAPTER SIX
1. Perón, op. cit., p.181.
2. Quoted in Esteban Peicovich, *El Ultimo Perón*, Barcelona 1976, pp.118–19.
3. *Time* magazine cover story, 23 June 1947.
4. *ABC*, Madrid, 10 June 1947.
5. Authors' interview, Father Hernán Benítez.
6. 23 June 1947.
7. 22 June 1947.

8. Perón, *Del Poder al exilio*, p.58.
9. Interview with Ricardo Labougle, Argentine Ambassador in London. The British Foreign Office archives dealing with the Perón period have by now been released, but the account of the negotiations surrounding Eva's visit was withheld under the fifty-year ruling applied to material judged likely to remain controversial.
10. Authors' interview, Hernán Benítez.
11. *Newsweek*, 3 August 1947.
12. *O Globo*, 21 August 1947.
13. *Observer*, 13 July 1947.

CHAPTER SEVEN

1. Philip Hamburger, *New Yorker*, 26 June 1948. For an entertaining account of Hitler and Eva Braun appearing on the pampas, see his article published in the *New Yorker*, 20 December 1948.
2. 'Z', *Argentina in the tunnel, Foreign Affairs*, 30 April 1951, vol. 30, no.3, p.391.
3. George I. Blanksten, *Perón's Argentina*, Chicago 1953, pp.332–5; Robert J. Alexander, *The Perón Era*, New York 1951, p.128; Pierre Lux-Würm, *Le Péronisme*, Paris 1965, p.124 *et seq*.
4. Authors' interview. Also, Pedro Santos Martínez, *La Nueva Argentina*, Buenos Aires 1976, vol. 1, pp.332–4. For Perón's own account, see Perón, op. cit., p.183.
5. Hamburger, op. cit.
6. Quoted in Lux-Würm, op. cit., p.130.
7. Authors' interview with Eduardo Colom.
8. Quoted in Blanksten, op. cit., p.118.
9. *Discurso de Eva Perón en el acto inaugural de la primera asamblea nacional del Movimiento Perónista Femenino*, Buenos Aires, 26 July 1949.
10. Authors' interview with Josefina Fulco.
11. Authors' interview with Maria Eugenia Alvarez.
12. Authors' interview with Delia Degliuomini de Parodi.
13. Philip Hamburger, *New Yorker*, 26 June 1948.
14. Elias Canetti, *Crowds and Power*, London 1973, p.19.
15. *Eva Perón habla a las trabajadoras del país*, Buenos Aires 1949, p.15.
16. Eva Perón, *Historia del Peronismo*, Buenos Aires 1951.
17. *Eva Perón habla*, p.14.
18. Virginia Lee Warren, *New York Times Magazine*, 3 June 1951.
19. Authors' inteview, María Rosa Calviño de Gomez.

CHAPTER EIGHT

1. *Sociedad de Beneficencia de la Capital, 1823–1936*, Buenos Aires 1936, p.15.
2. *La Nación*, 28 May 1926.
3. Diego Luis Molinari, *Diario de Sesiones de la Cámara de Senadores*, vol. 2, p.472.
4. e.g. Main, op. cit., p.102.
5. Authors' interview, Atilio Renzi.

6. Eva Perón, op. cit., p.225.
7. *Fundacion Eva Perón, Estatutos,* Buenos Aires 1955, pp.1–2.
8. All figures relating to the Foundation have been taken from the 1955 audit. The cited dollar equivalents do not give any real idea of the actual value of the Foundation's assets, since the peso had by that time fallen drastically against the dollar. Such sums would have been worth a great deal more in Argentina at that time.
9. Interview quoted in *Primera Plana,* 27 December 1966.
10. Authors' interview with Col. Hector Bolaños, administrator of the Foundation.
11. Authors' interview.
12. Prepared by Col. Bolaños at Perón's behest.
13. John Dos Passos, *Life* magazine, 11 April 1949.
14. José María de Areilza, *Así los he visto,* Barcelona 1970, p.190.
15. Milton Bracker, *New York Times Magazine,* 10 October 1948.
16. Rodolfo Walsh, *¿Quien mató a Rosendo?,* Buenos Aires 1969, pp.55–6.
17. Interview with Armado Olmos, secretary, sanitation workers' union, quoted in Borroni and Vacca, op. cit., p.225.
18. ibid., pp.211–2.
19. Father Benítez' memoir of Eva, *Careo,* July 1964, p.6.
20. Authors' interview with José María Castiñeira de Dios.
21. Perón, op. cit., p.144.
22. Authors' interview with Amérigo Barrios.
23. Authors' interview with Teresa Adelina Fiora.
24. Mary Main, op. cit., p.188.
25. *Documentación, autores y complices,* vol. 2, p.275.

CHAPTER NINE

1. Interview with Dr Oscar Ivanissevich, quoted in *Primera Plana,* 3 January 1967. In *Del Poder al exilio,* written in 1956, Perón observes that Eva's symptoms were first apparent in 1949. This is contradicted by all those who worked with her. In his later, tape-recorded memoirs, however, Perón implies that it was not until 1951 that he became aware of just how ill she was.
2. Gisèle Freund, *The World is My Camera,* New York 1974, p.190.
3. Perón, op. cit., p.106.
4. *Die Telegraaf,* 12 March 1976.
5. Fleur Cowles, *Bloody Precedent,* New York 1952, pp.171–2.
6. *ibid,* p. XI
7. Perón, *Del Poder al exilio,* p.54.
8. Jamandreu, op. cit., pp.80–1.
9. Authors' interview with Guillermo de Prisco.
10. Interview with Manuel Penella da Silva, quoted in *Primera Plana,* 17 January 1967.
11. Authors' interview with Hernán Benítez.
12. For an account of the railroad strike, see Samuel L. Bailey, *Nationalism and Politics in Argentina,* New Brunswick 1967, pp.130–5.

CHAPTER TEN

1. Hernán Benítez, *Careo*, p.17.
2. Authors' interviews with José Espejo and Atilio Renzi.
3. *Careo*, p.15.
4. V. S. Naipaul, *The Corpse at the Iron Gate, New York Review of Books*, 12 August 1972.
5. Interview with David Viñas, quoted in Borroni and Vacca, op. cit., pp.300–1.
6. Hernán Benítez, *Careo*, p.20.
7. Authors' interview with Pilar Madirolas and Irma Cabrera de Ferrari.
8. Perón, *Del Poder al exilio*, p.61.
9. Authors' interview with Atilio Renzi.
10. Perón, op. cit., p.62.
11. *Christian Science Monitor*, 25 October 1951.
12. Marie Langer, *El Niño asado y otros mitos sobre Eva Perón*, from *Fantasías Eternas a la luz del Psicoanálisis*, Buenos Aires 1957, p.73 *et seq.* Marie Langer also gives an explanation of the idealization of Eva. This was largely reflexive, in response to the attacks on her. 'For some, Eva was (thus) a saint, for others the devil; for some she was good, for others, evil. In reality everyone possessed two contradictory images of her ... but some promoted the good and repressed the evil and others did the opposite.' (Langer, p.89).
13. *Diario de la Cámara de Senadores*, Buenos Aires 1953, p.150.
14. Authors' interview with Atilio Renzi.
15. Authors' interview with Raúl Apold.
16. Authors' interview with Delia Degliuomini de Parodi.
17. Philippe Ariès, *L'Homme devant la mort*, Paris 1977, pp.555 *et seq.*
18. Perón, *Del Poder al exilio*, p.62. Perón's statement was made at a time when he had been much criticized for having made a 'spectacle' of his dying wife. One cannot be sure that Eva never requested to be embalmed but whether she did or not, the ultimate decision would have been Perón's.
19. This version of Eva's will was read by Perón to the assembled *descamisados* on 17 October 1952. According to Perón, it was to have been the first chapter of *Mi Mensaje*.
20. These other 'last wishes' were among the very few possessions which Perón was able to stuff into his suitcase on the night in 1955 when he went into exile. In 1973, just before he returned to Argentina, Perón handed them over for safe-keeping to his friend Jorge Antonio. Esteban Peicovich, op. cit., pp.124-5.
21. It has often been asserted that Evita had a great fortune and there has been much speculation as to what might have happened to it.

   In 1952 the Radical senator Silvano Santander published a series of documents which he claimed to have received from captured German archives in Berlin. For the most part these concerned the workings of 'Operation Land of Fire'. Perón and Evita had assisted in the shipment by submarine to Patagonia and subsequent concealment of a prodigious Nazi treasure looted from the European Jews. Evita, still an actress, had been responsible for hiding the money or ferrying it to other members of the ring. Through her friend Rudi Freude's father she had been made a beneficiary of the operation. The facsimiles of these documents were decorated with impressive-looking German stamps and festooned with gothic script, but in some important respects they were not convincing. First, they referred to Evita by her real, illegitimate name, Ibarguren, which she never used. Second, not only had she not met Perón at the time of this conspiracy, but Perón was in 1941 not in Argentina, but visiting the Alpine installations of the Italian Army. (Silvano: op. cit.)

It had been assumed by some of the opposition that the real motive of Evita's European tour had been to deposit money in Swiss banks. After Juan Duarte's visit to Zurich and suicide, the notion of a hidden fortune was once again popular. Perón did not behave like a rich exile, so it was assumed that he had failed to get his hands on the money. (On numerous occasions, he expressed a violent dislike for the Swiss and Switzerland which seemed to support this theory.) Perhaps the account had mistakenly been opened in the name Eva María Duarte de Perón; and perhaps the Swiss authorities now refused to give Perón the money on the grounds that this was not his wife's real name. The missing fortune was rumoured to be very large indeed. In 1970, Percy Foster of the *Los Angeles Herald Examiner* was told by 'an associate' of a former President that there was over $700 million in Evita's account – a sum equal to the assets of the Rockefeller Foundation.

In 1972 the tireless investigator Ladislas Farago arrived in Buenos Aires on the track of Martin Bormann, where he was welcomed by Argentine police officers and introduced to Juan José Velasco, an agent of *Coordinacíon Federal,* the Argentine secret service, who gave Farago what he would term 'the last word in the mystery of Martin Bormann's coming to Argentina'. This consisted of a number of documents purporting to come from a Father Egidio Esparza of AICA, the Catholic Information service of Argentina.

In these documents it was alleged that Evita had met with Bormann when she was in Rapallo, in 1947; and that she had personally arranged for his emigration to Argentina under the name of Eliezer Goldstein. (She had even introduced him to two Vatican officials as 'a distant relative of her family' – a philosopher of Jewish-Italian descent named Luigi Boglilio.) Evita had taken $800 million of the 'Land of Fire' hoard to Italy and she told Bormann he could only have a quarter of what remained. Yet what remained was enormous: 87 kilos of platinum, 2,500 kilos of gold, etc. etc. (Farago, op. cit., pp.239-247. Authors' interview.)

By 1972, Perón had begun the negotiations that led to his return to Argentina. A summary of what Farago was told had already appeared in *Ultima Clave,* a right-wing journal linked to the Navy, which opposed Perón's return. It seems likely that these documents were forged in the hope of re-kindling hostility to Perón.

Was there a Swiss account? It seems unlikely. If there was, it is likely that no one will ever know what was in it. Yet Evita did leave a sizeable, if not enormous fortune. This is adequately documented in real documents.

Shortly before his death in 1951, the shipowner Alberto Dodero gave Evita two pieces of prime real estate: a building in the Barrio Norte and an apartment house in Palermo Chico. These buildings were not mentioned in Evita's will. In Argentina in the event of a wife's death without leaving a will, property is usually divided equally between her parents and her husband; and that is what doña Juana now suggested should happen. But Perón by citing to her the spirit of Evita's public will, ultimately persuaded her to sign over her share to himself. The two buildings were then turned over to the Evita Foundation, created in 1954 with the statutory obligation of using Evita's legacy on behalf of the poor. They were supposed to become delinquents' homes.

When Perón fell from power in 1955, the buildings were 're-possessed' by the state on the grounds that they had been illegally acquired. Yet when Dodero's heirs, encouraged by this verdict, brought suit to recover them, alleging that they had been 'morally coerced' into giving them, their suit was rejected. The houses remained State property. One was sold, the other was converted and used for government office space.

In 1960 doña Juana took legal action against Perón to recover the half of the inheritance she now claimed had unfairly been taken from her. Her complaint made much of the fact that the document which she had signed had been improperly drafted, but doña Juana also said that Perón had promised and failed to support her. The case dragged on for many years, Perón refusing to settle. Yet in 1972, after doña Juana had died, Evita's two surviving sisters finally secured a judgement against Perón for the sum of 3,500 million pesos (about $3.5 million). (*La Opinión*, 6 September 1972.)

In 1973 Congress passed law 20,530, which gave back to Perón all that had been his and had passed into the hands of the State. It is not clear how these sequestered and sold assets were valued, but in 1974 Perón received 8,000 million pesos in compensation. It seems to have been after this happy resolution of his affairs that Peron decided to settle with Evita's sisters. Yet he did not accomplish this before he died in 1974.

On 23 July 1975, Isabel Perón, President of Argentina, signed a cheque for 3,151,150 pesos on the account of the Justicialist Crusade, a charity of which she was honorary president. The sum was to be transferred to the account of Perón's estate and paid out to Eva's sisters. But before this could be done a clerk at the bank copied the cheque and gave it to the press. Isabel's 'mistake', for it was thus she described what she had done, seemed outrageous even by the fiscal standards set by her government. There was a congressional investigation into the cheque and later, when Isabel had been removed from power, separate legal and military investigations. At this time the matter is not resolved, nor is the question of Eva's estate, since Blanca and Erminda have still not received their share. (*Redaccion*, 1976: *Somos*, 30 September, 1977.)

22. Hernán Benítez, *Careo*, p.19.

23. Dr Pedro Ara, *El Caso Eva Perón*, Madrid 1974, p.65.
24. Authors' interview with Sara Gatti, 'Sarita'.
25. *La Nación,* 29 July 1952.
26. *Life,* 11 August 1952.
27. Ara, op. cit., p.76.
28. Perón had planned to place Eva's body in the Convent of St Francis until the monument was completed. But at 3 am in the morning of the day after she died, a delegation of CGT officials, including José Espejo, asked for custody of the body. Doña Juana was opposed to this idea, but she ended by giving her assent, too.

Chapter Eleven

1. Pedro Ara, op. cit., p.120.
2. Perón, *Del Poder al exilio,* p.63.
3. *Un Año Más,* Buenos Aires 1953, p.1.
4. Ara, op. cit.
5. Authors' interview with Francisco Manrique.
6. Authors' interview with Admiral Isaac Rojas.
7. Authors' interview with Rojas and Manrique.
8. Ara, op. cit., pp.257-8.
9. Authors' interview with Mary Main. Other works with this perspective and in this vein are; Américo Ghioldi, *El Mito de Eva Duarte,* Montevideo 1952; Benigno Acossano, *Eva Perón, su verdadera vida,* Buenos Aires 1955; Roman J. Lombille, *Eva la predestinada. Alucinante historia de exitos y frustraciones,* Buenos Aires 1955; Ezequiel Martínez Estrada, *¿Que es esto?* Buenos Aires 1956.
10. Martínez Estrada, op. cit., p.241.
11. Luis Franco, *Biografía patria,* Buenos Aires 1958, p.154.
12. Ghioldi, op. cit., p.49.
13. Jorge Luis Borges, *Dreamtigers,* Souvenir Press Ltd., London, 1964. Borges has on many occasions referred to doña Juana as a whore, and more recently he has said the same of Evita. See, for instance, his conversation with Paul Theroux, quoted in the *New York Times Book Review,* 26 August 1979. He also told one of the present authors that Eva was a *puta.*
14. V. S. Naipaul's interview with Borges, *New York Review of Books,* 10 August 1972.
15. Julie Taylor, *Eva Perón, the Myths of a Woman,* Chicago, 1979.
16. Rodolfo Walsh, *Esa Mujer, Los Officios Terrestros,* Buenos Aires 1967.
17. David Viñas, *14 Hipotesis de trabajo en torno a Eva Perón, Marcha,* Montevideo 1971.
18. Juan José Sebreli, *Eva Perón Aventurera o Militante?,* Buenos Aires 1967, p.109. Since writing this book, Sebreli has changed his mind about Eva. He now identifies her with the 'extremist' wing of Peronism and believes that her *lumpen* origins did, after all, make her dangerously rancorous. 'Where Perón was prepared to negotiate, she

believed in the violent solution of problems.' Authors' interview.

19. The account of the abduction, interrogation and 'trial' of Aramburu comes from the guerillas' tape-recorded account of their 'operation'. It was later published in a Peronist underground newspaper. *Mario Firmenich y Norma Arrostito cuentan, La Causa Peronista,* 3 September 1974.

20. Authors' interview with Admiral Isaac Rojas.

21. Authors' interview with General Alejandro Agustín Lanusse.

22. Authors' interview with Francisco Manriqué. Detailed but frequently contradictory and confusing reports of the reappearance of the body were published in the world press. Both Lanusse and Manrique were involved in the operation and this is their version. Only such press reporting as appears to support their story has been used.

23. Ara, op. cit., p.266.

24. V. S. Naipaul, *New York Review of Books,* 10 August 1972.

BIBLIOGRAPHY

The bibliography is a list of periodicals and books consulted by the authors, not a complete bibliography of Peronism

NEWSPAPERS AND MAGAZINES

Crítica
Democracia
El Laborista
El Pueblo
La Capital (Rosario)
La Epoca
La Nación
La Prensa
La Voz del Interior (Cordoba)
Los Andes (Mendoza)

Antena
Así
Careo
Mundo Peronista
Primera Plana
Radiolandia
Sintonía

The New York Times
The Times
The Sunday Times
Time Magazine
Newsweek

WRITINGS OF PERON AND EVITA

Perón, Eva: *La Razón de mi Vida*. Buenos Aires: Ediciones Peuser, 1951. English translation: *My Mission in Life,* Vantage Press, New York 1952.

Historia del Peronismo. Buenos Aires: Editorial Freeland, 1951.

La ultima voluntad de Eva Perón. Buenos Aires: Servicio Internacional de Publicaciones Argentinas, 1952.

La palabra, el pensamiento y la acción de Eva Perón. Buenos Aires: Editorial Freeland, 1973.

Escribe Eva Perón. Buenos Aires: Ediciones Argentinas, 1973.

Perón, Juan: *Del Poder al exilio. Cómo y quiénes me derrocaron*. Buenos Aires, no date.

Conducción política. Buenos Aires: Ediciones Mundo Peronista, 1952.

La Fuerza es el derecho de las bestias. 1958.

Yo, Juan Domingo Perón. Barcelona: Editorial Planeta, 1976.

BOOKS ABOUT EVITA

Acossano, Benigno: *Eva Perón, su verdadera vida*. Buenos Aires: Editorial Lamas, 1955.

Ara, Pedro: *El Caso Eva Perón (Apuntes para la historia)*. Madrid: CVS Ediciones, 1974.

Barnes, John: *Evita: First Lady*. New York: Grove Press, 1978.

Boizard, Ricardo: *Esa Noche de Perón*. 4th edition, Buenos Aires 1955.

Borroni, Otelo and Roberta Vacca: *La vida de Eva Perón. Vol I. Testimonios para su historia*. Buenos Aires: Editorial Galerna, 1970.

Bourne, Richard: *Political Leaders of Latin America*. London: Pelican Books, 1969.

Copi: *Eva Perón*. Paris: Bourgois, 1969.

Costanzo, Francisco A.: *Evita. Alma inspiradora de la justicia social en America*. Buenos Aires 1948.

Cowles, Fleur: *Bloody Precedent*. New York, Random House, 1952.

Duarte, Erminda: *Mi hermana Evita*. Buenos Aires: Ediciones 'Centro de Estudios Eva Perón', 1972.

Ellena de la Sota, Julio: *La acción política de Eva Perón*. Buenos Aires, no date.

Franco, Alberto: *La mística social de Eva Perón*. Buenos Aires: Subsecretaria de Informaciones, no date.

Franco, Luis: *Biografía patria*. Buenos Aires: Editorial Stilcograf, 1958.

Ghioldi, Américo: *El Mito de Eva Duarte*. Montevideo 1952.

Lombille, Román J.: *Eva, la predestinada, alucinante historia de exitos y frustraciones*. Buenos Aires: Ediciones Gure, 1955.

Main, Mary (María Flores): *The Woman with the Whip: Eva Perón*. New York: Doubleday, 1952; Buenos Aires: Ediciones La Reja, 1955.

Martínez Estrada, Ezequiel: *¿Que es esto?*. Buenos Aires: Editorial Lautaro, 1956.

Martínez Payva, Celina R. and María Rosa Pizzutto de Rivero: *La Verdad. Vida y obra de Eva Perón*. 2 vols. Buenos Aires: Editorial Astral, 1967.

Paz, Carlos and Oscar Deutsch: *Eva Perón, peronismo para el socialismo*. Buenos Aires: Ediciones de Mirador, 1974.

Peralta, Jeronimo: *Semblanza heróica de Eva Perón*. Buenos Aires 1950.

Presencia de Eva Perón. Buenos Aires 1954.

Rodríguez, Angela Rina: *Eva de América. Madona de los humildes*. 1949.

Sacquard de Belleroche, Maude: *Eva Perón. La reine des sans-chemises*. Paris: La Jeune Parque, 1972.

Sebreli, Juan José: *Eva Perón ¿aventurera o militante?* 4th edition, Buenos Aires: Editorial La Pléyade, 1971.

Storni, Julio A. *Grandeza y proyección de Eva Perón*. San Miguel de Tucumán 1952.

Tettamanti, Rodolfo: *Eva Perón*. Buenos Aires: Centro Editor de América Latina, 1971.

BOOKS ABOUT PERÓN AND PERONISM

Alexander, Robert J.: *The Perón Era*. New York: Columbia University Press, 1951.

de Areilza, José María: *Así los he visto*. Barcelona: Editorial Planeta, 1970.

Bailey, Samuel L.: *Labor, Nationalism and Politics in Argentina*. New Brunswick: Rutgers University Press, 1967.

Beveraggi Allende, Walter: *El fracaso de Perón y el problema argentino*. Buenos Aires: Editorial Rosso, 1956.

Blanksten, George I: *Perón's Argentina*. Chicago: Chicago University Press, 1953.

Braden, Spruille: *Diplomats and Demagogues.* New York: Arlington House, 1972.

Chavez, Fermín: *Perón y el peronismo en la historia contemporanea.* Buenos Aires: Editorial Oriente, 1975.

Ciria, Alberto: *Perón y el justicialismo.* Buenos Aires: Siglo XXI, 1971.

Colom, Eduardo: *La revolución de los descamisados.* Buenos Aires: La Epoca, 1946.

Fayt, Carlos S.: *La naturaleza del peronismo.* Buenos Aires: Viracocha, 1967.

Gambini, Hugo: *El 17 de octubre de 1945.* Buenos Aires: Editorial Brújula, 1969.

García Lupo, Rogelio: *Historia de unas malas relaciones.* Buenos Aires: Jorge Alvarez, 1964.

Godio, Julio: *La caída de Perón.* Buenos Aires: Granica Editor, 1973.

Greenup, Ruth and Leonard: *Revolution before Breakfast.* Chapel Hill: University of North Carolina Press, 1947.

Guardo, Ricardo: *Horas difíciles.* Buenos Aires: Ediciones A. Pena Lillo, 1963.

Halperín Donghi, Tulio: *Argentina en el callejón.* Montevideo, Arca, 1964.

Hernández Arregui, Juan José: *La formación de la conciencia nacional: 1930-1960.* Buenos Aires: Ediciones Hachea, 1960.

Imaz, José Luis de: *Los que mandan.* Buenos Aires: Eudeba, 1964. English translation, *Those Who Rule,* Binghampton N.Y.: New York State University Press, 1969.

Josephs, Ray: *Argentine Diary.* New York: Random House, 1944.

Libro negro de la segunda tiranía. Buenos Aires, 1958.

Luna, Felix: *El 45. Crónica de un año decisivo.* Buenos Aires: Editorial Sudamericana, 1971.

De Perón a Lanusse. Buenos Aires: Editorial Planeta, 1972.

Lux-Würm, Pierre: *Le Péronisme.* Paris: Librairie de Droit et de Jurisprudence Pichon et Durand-Auzias, 1965.

Mafud, Julio: *Sociología del Peronismo.* Buenos Aires: Editorial Americalee, 1972.

Monzalvo, Luis: *Testigo de la primera hora del peronismo.* Buenos Aires, Editorial Pleamar, 1975.

Murmis, Miguel and Juan Carlos Portantiero: *Estudios sobre los orígenes del peronismo.* Buenos Aires: Siglo XXI, 1972.

Navarro Gerassi, Marysa: *Los Nacionalistas.* Buenos Aires: Editorial Jorge Alvarez, 1969.

Owen, Frank: *Perón, His Rise and Fall.* London: Cresset, 1957.

Pavón Pereyra, Enrique: *Perón (1895-1942).* Buenos Aires: Espiño, 1952. *Colloquios con Perón.* Buenos Aires 1965.

Peicovich, Esteban: *El Ultimo Perón,* Barcelona: Editorial Planeta, 1976.

Perelman, Angel: *Como hicimos el 17 de Octubre.* Buenos Aires: Editorial Coyoacán, 1961.

Potash, Robert: *The Army and Politics in Argentina, 1928-1945. Yrigoyen to Perón.* Stanford: Stanford University Press, 1969.

Project of Oral History. Di Tella Institute, Buenos Aires.

Rabinovitz, Bernardo: *Sucedió en la Argentina, 1943-1956*. Buenos Aires: Editorial Gure, 1965.

Reyes, Cipriano: *¿Que es el laborismo?* Buenos Aires: Ediciones R. A., 1946.

    Yo hice el 17 de octubre. Buenos Aires: GS Editorial, 1973.

Rouquié, Alain: *Pouvoir militaire et société politique en république Argentine*. Paris: Presses de la Fondation Nationale des Sciences Politiques, 1978.

Sábato, Ernesto: *El otro rostro del peronismo*. Buenos Aires: Gure, 1957.

Santander, Silvano: *Técnica de una traición. Juan D. Perón y Eva Duarte agentes del nazismo en Argentina*. Montevideo 1953.

Santos Martínez, Pedro: *La Nueva Argentina*. Buenos Aires: Ediciones de las Bastille, 1976.

Various: *Asi cayó Perón*. Buenos Aires: Editorial Lamas, 1955.

Whitaker, Arthur P.: *Argentina*. Englewood Cliffs, N. J.: Prentice Hall, 1964.

    Argentine Upheaval. New York: Praeger, 1956.

MISCELLANEOUS

Ariès, Philippe: *L'Homme devant la mort*. Paris: Editions du Seuil, 1977.

Borges, Jorge Luis: *Dreamtigers*. Austin: University of Texas Press, 1964.

Canetti, Elias: *Crowds and Power*. Harmondsworth: Penguin Books, 1973.

Canton, Dario: *¿Gardel, a quién le cantás?* Buenos Aires: Ediciones de la Flor, 1972.

Clemenceau, Georges: *Notes de voyage dans l'Amérique du sud*. Paris: Hachette, 1911.

Discépolo, Enrique Santos: *Cancionero*. Buenos Aires: Torres Agüero Editor, 1977.

Farago, Ladislas: *Aftermath*. New York, Simon and Schuster, 1973.

Frank, Waldo: *America Hispana*. New York: Scribners, 1931.

    South American Journey. New York: Duell, Sloane and Pierce, 1943.

Freund, Gisèle: *The World is My Camera*. New York: Dial Press, 1974.

Huret, Jules: *En Argentine: De la Plata à la Cordillère des Andes*. Paris: Fasquelle, 1913.

Jamandreu, Paco: *La cabeza contra el suelo*. Buenos Aires: Ediciones de la Flor, 1975.

Korn, Francis: *Buenos Aires: Los Huéspedes del 20*. Buenos Aires: Editorial Sudamericana, 1974.

Langer, Marie: *Fantasías eternas a la luz del psicoanálisis*. Buenos Aires: Editorial Nova, 1957.

Martínez Estrada, Ezequiel: *Radiografía de la pampa*. Buenos Aires: Editorial Losada (4th edition), 1952.

    La Cabeza de Golíat. Buenos Aires: Centro Editor de América Latina, 1968.

di Nubila, Domingo: *Historia del cine argentino*. 2 vols. Buenos Aires: Edicion Cruz de Malta, 1959.

Oliver, María Rosa; *Mundo, mi casa*. Buenos Aires: Editorial

Sudamericana, 1970.

Ordaz, Luis: *El teatro argentino.* Buenos Aires: Centro Editor de América Latina, 1971.

Rennie, Ysabel F.: *The Argentine Republic.* New York: Macmillan, 1945.

Scalabrini Ortiz, Raúl: *El hombre que esta solo y espera.* Buenos Aires: Editorial Plus Ultra, 1974.

Walsh, Rodolfo: *¿Quién mató a Rosendo?* Buenos Aires: Editorial Contemporaneo, 1969.

   Los officios terrestros. Buenos Aires: Editorial Contemporaneo, 1967.

Warner, Marina: *Alone of All Her Sex: the Myth and Cult of the Virgin Mary.* New York: Knopf, 1976.

INDEX